BLINDFOLD GAMES

ALAN ROSS

BLINDFOLD
GAMES

COLLINS HARVILL
8 Grafton Street, London W1
1986

William Collins Sons and Co. Ltd.
London · Glasgow · Sydney · Auckland
Toronto · Johannesburg

BRITISH LIBRARY CATALOGUING IN PUBLICATION DATA

Ross, Alan
   Blindfold games.
    1. Ross, Alan—Biography   2. Authors, English
  —20th century—Biography
  I. Title
  828'.91409   PR6035.0673Z/

ISBN 0 00 272773-0

First published by Collins Harvill 1986
Reprinted 1986

Set in Linotron Baskerville by
Rowland Phototypesetting Ltd
Bury St Edmunds, Suffolk
Made and printed in Great Britain by
St Edmundsbury Press
Bury St Edmunds, Suffolk

They bear, in place of classic names,
   letters and numbers on their skin.
They play their grisly blindfold games
   In little boxes made of tin.

RUDYARD KIPLING

And time is a froth of such transparency
His drowning eyes see what they wish to see
A girl laying his table with a white cloth.

ALUN LEWIS

CONTENTS

Preface   11

PART I

Dreams of Bengal   15
Indian-Breds   26
A Stitching of Track   32
A Survivor   40
Gardens of Eden   47
Landscapes Into Art   50
Bengal Lancer   58
Strangers' Child   68

PART II

First and Last Gods   75
Rectory Life and Stolen Silver   84
The Worsley Summer   96
Housemasters and Others   103
Success, My Dears   113
Crusoe   131
Oxford   142

PART III

JW51B   161
East Coast Routines   201
Second Front   232

PART IV

Occupying Germany   255
A Bad Man   264
The Pied Piper   278
Demob Suit and Bell-Bottoms   287

POSTSCRIPT   301

PREFACE

These pages are only incidentally an autobiography; more accurately, they represent the raw material out of which I began to write poetry. They begin in Bengal and end in Germany in 1946, when I was 24.

War, India, cricket: these were my first subjects as a writer and they remain the preoccupations of this book. In due course, the playing of games was replaced by writing about them, and it was to the belief that the best characteristics of each derive from the same source that I nailed my colours. The searching for 'suitable similes', in Marianne Moore's phrase, from her elegy to Pierre Etchebaster – the Real Tennis champion – whether for Hammond's off-drive, Stanley Matthews' mesmeric dribbling, or a racehorse's action, was as good a way as I could imagine of relating techniques to aesthetics.

Before the 1914-18 war the Futurists and Vorticists evolved a style of painting that reflected their delight in machines and machinery – aeroplanes, ships, trains, factories. If I could achieve, to similar effect and in a similarly contemporary idiom, poems that used the playing of games as their subject-matter, then that, I felt, would be enough of an antidote to war to be going on with.

Perhaps, as much as anything, writing this book has been an attempt to reconcile differing definitions of style and to trace the manner in which a single-minded devotion to sport developed into a passion for poetry.

A.R.

PART I

Dreams of Bengal

ABOVE MY DESK, two views of Calcutta, dated 1798; four years after the Daniells, uncle and nephew, had left India. Entitled 'Garden Reach' and 'Hooghly' they show a similar sweep of river, that elbow of the Hooghly before it glides between the Botanical Gardens, with its Great Banyan Tree, and Kidderpore Docks. Soon it will straighten out past Fort William and the Racecourse, Eden Gardens and Strand Road. On the north bank the Grand Trunk Road, parallel to the river, leads out, behind Howrah station, to Belur Math, many-domed headquarters of the Ramakrishna Mission founded in 1897 by Vivekananda and so designed to resemble from different angles a church, a mosque and a temple. Not far off, at Chitpur, is the house where Tagore was born and where, in 1941, five years after the last of my childhood ties with India had been dissolved, he died.

What the engravings show are expanses of water under scattered cloud. Boats drift under lateen sails or are laboriously poled to new fishing areas. Lawns slope to the river edge. At intervals steep, narrow steps run down to bathing *ghats*. Landing stages glint behind clusters of bamboo and mango. Spindly mop-like palms shade the infrequent domed buildings, outposts of an invisible city. Between the huge sky and the wide waterway the land seems barely to have broken surface.

This same scene appears more elaborately in View of Calcutta from the Garden Reach, in the Daniells' *A Picturesque Voyage to India*. The river jostles with sailing vessels and small craft and in the distance the sky-line of Calcutta suggests Venice. The Garden Reach of East India Company princelings set its mansions to catch the breeze coming off the Hooghly, some far scent of the sea lost in its muddiness.

Thomas Daniell's drawings, particularly those of excavations, give India an Italian look. Doomar Leyna, or the ruins at Rameswara, might be Pompeii, the Esplanade in Calcutta, Naples. The illusion derives from architecture divorced from climate.

The Calcutta that emerges from the engravings of late eighteenth-century travellers is white and stately, a far cry from Kipling's 'City of Dreadful Night'. That is how I remembered it, too, sheltered from its *bustees* and bustle. It does not matter how often I have experienced it to the contrary, I have only to look at a map of the skull-shaped city – the Hooghly running from temple to upper lip – for it to detach itself into a series of frozen images bereft of people: the Victoria Memorial; the Kalighat temple; South Park Street cemetery; the Ochterlony Monument; Dalhousie Square; the High Court; the Jain Temple; the Nakhoda Mosque; the Marble Palace. These are the conventional 'sights' of Calcutta but they were nevertheless also the spoils of childish photographic expeditions that, so soon separated from the originals, were my only sources of comfort. They were 'picturesque' views, just as the Daniells called their journeys 'picturesque' – chosen for their suitability as subjects for pictures. From the ages of seven to twenty they had to stand in for me as icons.

The eyes open to the eyes of an ayah, lifting a mosquito net, become bridal. From downstairs the ebb and flow of talk as doors open, shut. Clink of glasses, smell of cigars. In a shaft of light beyond the bed a woman raises her dress to pee: silk stockings, band of bare flesh, dark triangle of hair. She gets up, pulls the plug, and before lowering the dress, a pale almost transparent green silk, examines herself in a mirror, turning this way and that, flattening her abdomen. Later I see her often, a friend of the family, but am conscious only of that moist delta, an image incongruously revived by any map of the Hooghly estuary.

The Sundarbans, where during monsoon tributaries of the Ganges and the Brahmaputra flood the estuaries between

Calcutta and the sea, are haunts of the white tiger. On Sagar Island the Hooghly is fifteen miles wide and there, picnicking during the Daniell's visit, the heir to Sir Hector Munro was hauled headfirst into the jungle by a tiger. The Hooghly river-pilots whom I knew as a child used to report on the number of tigers seen swimming between the islands. It was one of these pilots, Lew Borrett, who used to sing 'Leaning' in his tenor voice when home on leave and staying with us in Cornwall. He was burly and good-natured, with black gleaming hair worn *en brosse*. There never was such a romantic-looking woman as his wife Anna. Years later, on my return to India for a holiday from school, I met her again on board ship; she had left her husband, married an Indian school teacher, thin, bespectacled, timid, and lived the genteel occluded life of those in her situation. I was travelling first-class; she was now in steerage, a nominal Indian. I could not bear it. Lew took to the bottle and picked up with a pretty Eurasian secretary who looked like Merle Oberon, herself a product of Eurasian Calcutta. Lew took me out from school in Falmouth, where I had been sent at the age of seven.

Childhood addresses: 7/1 Burdwan Road, 11 Camac Street, 22 Lee Road, 226 Lower Circular Road. It was in the last of these streets, in the Presidency General Hospital (now S. S. Karnani Hospital) that Surgeon-major Ronald Ross in 1898 developed the cure for malaria. A plaque records the fact, but not that Mohamed Bux, Ross's servant, was sent out to catch mosquitoes in order that they could bite him. Ross was a good name to have in Calcutta.

These houses have merged in my mind into one house: a two-storied, porticoed building of grey stone, its wide verandah opening on to a neat lawn. There is a short sweep of drive, a compound to one side. An iron gate bars the entrance to the drive; beside it a hut for the doorman is festooned by some kind of creeper.

When my Indian childhood came to an end and I was sent to England – the first step in an alienation from all family life – it was for this composite house that I mourned. The bearers with whom secret alliances were joined against parental instructions, their lips stained with pan and betel as if they were bleeding; the mali alongside whom I would squat while he watered and weeded; the various drivers and kitmagars with whom I played cards on the verandah while increasing numbers of dependants would peer out from the compound. The authorized staff, including cooks and sweepers, amounted to about ten, their duties strictly delineated according to rank and caste. Trade Union members today have nothing on Indian domestic servants. In addition, platoons of relatives lurked in the shadows, swelling in numbers until the food bills grew out of all proportion. The servants' food always smelt more interesting than our own, and the nasal whine of Bengali popular songs never stopped. Every so often my mother would remonstrate and for a few weeks there would be a reduction in intake. Then, after a decent interval, they would drift back.

Sometimes curious antipathies and hostility would develop between various servants, presumably because of family encroachments or unfair shares of the spoils. Bearers would glide about with stony faces, doing the least they could get away with, or go unaccountably missing. Even the games with me would be reluctantly played. Then, without explanation, everything would be sweetness and light again. There was nothing to be done during these periods of tension: questioning resulted only in withdrawal. No one knew anything: heads would just be wagged from side to side in the familiar gesture.

It was this shifting, shiftless surrogate family whose loss I found most hard to bear in England. They appeared nightly among the squawks of mynahs and the flapping of crows. Their bare feet trod dry mango leaves and the sound of doves was drowned by the mali's mower. Calcutta came to me as a series of glints: glint of eyes and of hair and of saris, of cycles and rickshaws, of cinema hoardings and punkahs, and always of the Hooghly. There was no heat or oppressiveness in these Bengal images. Discomfort had no part in that interior cinema whose colours were fusions of brown and green, the brown of bodies and water and earth, the green of palm trees and lawns, of the racecourse and Eden Gardens cricket ground, and the swarming maidan that contained both. Between now and then a thick glass pane muffles the misery. At the time it cracked and the splinters were embedded around my lungs.

I had a childhood in India and a brief period of adolescence there. What I left behind I came to understand less and less, but all the more to need. The childhood is real though scarcely remembered, as if memory itself was blindfolded. All the sounds of those years, jackals and pi-dogs howling into the dawn, the whistle of long distance trains and shunt of engines at Howrah, the sirens of Hooghly steamers and tinkle of rickshaw bells, were melancholy, intimations of departures I had no part in. Through those boarding-school years what was most loved and familiar was oceans away, though it was the brown hands that I craved, and not the alternately distant and crowding affection of parents.

Calcutta began, for all practical purposes, in 1690 with Job Charnock moving up the Hooghly in monsoon rain. It was his tomb, squat octagonal mausoleum among the dusty scrub of St John's Churchyard behind Dalhousie Square, that became the most visited site of that adolescent season. It was only a short distance from my father's office in Bankshall Street and if I was early I would hang about in the churchyard looking at tombstones before going to meet him after work. To anyone born in Calcutta Charnock must figure as the archetypal romantic hero. Not only was he responsible for the founding of their city, but at Patria, in 1663, he performed an act of wonderfully spontaneous chivalry. Having gone out of mild curiosity to watch a young Hindoo widow commit suttee on her husband's funeral pyre, he was so taken by her beauty that he snatched her from the flames and later married her. The marriage was a supremely happy one. Charnock's mausoleum was built by Charles Eyre, later Governor of the Bay of Bengal, who married one of Charnock's four daughters in the first-ever recorded English wedding in Calcutta.

Desmond Doig in his Calcutta sketch-book imagines Charnock's arrival: 'a monsoon day, grey river, grey sky, and a small armada of sailing ships battling up the Hooghly. I fancy tigers watching from the dank jungle on the river banks, crocodiles fatly scurrying as the ships' boats pulled for shore. A lumbering take-off of adjutant cranes . . .'

The familiar image of Charnock, derived largely from the unfriendly and disapproving accounts of Captain Alexander Hamilton, author of *A New Account of the East Indies*, has him holding court under a large neem tree. He wears loose shirt and pyjamas, puffs at a large ornamental hookah, and sips arrack.

Hamilton, captain of a ship frequently in and out of Calcutta, disapproved of most things going on round the banks of the Hooghly; the unhealthy site, chosen simply because Charnock took a fancy to 'a large shady tree'; the greedy merchants and their lewd wives; the debauched Dutch and their seminary for prostitutes at Barnagul; the despotic methods of Charnock himself who, according to Hamilton, had natives whipped near his dining room so he could hear their cries.

Even accounting for Hamilton's puritanical dislike, there is nevertheless something disconcerting about Charnock, as if there were two of him. On the one hand the ruthless trader exhausted by work, subject to fevers, a merchant chieftain reclining at dusk while go-betweens and supplicants attended on him; on the other the noble savage, the patriarch, living, as a contemporary report stated, 'in a wild and unsettled condition at Chuttanuty, neither fortified houses, nor gardens, only tents, huts and boats. Thieves and wild animals roam the area at night.' The hard-headed administrator and the unconventional visionary appear to have been occupying the same skin.

Charnock, on one of his earlier spells on Company duty in Bengal, was flogged by local Muslims with whom he had got into dispute. Not surprisingly, when he returned for his third visit at the request of the Emperor Aurangzeb's Viceroy,

Nawab Ibrahim Khan, Charnock demanded favourable trading terms and personal guarantees, which he got. He had already been made Governor of the Bay of Bengal in 1686, but illness and continuous Muslim hostility had eventually driven him out.

Charnock – why is there no great Life of him? – died in 1692, aged 62. He was buried one night 'by the glare of a procession of fiery torches'. The settlement he founded, that was to become the great city of Calcutta, had only been going two years. Whatever he was, he epitomized for me the hero as both survivor and outcast leader and dreamer.

Bengal

Against the betel-stained violence
The senseless murders that appal
The oppression of words and climate
That breathe Bengal

You must set the softness of heart,
A querulous literacy,
And the old ox-eyed gentleness
That rips them apart.

Indian Childhood

The house, whose wings glowed white in heat,
Had shutters through whose slits the striped
And ochre river silvered into fields of wheat.
The mud flats and the natives gave a look
Of coiled repression and of power
That always stuck – a legend in a book.

Time sifted the images, yet upsetting things,
Like falling fortunes, lingered to remind
– A chance remark, a suicide,
A door one dared not look behind –
Reappearing in sleep, a false world
With dreams mysterious and deep.

But they no longer mattered or disturbed.
What occurred in the billiard room,
The nursery at night, or at the river's edge,
Were sooner or later, by experience, curbed,
Though the most serious repression
Was glossed over and remained unheard.

A Grandmother in Calcutta

It was always afternoon
When we went there, everything in shade,
The palms like splayed umbrellas, the frayed
Banana leaves the same colour
As the bead curtains rattling on the verandah,
My grandmother rocking back and forth.

Huge and handsome, she seemed
Physically as rooted as indeed she was
By birth and tradition, growing
Out of the floorboards like a vast lettuce
Gone to seed, but entirely there
In her frail finery, about her a kind of glowing

Nostalgia that bred images
Of eminence, in which she washed us
As if they were a stream still flowing
– French planters of indigo, Irish colonels dead early
Of drink or dysentery, East Indiamen, judges,
Directors of jute mills, surgeons, burly

Impresarios of the railway, moustaches
Venomous but with a family stutter.
Now at last they had run out, too many
Killed too young, and what flowed
Or flowered were the stains and gashes,
Dry rot in the floorboards where Granny

Pat rocked under the insults of mynahs,
One loopy daughter puffing from a green holder,
Banging out preludes on a tinny piano,
The other, a saint in her way, never back
From tending the backward, and always the smell
Of bananas and cigarettes, poverty growing bolder.

South of Madras

At Mahabalipuram
There is only the temple
A dead cobra draped on the rocks like a belt
The man having his hair cut
Three women in saris.

The beach runs for ever,
Salt spraying the pagodas,
The lion, the bull and the elephant
Halted in their tracks,
And the stone chariots hub-deep in sand.
The Pallava empire ended here,
Where Durga and the buffalo wrestled
And the hoofmarks of a horse
Cantering along wet sand contract
And expand like the valves of a heart.

The Swimmer, Udaipur

Daily at noon the solitary swimmer
Measures his distance to Jag Nivas,
Island of parrots and palace ruins.
His oiled topknot slits the lake
Like a periscope or bird's crest.
Blurred eyelids dissolve to houseboats,
Open to hills and smoke-gold temples,
And on the way back the reverse.
This obsessive curving of one arm
After the other through brown water
Is an act of love and penance.
Pink saris are music to him.
He wades out past masseurs and dhobis
Reducing flesh and cloth to essentials,
Waste like colour seeping from linen . . .
At dusk, sometimes, sadness like smoke
Or mist veils the islands, there is the sound
Of sitars, voices that fall or wail.

Yogis at Chowpatty Beach

Only their heads are visible
As if decapitated, or on cocktail sticks,
Bodies in coffins of sand, beards floating.
It is a way of detachment. Bhelpuri stalls,
Their awnings striping the beach
Like bathing huts, do not disturb them.
They are immune to the smells of spices.

The ocean is bronze, the horses
And cows plodding its edge, black.
Tonight, sunset has silenced politics,
There are no speakers
In the shadow of Tilak, stone orator,
No cries of corruption, fist-shakings.

24

Instead, the dynamic of silence,
Vertical yellow disposed
By saddhus. On Tilak
Marigold wreaths are bruised to saffron.
And, hoisting their dhotis,
Clerks open umbrellas as insurance,
Wading to a backcloth of dhows,
The Arabian sea under surveillance.

In Cochin

On the verandah, at the water's edge,

A dark man in a white suit,
Pink gin, and an airmail *Times*

Or a white man in a dark suit
Reading the *Cochin Gazette*,

Depending on the day or the light.

He is without identity,
A fingerprint on a door, or shape in a cane chair

Like myself, watching the fishing nets
Strain sunset through mesh claws.

The cemetery is full of our ancestors.
On a torn cloth we play snooker,

The marker a connoisseur of potholes.

White Jews came here, and Vasco da Gama.
The canals swell with suicides.

Brides of empire, of Malabar.

25

Indian-Breds

MY FATHER HAD LITTLE INTEREST in the founding merchants of Calcutta. He knew and had to deal with Portuguese and Dutch, Armenians and French, many of whom descended from families who had preceded the British. At one time or another the British had quarrelled and fought with all of them. During my childhood, when the British seemed only dimly aware that their own era was closing, the part played by other Europeans in India was negligible. My mother's great grandfather, Edward Budd, captain of an East India merchantman, had married an Armenian Begum, and through her acquired vast indigo estates in Nepal. When synthetic drugs were discovered these estates, which took three days to cross on horseback and whose revenues were sent away in bullock carts guarded by Gurkha mercenaries, became virtually valueless. The Armenian connection in my family was not regarded as something to boast about. The subsequent history of my mother's family was one of general extravagance and decline: extravagance in good living, Afghan horse-dealing, and women: decline through early deaths hastened by climate and drink. My maternal grandfather, Captain Patrick Fitzpatrick, a surgeon in the Indian Army, died in his thirties, leaving five children, four of them girls. His brother James, an Inspector of Police, strikingly handsome and a brilliant Indian linguist, was the model for Kipling's character Strickland.

My grandmother lived at No. 1 Pretoria Street, a central but dilapidated lane that had a country air. Its surface was unmade-up and cows lay around in the shade of banana trees. One of her brothers had married a Burmese woman, had disappeared off to Rangoon and was never heard of again. I remember my grandmother as being hugely rooted in shuttered rooms, the house, itself in the shade of a huge tree, in permanent twilight. My aunt Freda chain-smoked from a green cigarette holder, banging incessantly on a tinny piano; the other sister, Beryl, taught in a convent. There was no money to spare, few visible servants. The house smelt of damp and bananas. Vere, my mother's only brother, was thin, febrile, wild, a dashing horseman. He stammered, like most Fitzpatricks, made and lost large sums of money in America and the Caribbean, and died in Calcutta, after a bad motor accident, impoverished.

During my holiday visit to India in 1936 it was racing that brought my father and I closest together. Although my father was little interested in breeding, or indeed in Indian history, there were those among his friends who knew Indian affairs and their inter-relationship with the development of racing in India. Sometimes at night on the verandah, cards being shuffled under the punkahs, cigar smoke drifting into the garden, I would get history lessons *in situ*, learning about the Mysore and Mahratta wars, about Dupleix's vision of a French Empire in India, about Hyder Ali and Tippoo Sultan, about Clive and Warren Hastings, Scarcely had the noise of battle from the Mahratta wars died away and Tippoo Sultan been laid to rest at Seringapatam than racing started up formally in Calcutta. The first actual report of a race in Calcutta is in 1769, thirty years before the death of Tippoo. The horses were either Arabs or Capes, and they had to race two miles, sometimes three. Akra Farm, beyond Garden Reach, was where the first races were held. The Nabobs could, if they wished, sail to the course in their own budgerows, boarding from their garden jetties and being rowed by their own crews in gleaming livery.

W. G. C. Frith in his history of the Royal Calcutta Turf Club describes the late 1920s as the most prosperous period the club had ever known. My father had yet to graduate to the owner-ship of horses, but his cronies used to talk about legendary racecourse figures like 'Owl' Marshall, owner of Kipling who won the Indian Grand National twice, and Captain 'Rattle' Barrett, the polo player, who rode it. I can still remember the names of the famous horses of the time, Orange William and Star of Italy, Nightjar and Roubaix. The racecards sold in Clive Street, of which I collected copies, listed such exotic-sounding owners as the Kour Sahib of Patiala, H. H. General Nawab-zada Obaidulla Khan, the Aga Khan, the Maharajah of Cooch Behar, the Maharajah Scindia of Gwalior, Nawabzada Yemin-ul-Mulk of Bhopal, the Honourable the Rajah of Ramnad. Among such names, and the wealth they represented, British owners – Army officers, the senior members of leading Calcutta firms, an occasional civil servant – found it hard to compete.

There would be gossip about goings on up-country – in Lahore and Meerut, Dehra Dun and Rawalpindi – about the unsolved Monsoon Cup Day Tote Robbery, when the tin box containing the takings was found on being opened to contain bricks; about 'remounts' and 'Indian-Breds', about the respective merits of the jockeys, Huxley, Bullock, Dobie, Sibbritt, and the importation of Australian horses.

In my mind the bearers still glide round in their navy blue monogrammed puggrees and cummerbunds dispensing burra pegs, the dogs whine in the compound, the old familiar smells of the bazaar and the river drift across the lawn. The voices rise and fall, some of them with the softest of Scottish accents. The figures of the trainers, the moustached and check-waistcoated Harper, looking like an old farmer, Jimmy Robinson, with clothes and demeanour of a diplomat, Alec Higgins in his co-respondent shoes, stalked my dreams when I had been removed from them for ever. Race days, the turreted stands gleaming under flags and brilliant with saris, were the high point of the week, the start of the week-end ritual for my father that continued with dinner at Firpo's, golf the next morning and curry lunch at Tollygunge, siesta and finally a visit to see the latest film at the Empire. It was a ritual that never changed.

But when I look now at photographs of the Turf Club with its Palladian entrance and colonnaded verandahs, I am back driving before breakfast on days when there was no racing up Theatre Road and across Chowringhee into Queen's Way, the maidan on one side and the Victoria Memorial on the other. Except for the white of the stands on the far side of the course there is nothing between us and the Hooghly but grass and trees. The greenness catches at the throat. Beyond the clubhouse a circular road leads past the docks out to Garden Reach; to the right, marked by the spires of St Peter's Church, lies Fort William. Ringed by trees Eden Gardens cricket ground links Outram Ghat and Baboo Ghat, Government House and the High Court faintly discernible in the distance. Once the mist has cleared off the maidan, Calcutta at exercise and at its ablutions, meditating and manoeuvring, is laid bare. Hooves thud, troops and police drill, holy men pray, whole families sluice themselves at stand-pipes or in fountains or on the steps of Prinsep Ghat. Later, goats will be herded between games of cricket and round political meetings. During all this activity, carried on from dawn till dusk, the racecourse itself remains silent, a shuttered stage whose drama is being rehearsed out of sight. Whenever now I drive past an empty racecourse I am transported back to those childhood mornings in Calcutta. Nothing has ever smelled fresher or promised more in retrospect.

Shaw, Wallace, my father's firm, owned numerous coal mines in northern and western Bengal and often my father, who was responsible for them, would be absent on tours of inspection. Sometimes he took me with him, usually to Asansol, where we would stay with the manager. Mining towns, apart from the pits themselves and the workers' quarters, consisted of a club house, a handful of bungalows with neat gardens, and a single street containing shops, offices, a bank and a market. Coal dust lay everywhere like black talc. Everything had to do with the extraction and transporting of coal. Although Asansol, on the junction of the Grand Trunk Road and the Bengal-Nagpur coalfields line, is only 130 miles from Calcutta, the journey by road or rail took many hours, so that the people working there lived an outpost life, as far removed from that of Calcutta as imaginable. Going there seemed a great adventure. Since then Asansol, through the damming of the Damodar river, has developed into a great iron and steel centre.

These journeys north, my father, myself and bearer, were my first taste of adult masculine society. I had, *en famille*, travelled often from Calcutta to Bombay by rail to board ship. My sisters were at school in France and every two years, until I myself left India to go to school, I would be taken 'home'. These 'business' trips were another matter, preliminary sorties into the world of affairs where serious issues were debated and women were not admitted. Lost under my solar topi I felt it sufficient simply to be present when prices, wages and equipment were discussed and coolies scuttled between shunting freight cars.

There was one other journey that I made regularly in those days, and that was to Kurseong, in the foothills of the Himalayas. There I would be sent to avoid the worst of the hot weather, either alone with my ayah, or with my mother. I have never been back there, but photographs suggest a place of woodsmoke and bells, everything on a steep slant, with ponies stumbling towards the skyline or down to the valley. Kanchenjunga was that jagged peak among so many others on the icy wall that shut India in, and which even rickshaws could not scale.

The sweet Himalayan air must have been wonderful after the humidity of Calcutta. My breath in photographs forms transparent balloons against the dark hillsides, the women curved over the tea plants like waves about to break. The one image in all Indian life that stands for the others is that row of saris – cerise, turquoise, orange – embedded in green; whether it is imposed on the memory or real, it carries over from childhood as if it had been tattooed.

Is it memory, or what one has since read or been told, that restores the red-and-blue striped Buddhist monastery on the way back from Tiger Hill, the tiny mountain railway station at Ghoom, the leeches that seemed to stick everywhere in damp weather, the waterfalls and streams pouring through forest clearings as we chug our way, pulled along by the B-class 0-4-0 engine, up from Siliguri?

Where did we stay, my mother and I, on those flights from the heat on to the very edge of the world? *Murray's Guide* only owns to a Rest House and a Dak bungalow, but there must have been hotels, surely. I do not remember my father ever accompanying us nor how long we stayed, but the preparations for the journey, the picnics, the excitement of changing trains on to the narrow gauge tracks, seem real to me.

Darjeeling, although a few miles to the north, is nearly 1000 feet lower than Ghoom, but on the last lap of the journey, the toy-like train chasing its own tail at walking pace, children jump on to the running boards for free rides. For years afterwards I was surrounded by the clutter bought in the bazaars of Kurseong and Darjeeling – a fur cap, carved boxes, gongs, swords. There is a photograph of me holding the hand of one of our bearers while behind us, grouped like a football team in full climbing regalia, stand Tibetans, Lepchas, Nepalese and Bhutias. In another one women porters, rings in their noses, bangles and necklaces gleaming, hump trunks out of the carriage into the pony and trap in which, curiously Tibetan looking, I am already installed.

'The roof of the world'; 'the land of the white orchid' – you come upon these phrases in geography books, and later, at school in England, they would bring me near to tears. For the white orchids in those months were all around us, I would be woken to watch the sun spill over Kanchenjunga, we could hear tigers stalking the undergrowth of the forests of Cooch Behar. Sikkim; Lhasa; the returning travellers and traders from such places were the ordinary passers-by of our daily pony rides, and I had only to bring the teak objects out of my desk to summon them up.

A Stitching of Track

THE RAILWAYS and railway stations of India; one did not need to know Kipling to feel their romance, though Kipling defined it more than anyone. 'The railway', Paul Theroux wrote in his foreword to *Railways of the Raj*, 'was the imperial vision on a grand scale . . . India was the proving ground for the Victorian imagination: the railway builders sewed together the entire sub-continent with a stitching of track.'

They certainly did that, but in the 1920s the police and the railways were a step down from the ICS, the Army, and big business, though most families with real ramifications over a period of time in India were likely to be involved with both. Fitzpatricks – my mother's family – were mainly Army surgeons, though also Police inspectors and Railway impresarios at the same time as a Fitzpatrick was Governor of the Punjab. Rosses of one kind or another were surgeons, military architects, soldiers, tea-planters, bankers, administrators. Their inter-marriages, some with Indians (like those of the Gardner, of Gardner's Horse, and Skinner, of Skinner's Horse, families) are impossible to unravel. But if socially those who worked in railways for the most part inhabited a world separate from the 'society' of the big cities – isolated as much by circumstance as by rank – they saw a lot more of India. The 'iron horse' had pushed its nose into every corner of India by the time I made the first of a dozen subsequent crossings; what had once been pioneering had become commonplace.

To a child sent home to England the railways provided the last indelible glimpse, stored in the most private recesses of the heart, of the landscapes of innocence – where the words 'friend' and 'servant' were interchangeable, where sadness was simply separation, and it was unthinkable that the brown arms that had always meant security should ever be absent. 'Growing up' was something that took place in England; in India time stood still. Elizabeth Hardwick observed in her book *Sleepless Nights* 'The stain of place hangs on not as a birthright but as a sort of artifice, a bit of cosmetic . . . it is not true that it doesn't matter where you live, that you are . . . merely yourself. Also it is not true that all are linked naturally to their regions. Many are flung down carelessly at birth and they experience the diminishment, and sometimes the pleasant truculence of their random misplacement.'

There was diminishment but no truculence in that last journey almost due west – Midnapore, Jamshedpur, the long night rattling and winding through West Bengal, Bihar, Orissa, dawn over the dusty plains of Madhya Pradesh, and then the last dip south past the caves at Ajanta and Ellora to Bombay. Kipling's railway stories are strong on detail and the excitement of travel – the pampered seclusion of first-class, the pandemonium and chaos of Intermediate – but for me on that one-way journey there was no excitement, no exhilaration. The land was drained of its colour, the pounding of the engines did not say 'going home' as they were doing for others but 'going away', 'leaving behind' – leaving behind everything that mattered. The bearer sat out in the corridor, sidling along from time to time to bring *nimbu pani*, make up and turn down beds, lay out meals. That feeling of dread and emptiness, as if one's blood had been watered, returned at regular intervals over the years with no lessening of impact.

The many adult journeys across India, taking in Delhi and Benares, Lucknow and Calcutta and Puri, Bangalore and Ooty, that veered south across Rajasthan and Gujerat, to Cochin, and Trivandrum, revived the excitement and shed the misery. At the end of them there were no familiar old bearers and malis, ayahs and kitmagars, and there was no family house to go to. But this was still what 'coming home' meant in a way far profounder than I had ever realized. At fifteen I had sat opposite my father, an almost total stranger to me, while we travelled from Bombay to Calcutta: Poonia, his bearer, hung

33

up my father's business suit, poured out the whisky, produced shorts and sandals for him. He himself sat cross-legged outside the door, chewing pan. My father read papers, studied reports. So we remained for two days while India pasted itself – plains, rice-fields, banyan trees, bullock carts, clumps of palm and bamboo, parrots, dried-up rivers – onto the windows. At dilapidated, shanty-like stations we would get out and stretch our legs, and my father would smoke a cigar. Water-vendors, men selling rotis, oranges, sweetmeats, passed up and down the platform making their cries. Then, without warning, we would glide off again, through small mud villages, past women in saris bending at their tasks, old men squatting at candle-lit door-ways. That train-magic has not changed and repetition has never dulled the experience.

What I had forgotten was the extravagance of India's railway architecture. Brunel's Italianate Sealdah station in Calcutta, built in 1862, unfortunately no longer exists, but there is scarcely a station in India, down to the most obscure wayside halt, which is not in some way uplifting. The quality of travel may have declined and the buying of a simple ticket turned into a Kafkaesque nightmare, but the stations them-selves, fortresses, palaces, or colonial villas in style, do not disappoint. Platforms and halls gleam under constant polishing, stalls heaped with carnations and roses, mangoes and papayas, sweetmeats and spices, reflected on them as if on water.

Victoria Terminus, Bombay, administrative head office of the old Great India Peninsula Railway, no longer stands in such splendid isolation as it did at the turn of the century, but Stevens's huge Venetian gothic 'cathedral' with Islamic and Saracenic embellishments – domes, towers, gables, spires, arches – seems, as you approach it from Ballard Pier after landing, to float in the haze like something remembered or imagined rather than realized. This was the station from which the dust of India was finally shaken. In contrast, Howrah, barrack-like and dumpy, always seems a place of arrival, frenzied, jammed, initiatory. Long ago the present, single-span cantilevered bridge which you have to cross to enter Calcutta proper, may not have been quite the bottleneck it now is, but it is hard to believe there was ever a time when it was much of an improvement on its predecessor, the old Pontoon Bridge which lasted until the war. This used to open for river traffic and then bullock-carts, taxis, rickshaws, cyclists, buses and coolies piled up on either side in impossible confusion.

The great stations – Islamic, pith-helmeted Lucknow, turreted Lahore, cloistered Madras Central – assumed for the travelling Indian, expecially the poor, the status of secular temples. Their architecture, whether nobly military or civic, was on a scale to catch the imagination in a way Christian buildings could not hope to emulate. They were not only objects of awe, but acted as ante-rooms to reunion, providing shelter as well.

I took to England with me, a farewell present from an admirer of my mother's, a frog-faced tea-taster called Harry, a stack of railway magazines. Inside were pictures of rickety-looking bridges on the Darjeeling line, aqueductal arches over terrifying gorges linking Kalka and Simla, sturdy engines clinging precariously to the cliff-face between Colombo and Kandy, trains like vertical slow-worms on the steep gradients to Poona and Ootacamund. There were photographs of fantastic bridges constructed through jungle, of tracks flooded by monsoons, of workshops looking as intricate as the interior of clocks, of steam railcars and shunting engines, of captured elephants embarking at Mysore and camels with the air of elderly memsahibs waiting to be loaded. The railway map of India – that unrealized dream of Dalhousie to have India linked by lines of only one gauge – was pinned on the inside of my school desk and from it I could make imaginary journeys from Delhi to Amritsar, Cochin to Ooty, Calcutta to Patna and Allahabad. I saw myself lazing in princely saloons as the mail trains hooted through the afternoons or leaning out of toy-like carriages as they wriggled their way into the cool of the hills. In due course I made most of these fancies come true, but even when they must have seemed more remote possibilities than journeys to the moon I knew in my bones that they really lay before me.

Harry was more interested in locomotives than locations, I think, and in my mother more than either. But he knew the railway system backwards. He knew what class locomotives were used on what lines, he'd travelled on the private trains of Maharajahs and was an authority on time-tables. He could imitate the noise of bulb horns and steam trains struggling up steep gradients and he knew all about the 'stink expresses' used to cart away rubbish. The Rail Transport Museum in Delhi and Michael Satow's *Railways of the Raj* could not have taught Harry a thing.

For most Indians the railways are lottery and excitement, frustration and discomfort. They travel them passively, becoming one with the movement, over long hours seeming scarcely to be alive. No wonder, for those who could read, Wheeler's Indian Railway Library, publishers of Kipling's early stories, seemed so enticing, for here were adventures deriving from situations similar to their own. In the lulling hypnotic rhythm, dream and reality were separated by scarcely more than a pane of glass. The characters that sprang from the page and looked out at country much like the one they were passing spoke their own language.

Harry was no reader but an acquirer of arcane information. Tea-tasting is not a career that offers much chance to shine in society, but Harry's railway expertise made him an asset. His present to me meant more than he could ever have imagined.

The Taj Express

Night expresses hooting across India,
The clank and shunt of an empire

Outstaying its welcome. I open eyes
To an ayah's eyes, the shuffle of cards.

Coaldust on my tongue like a wafer,
And in a swaying lavatory a woman's

Knees slanting moonlight at her belly.
The engines hiss and spill.

The Deccan moored to huge mango trees,
Mosquito nets like child brides.

Stations are marble dormitories, fruitstalls
Inset like altars, wax dripping –

An air of the morgue, all these sleepers
Huddled like mailbags without addresses.

Dawn of papaya and fresh lime.

A Wartime Present

A map of India carved,
As it might be a heart, on the back
Of a cigarette case. In uniform pockets
I could trace the shape of Bengal,
Calcutta alive at my fingertips,
The Hooghly through ice. On deck
After dinner, nights mild or atrocious,
I'd inhale childhood – drifts
From the compound of curry and *pan*,
Smells of the racecourse, betel-stains
Like blood in the speech of bearers –
All that remained to set against drowning,
Tall seas turned on their backs
Like doped tigers, allegiances of the exile
Without family, without family feeling.

The boundaries became wrong, ghosts
Of a forfeited unity, but their fading
Disguised it. The rub of materials,
Naval serge, flannel, white duck,
Had worn out the heart, the old essences
Thinned into nothing. And the case,
Lying in a drawer for years, had lost
Its suggestiveness. Only now,
Coming on it suddenly and carrying it
Back to Bengal, do I feel
Under my fingers like braille
The frontiers begin to come true,
The heart beat from the gold. I take
The case from my pocket and here,
In Calcutta, open it to the air,
Hoping that more will adhere
Than the stew of corpses and cowdung –
Something of the old power to evoke
Images that might last out a life.

The Gateway of India

The first addictive smell
And that curiously sated light
In which dhows and islands float
Lining the air with spices.

The beginning and end
Of India, birth and death,
The bay curved as a kukri
And on Malabar Hill the vultures,
Like seedy waiters, scooping the crumbs off corpses.

Rush-hour, Calcutta

'The hour of the cowbells' is what
These sometimes abstemious Bengalis,
Camped in their homeless dusk

Call that delirious moment
When light melts and car-horns mellow,
And we in our whisky culture

Fret in the traffic, smoke
From the jute mills coating the Hooghly,
Faces like pebbles bleaching the maidan.

It is the moment when saris
And soft drinks, sweetmeats and sweet eyes,
Take on the colour of sunset,

Expresses hooting out of Howrah,
Tent-flaps opening like mouths.

A Survivor

FANNY PARKS'S *Wanderings of a Pilgrim in Search of the Picturesque* was published in two volumes in 1850. It bears the sub-title 'Revelations of life in the Zenana'. The numerous sketches are mostly done by herself on the spot and drawn on stone by her husband, Major Parlby. Fanny Parks arrived in Calcutta about the same time as the first of my mother's ancestors, in 1822, exactly a century before I was born there. She was one of that splendid and disparate group of Victorian women travellers in India, the Eden sisters among them, who were surprised by nothing.

'I have seen Bengal,' the proverb runs which she quotes. 'There the teeth are red and the mouth is black.' The red teeth became in my nightmares the blood of my father's bearer, Poonia, who cut his throat soon after I left for England, and whose lips and teeth had always been pan-smeared. Calcutta in 1822 was known as the city of palaces; 'It well deserves the name,' Fanny Parks observes, describing the large gardens, the verandahs, rising from basement to top floor, which give, with their pillars, 'an air of lightness and beauty to the buildings.'

Arriving in November after a five-month voyage, she is at first charmed by the climate. Calcutta, from November to March, has sparkling weather, cloudless and rarely humid. She is struck by her first sight of the native fishermen in their dinghies off Garden Reach. 'In the cold of the early morning they wrap themselves up in folds of linen, and have the appearance of men risen from the dead.' She goes ashore and sets up house in Park Street, off Chowringhee, presumably with her husband, though he gets few mentions in her narrative.

Fanny Parks came to India totally receptive, open to every kind of experience. Within a month she is describing a ball given by the Marquis of Hastings at Government House, scarcely reachable owing to thick fog: present were 'Nawabs, Rajahs, Mahrattas, Greeks, Turks, Mussulmans and Hindoos'. She learns Hindustani and gets given a beautiful Arab horse which she rides on the racecourse at six in the morning, observing the hundreds of adjutant birds stalking the maidan. She comes to terms with the tax system of dustoorie; she sets herself to understand the tasks, characters, religions, styles of dress and habits of all her servants.

By May her idea of the climate is changing. From Calcutta being 'so delightful, it rendered the country preferable to any place under the sun' it has become very oppressive. 'If you go out during the day I can compare it to nothing but the hot blast you would receive in your face, were you suddenly to open the door of an oven.'

Even so commonplace an object as a punkah is seen by her with new eyes, and described in meticulous detail. She begins to realize how enervating the climate becomes, 'I find myself as listless as any Indian lady is universally considered to be.' The bearers do nothing but eat and sleep, her ayah dresses her, 'after which she will go to her house, eat her dinner, and then returning, will sleep in one corner of my room on the floor for the whole day.'

This listlessness of the Indian, often contrasted with the energy of the Europeans, was a constant feature of my own mother's conversation. A mixture of resentment and indifference exaggerated it in the case of servants on whose behaviour most European women based their generalizations. Yet, after a lifetime in India, the same complaining and vigorous Europeans tended to be as debilitated as the servants they harried. My father, after forty years in India, left at a week's notice, suddenly unable to face another monsoon and the lowering effects of amoebic dysentery. Indians, often equally exhausted by the climate, had no such options.

As a child, when my daily rituals were mainly shared with Indians, when I spoke Hindustani better than English, I was aware of that dark region of non-involvement into which the

41

male Indian would withdraw without warning. The affectionate companion turned into a sleepwalker, hardly able to respond, beyond caring. For a child a *volte-face* of this kind was
the more hurtful because it was incomprehensible.

Twice, as a child, I nearly died of the strange fever that comes
without warning in Calcutta and to whose effects the South
Park Street cemetery bears witness. Often, it was said, you had
lunch with a man and buried him before dinner. Major Parlby,
Fanny's husband, was struck down by such a fever their first
July but 'happily he was saved from a premature epitaph'.
Fanny Parks records wryly that she had great trouble with the
servants. Her ayah reported 'It would be a great pity if the
sahib should die, for then – we should all lose our places.'

Fanny Parks's journals, though describing life a hundred
years earlier, fill out my own childhood. Nothing was written of
interest, little curiosity about India or initiative shown, by
women of my mother's generation. Yet these early Victorian
women, with much less ostensible freedom of movement and far
more natural hazards to overcome, showed a zest for the
country I cannot remember among any of my parents' friends.
For these latter India, for no good reason, had ceased to be an
adventure; it was merely the place where they were obliged to
spend their lives. In the eighteenth century and at least the first
half of the nineteenth there was a fair chance that most
Europeans would die in India before they could enjoy their
spoils at home. That was hardly the case in the 1920s.

Few European merchants or officials travelled much in India
outside their line of business, their wives hardly at all, except to
go to the hills. The country – its inhabitants, customs, landscape – was not considered an object of interest. There may
have been reasons for this immobility – economic, social,
domestic – but it contrasts badly with the excitement that
comes off the pages of these Victorian memsahibs, travelling
wherever they could, taking notes, drawing.

On any page of *Wanderings of a Pilgrim* you find the kind of
rapid, intelligent observations that bring a place alive: nautch

girls dancing at a rich Bengalee Baboo's party; the rains; an
outbreak of robberies; a trip on the Ganges; rates of interest and
the high cost of life insurance, resulting in many 'poor miserable invalids unable from their debts to leave India'; the skill
with which clay images of all types of Indian are made in
Calcutta; the first races of the season. Half a dozen brief entries
may cover six months, but a Calcutta season is made to come
alive in the process.

I had a sense, as a child, of caste in India, but none of
religion. Fanny Parks records: 'An European in Calcutta sees
very little of the religious ceremonies of the Hindoos' and that
remained the case. She herself describes such things as the
worship of the *toolsee* with a thoroughness and a sympathy that
would have made her seem eccentric in the eyes of my mother,
for whom all Indian superstitions and devotions were time-
wasting and ridiculous.

'I observe the motion to prevent the necessity of sending their
sons to Haileybury has been lost,' Fanny Parks writes. 'The
grand object of the students should be the acquisition of the
oriental languages, here nothing else tells.'

The smoking of hookahs; the death of Lord Byron 'the other
evening, as we were driving past a Greek chapel on the banks of
the Hooghly, prayers were being offered for the repose of the
soul of the departed'; the dullness of local food in comparison
with the menus in a French 'almanach des gourmands'; water-
parties to the botanical gardens 'my beautiful Arab carries me
delightfully; dove-like, but full of fire'; the impossibility of
making fortunes any longer – these are some of the subjects
during her 1824 journal.

An Indian Civil Servant was required to serve twenty-five
years for his pension, twenty-two of these in India. Mrs Parlby
doesn't think much of that. 'I should like first to know, how
many will be able to serve their full time of bondage? Secondly,
what the life of a man, an annuitant, is worth who has lingered
two and twenty years in a tropical climate.'

Her remarks about money have a familiar ring. 'Provided

there is a good bulky dividend at the end of the year upon India Stock, the holders think the country flourishing in the greatest security.' That sentence could have stood for the whole philosophy by which I was brought up.

Hundreds die daily of cholera and fever in the hot weather. Yet Fanny can write 'We now consider ourselves fairly fixed in Calcutta; the climate agrees with us; and though we hold existence upon a frailer tenure than those in England, we still hope to see many happy years . . . Furlough and the pension must make amends.'

Whomever one reads about European life in Calcutta the sentiment remains the same: there is a season in hell, and a season 'in which we live, and breathe, and have our being'. Bishop Heber, after preaching twice in a day, is found dead in his bath, presumed to have suffered apoplexy.

In Calcutta, Fanny observes, 'we do not die of the blue devils, *ennui*, or from want of medical attendance, as those do who are far removed.'

Unexpectedly, the Parlbys are posted to Allahabad, but not before Fanny can report 'Killed a scorpion in my bathing-room, a good fat old fellow; prepared him with arsenical soap, and added him to the collection of curiosities in my museum.' Soon they are settling their furniture and their horses, sending their heavy baggage up-river, and themselves setting off on the Grand Military Road, first on horseback, then by buggy.

The Parlbys spent much of the next ten years in Allahabad and Cawnpore. When Fanny in 1836 takes a river trip back to Calcutta she cannot restrain her pleasure at her first sight of an English vessel for a decade. The variety of Hooghly shipping enchants her. 'The fine merchant-ships, the gay, well-trimmed American vessels, the grotesque forms of the Arab ships, the Chinese vessels with an eye on each side of the bows to enable the vessel to see her way across the deep waters, the native vessels in all their fanciful and picturesque forms, the pleasure boats of private gentlemen, the beautiful private residences

44

in Chowringhee, the Government-house, the crowds of people . . .'

The Calcutta fogs seem much in evidence, 'a deep, white, thick fog, so usual in the early morning in Calcutta'. At the races the horse winning the Auckland Cup – designed by Emily Eden, sister of the Governor General – dies as it passes the winning post; guests dining in Alipur two miles away take two hours over the journey because of the poor visibility; Fanny is too ill to attend a ball given to the Eden sisters.

Fanny returns to Allahabad by steamer, normally a journey of 800 miles by river, but because of low waters they have to go via the Sundarbans, an extra 300 miles through 'short thick jungle and dwarf trees . . . an assemblage of islands, the tides flowing between them . . . A more solitary desolate tract I never beheld.'

They pass a spot where an oar is stuck up on end, the sign that a native had been carried off there by a tiger, a frequent occurrence among the woodcutters.

It is eight years before Fanny sets foot in Calcutta again, having returned home ill meanwhile, travelled in Europe and rejoined her husband, invalided from India, in Cape Town. She arrives off Baboo Ghat, Calcutta, after a long voyage from the Cape on 1 April, 1844. Cholera and smallpox are raging, but the mango-fish, smoked for breakfast, is perfection.

Soon she is on her way again up-river to Allahabad, for her last spell in India. Calcutta she sees only once more, on her way home. Twenty-four years separate the first and last entries in her book.

Fanny Parks was a survivor, a natural traveller only happy on the move. Baudelaire in a famous poem observes that the real traveller sets out from the need to travel, without specific ends in view. She is of their number. There is scarcely an entry in the two volumes of her diaries – nearly 1000 pages – which does not, by its show of natural curiosity, candour and desire to be informed, interest the modern reader. She rarely writes about herself, except in the detached fashion in which a nurse

45

might record the humours, fevers, or well-being of a patient. There is precious little gossip of the social kind. She would, in consequence, have made no mark in Calcutta society of the 1920s, with its ignorance of and disinterest in almost everything to do with Indian history, religion, architecture, art. Such a lack of involvement would not have offended Fanny Parks but she would have taken note of it.

Gardens of Eden

INDIANS ARE CRAZY about cricket but the passion I developed for it dated from my arrival in England. Rugby and golf were my father's games; and cricket, I think, he only came to like through me. In any case I was too small to hold a bat when my childhood in India came to an end. It was only many years later, when I began my biography of Ranjitsinhji, that India and cricket came together for me. Nevertheless, I had been to Eden Gardens, where the Calcutta Cricket Club had been founded in 1792, and where Test Matches are still played within sound of the Hooghly. The ball swings there because of the moisture almost as much as at Hove, a rare occurrence in India. Almost exactly a hundred years after cricket was first played by garrison soldiers in Calcutta, Ranjitsinhji, an Indian prince, made 154 not out for England against the Australians at Manchester in his first Test match. The cricket connection he established with Sussex continued through his equally graceful and talented nephew Duleepsinhji, captain of Sussex when I first went to live there.

Eden Gardens, only separated from the racecourse by the star-shaped enclosure of Fort William, is now the second largest Test ground in the world, holding 80,000. During my childhood India was slowly working her way towards Test status. The winter after I left for my first school in England – 1930–31 – was scheduled for the first official Test Match involving India. Ironically the tour coincided with a particularly vocal wave of nationalist feeling and was postponed. In 1932, a year before Ranji's death, India played her first Test Match at Lord's, under C. K. Nayudu. Duleepsinhji, by now seriously ill with tuberculosis, was ending a brilliant career with Sussex and England. The Indian stars of those days, some of whom I saw at Eden Gardens, were the burly, crinkly-haired Mohamed

Nissar, the fastest and strongest bowler India has produced, the tireless and accurate Amar Singh, the great opening pair of Vijay Merchant and Mushtaq Ali, and the dashing all-rounder Amarnath. On 5 January 1934, the first ever Test was played in Calcutta, a draw, England having already won in Bombay.

Considering the problems of caste and religion it's amazing that India produced a national side at all. Yet before the Great War Europeans, Parsees, Hindoos and Mohammedans had all fielded individual teams in an All-India tournament. Subsequently Christians and Jews combined and a new championship competition was started called the Pentangular.

India's captains in the early days tended to be Maharajahs of greater wealth and girth than ability. In 1911 the Maharajah of Patiala, a Sikh who sported a diamond earring, financed a side to travel to England. The Maharajah of Porbandar was India's official captain on the tour of 1932, but, unlike the Maharajkumar of Vizianagram four years later, sensibly stood down for the Tests.

Some fine English players came to Eden Gardens in the 1930s: D. R. Jardine, Charles Barnett, Cyril Walters, Hedley Verity, James Langridge, Brian Valentine among them. I missed them there, and though I later watched Test cricket in Australia, South Africa and the West Indies, I never had the chance of doing so in India. In England, though, I would always identify with India.

When I used to be taken to Eden Gardens it was still essentially the home of Calcutta Cricket Club, a lush domestic circle squeezed out of the maidan, not the immense concrete stadium it has since become. The sound of bat on ball came through against river noises, sirens, cranes, hooters. Masts moved on the horizon, the sails of dhows flapped, funnels puffed black smoke against the drained sky. At dusk, when the cricket was over, we would drive back to Alipur along Strand Road, the river to our right. Beyond Fort William we would cut in past the entrance to the racecourse, crossing Tolly's Nala by the zoological gardens and entering the calm of Alipur by way of

Belvedere House and the spot where Warren Hastings and Philip Francis fought their duel in 1780. This was an altogether more rural and peaceful Calcutta, bullock carts trundling back to the country, tall palms hardening against saffron sky, house after house, beyond its sweep of drive and *porte-cochère*, its lawns and lit verandahs, preparing for dinner. Thus a day that began in the compound with the kitmagar bowling, the cook and mali fielding, would end with me clutching the score-card from Eden Gardens. Some of the famous players then on view, both Indian and English, I would play against myself in odd matches during the war, and a few were still around when I began to write about cricket in 1950.

The Indians, when they came to England, often seemed fragile in the face of fast bowling and in the earlier days their fielding was often shocking. Their best players, nevertheless, had a lovely grace and ease of movement. C. K. Nayudu, Merchant, Mushtaq Ali, Mankad, Manjrekar, Hazare were beautiful, wristy strikers of the ball. But it was soon apparent that not all Indian cricketers, contrary to one's imagination, were the embodiment of grace and elegance. They ranged from the portly to the bony, from the tall to the squat, their differences in physique even greater than in any English team.

Years later, looking through Company drawings in the India Office Library, I came across two pictures of washermen at Murshidabad, done in the 1780s. Although they are holding damp clothes in their hands, not bats, their postures and the position of their feet and arms are those for batsmen at the finish of classic strokes; the cover drive and offside hit off the back foot. Both wear white turbans, one has on a pair of drawers, the other a kind of tunic and dhoti. A river runs behind the figures and temples can be glimpsed through palm trees on the horizon. No coaching manual could better illustrate two basic cricket strokes.

49

Landscapes into Art

My PARENTS, unfortunately, never bought either Indian paintings or paintings of India, but instead collected the kind of teak and brass objects that litter the villas of old India hands. The 'Company' painters, so-called, were Indians working to commission. They flourished throughout the nineteenth century, those in Calcutta mostly emigrés from the courts of the Moghul Viceroys in Murshidabad. Their main tasks were the recording of flora and fauna, scenery, monuments, varieties of clothing and transport, for employees of the East India Company to take home as mementoes. The camera put an end to their usefulness, but for a century or more, influenced sometimes by the aquatints of such artists as William Hodges, whose 'select views' were published in 1785–88, and commissioned by enlightened patrons like Lady Nugent, wife of a Governor, Indian painters produced versions of Indian life that increasingly made their way to Europe. The fine new buildings of Calcutta and illustrative sets of servants and native occupations were the mainstays of this trade. Most of the individual painters were unknown, but two of them, Shaik Muhammad Amir of Calcutta and Latif of Agra became recognized as being outstanding. Fanny Parks used some of Latif's drawings to illustrate her *Wanderings*.

There was certainly no shortage of activities to record: there are Company drawings of ayahs, baborchees (cooks), shopkeepers, water-carriers, box-wallahs, chowkidars, armed retainers, tent-pitchers, dandies (boatmen), dog-keepers, hookah burdars, women sweet-meat sellers, sweepers, munshis (clerics or language teachers), mendicants, pundits, sepoys, sawars, peons and sirkars. Sometimes artists were employed by Government departments; for example, a drawing of a man with elephantiasis of the scrotum was sent back to the East India Company in London as an illustration of a condition described in a doctor's letter. What an opportunity was missed by Europeans of my parents' generation, for Company works, available for almost nothing before the war, fetch huge sums today.

I know of no paintings or water-colours by Edward Lear of Calcutta, though he stayed there for 3 weeks with the Governor on his Indian trip. But I possess a coloured drawing by him of the Temple of Khardah, a multi-domed place of pilgrimage for Vaishnavas twelve miles upriver near Barrackpore. All Lear's Indian work has a marvellously evocative freshness, the mist as here seeming just to have risen off the water and the foliage, boats, animals to be scarcely realized. The burden of the day's heat has yet to descend and in consequence there is a sense of lightness and energy.

During his fifteen months in India Lear made over 2000 watercolours. He had gone on the invitation of Lord North-brook, an old friend and now Viceroy. Evelyn Baring, Northbrook's cousin and secretary, was an even older friend of Lear's from his Corfu days.

Lear's Indian journals are full of grumbles. Accounts of illness, complaints about the heat and food, the general discom-forts of travel, fill up most of the entries. He found his lodgings too wretched on some journeys, too formal and grand on others. The Indians exasperated him, the British, the women es-pecially, got on his nerves. He flew into rages with Giorgio, his loyal and much put-upon servant.

Yet the best of Lear's Indian drawings are among his most beautiful, for he was often exhilarated to a point of euphoria by the landscape. He didn't care much for life at Government House in Calcutta, calling it 'Hustlefussabad', a consequence, possibly, of his having eaten and drunk more there even than usual. He was always on the look-out for the 'Indian-ness' of India, and Calcutta seemed to him essentially British in spirit. Darjeeling engaged his interest more, but the cold, the remote-

51

ness of the high peaks, and the silence of the few birds depressed him. Only in the Dak bungalows up-country did he find the repose he wanted.

The rains kept Lear in Poona for two months and there he did several fine river views as well as detailed drawings of flowers and trees – ferns, poinciana leaves, lotus plants. Most of his work was done around sunrise or sunset, on the spot, which accounts for the generally cool atmosphere of all his Indian works. The contrast between the sweating belligerence of his notes and the detached elegance of his draughtsmanship was due as much to technique as to mood. Lear's India is exotic rather than tropical; pearly sunrises over limpid rivers, temples among graceful palm trees, mountain peaks flushed by sunset. What he did best were trees and water: the people have little presence, the monuments are dutifully rather than intensely drawn, the bustle has been abstracted. You would imagine, looking at Lear's India, that it was an empty place, short of people, and rather silent. Empty, parts of India are, but rarely is it silent. The life of the bazaars and the *bustees*, the crowded streets and alleys, the vast throngs at religious festivals and political meetings, find no place in Lear's art; nor does the amusement he found wherever he was.

Yet there were many compensations for him and when finally he shook the dust of Ceylon – 'a bore of the first quality' – off his feet he was already planning to return. He never did; and while many places had, at the time, seemed uncongenial to him – Ooty too much like Leatherhead, the Malabar coast too humid, Delhi ruined by 'hideous British utilities' – in retrospect, in the fashion I came to recognize only too well, the enchantments of India grew on him. Ten years after he had left in 1875 he was working up drawings of the Travancore coast, of elephants under huge banyans at Barrackpore, of storks wading the waterfront before the temples of Muttra.

There were many British traveller-artists before Lear, but only a handful – Hodges, George Chinnery, D'Oyley, Prinsep, and the Daniells among them – contributed as much towards turning the landscape of India into art. Few Anglo-Indians had much use for it.

On either side of the front door in the hall of my mews house in Chelsea hang two small Indian watercolours by the same unknown artist. In both, a mournful, pampered and moustached gentleman is portrayed against a cobalt sky. In the left-hand picture he is standing, clad in a white, long-sleeved frock-like garment, with under it a white lunghi reaching to his ankles. His feet are encased in black slippers with prominent heels. A white headcovering, half-way between a matelot's cap and a bishop's hat, sits rakishly on unevenly protruding tufts of black hair. His right hand holds a red rose as if it were a candle. A pink scroll is clutched in the other hand. Behind him a servant, bare-headed and bare-chested, protects his master's head with a long, cerise-lined, green parasol. The servant wears clog-shaped maroon slippers and a solicitous expression. The most noticeable things about both the moony, decadent-looking master and the attentive bearer are their coal-black eyes, eyebrows and hair.

In the second picture the master has a dandyish man-about-town expression. He, too, wears black slippers below white trousers of some form-fitting material, but is seated and shirt-less. Instead of a rose he carries in his right hand a pineapple-shaped holder containing the tall stem of a blue glass lamp. At his side an attendant, dressed in identical fashion, except that he is wearing sandals instead of black slippers, appears to be poking the wrong end of a toasting fork into his ear.

These 'Kalighat' paintings were done around the turn of the century for sale to pilgrims visiting the Kali temple off Tolly's Nala, that sewer-like stream which, by way of Tollygunge and Alipore, runs into the Hooghly just south of the racecourse. In their way the most accessible of all Indian paintings, they combine the traditional methods of Bengal scroll-painters with those of eighteenth century British water-colourists. The result is a form of bold, visual journalism in the manner of Léger.

Much Kalighat painting is plainly anecdotal, relating local scandals and incidents; other pictures illustrate the activities of courtesans, the recreational pursuits of Englishmen, horse-racing, animals, fishes, natural history. A third group is concerned mainly with mythology and religious themes: the depiction of gods and goddesses, the misdemeanours of priests. What distinguishes all of them is their strong, simple colours and compressed rhythms, the bounding line that relates both to Ajanta cave painting and to Cubism.

By the time I was driving round Kalighat at the age of fifteen taking photographs, the temple painters had mostly departed. They seem to have reached their peak in the 1890s, gradually fading away as modern printing techniques rendered their wares uneconomical. But the best of them, influencing Jamini Roy and Gopal Ghose in the 1930s and 40s, had an economy of method and a sense of humour that make their work as engaging now as when it was done. Clothes, hair-styles, domestic upsets, crimes, are illustrated in meticulous detail.

There may have been a few Kalighat paintings on view or for sale in the 1930s but I doubt it. Interest in them, mainly due to W. G. Archer's book on bazaar painting, published in 1953, belongs to a later period. In any case the mildly satirical outlook of certain Kalighat artists in whose work the British appear as both foppish and comical, either lying down being waited on hand and foot by bearers or on animal-back shooting things, would not have endeared them to my father. I, certainly, would have known no better. It was not, though, only the British who were caricatured; what Archer called 'the new Babu' or westernized Bengali-about-town came in for his share of ridicule.

Curiously, the master figures in my two paintings bear an uncanny resemblance to the aggrieved husband in certain Kalighat representations of the celebrated Tarakeshwar murder of 1873. The trigger for this violent event was the seduction of the sixteen-year-old wife of a young Brahmin civil servant by the chief priest of the Shiva temple at Tarakeshwar in the

54

Hooghly district of Calcutta. The girl's family seems to have connived at the relationship which ended with the husband hacking his wife's head off with a fish knife. He was convicted of murder and sentenced to transportation for life. The chief priest, charged with the criminal offence of adultery, was given three years' hard labour and fined two thousand rupees. It is hard to see the gentle dandy of my pictures as the hero-victim of such passionate events, but if he is not then he must be a physical prototype used by the same artists in different situations.

Erotica in its various forms was more accessible to me at the time than art. The famous erotic sculptures at Konarak and Khajuraho, in which copulating figures form an endless daisy chain round the temple walls, were tirelessly reproduced in badly printed booklets on sale in the bazaars. These serenely smiling and inventive creatures, handsomely endowed, were to be sources of envy and surprise, rather than of lust. When later I dutifully went to the Temple of the Sun at Konarak, a testament to sexual ingenuity and perseverance, gazing at the external friezes of couples whose mouths and hands were as simultaneously engaged as any juggler's, produced neither a sense of novelty nor desire. The patience and technique seemed admirable, but flair and passion were not communicated.

More to my taste were pamphlets of Rajasthan and other eighteenth and nineteenth-century paintings, printed in hideous colours on the shiny paper associated with the magazine called *Health and Efficiency* – hitherto the sole source known to me of the naked, though shaven, female figure. Some of the illustrations, depicting women being mounted, symbolically or not it was hard to tell, by stallions and monkeys, seemed to me to be fantasy of too improbable a kind, but certainly they were realistically painted and the women in them wore blissful expressions.

Sometimes during the cold weather of 1936-37 I would play squash in the late afternoons with a girl who worked at

Government House. She would pick me up from Lee Road in her car and drive me to the Saturday Club. She had, I imagine, some slight Indian, or possibly Chinese blood, the result of which was a skin of pure ivory, her loins and breasts, where they had been covered against the sun, scarcely paler than the rest of her.

After charging around for an hour, we would return, wringing with sweat, to her flat in Bhawanipore Road. Calling out to the bearer to bring fresh lime sodas she would set off towards the bedroom, asking if I wanted first shower. Always I declined, and quite unselfconsciously she would pull off her shirt and shorts, throwing them on the floor on her way to the bathroom.

She never fully shut the door and through it we carried on some kind of conversation. Eventually she would emerge, her long dark hair dripping, swathed in turquoise towelling. She would light a cigarette at once and lie back in a cane chair. Then it was my turn, though more shyly I took off my clothes in the bathroom. Occasionally she would join me, squatting on the lavatory top and gossiping while I showered.

'Look at me, if you like,' she said once, letting her towel fall open, 'we're all the same.' But it was quite evident that women were not all the same, and the breasts and bottom of which I got tantalizing glimpses belonged to one whose sexual eloquence would be hard to match in a lifetime. If there was an element of teasing in her behaviour, it was gentle, not mocking. She wore her body rather than displayed it, without provocation. As the smell of sweat was exchanged for the oil she anointed herself with and the scent she lavished on herself after dressing, so did the atmosphere between us change from the fraternal to the distantly romantic. But whereas in the first state we were equals, afternoon participants in an energetic game, once she was clothed she put herself unmistakably out of reach, a mysterious creature whose nocturnal activities were enjoyed by others than me.

Her favours to me were those granted to a boy of fifteen. The fact that I was allowed to enjoy the privilege of gazing at that

56

alabaster body, the veins of which, running up breasts and wrists, behind knees and over ankles, later mapped so many of my nights, was due entirely to the disparity between our ages. It was in fact less than ten years, but the difference in experience was immense. Yet while her body was infinitely more appealing than anything I had observed in erotic sculpture or bazaar pornography the sexual element at the time was diminished by the friendliness of our relationship.

Despite the opportunities so innocently afforded me, there were unspoken limits. Any time during the afternoon hours – had I dared – I might have been allowed, in the nature of experiment, to touch. And who knows what then? But I was afraid to spoil everything. Once dressed, though, her make-up replacing outdoor simplicity with sophistication, we were not merely years apart, but alienated. The telephone would ring and I would hear arrangements for the evening being made, her look and sound taking her hopelessly away. Her driver always drove me home, but by then her thoughts had already left me; her interest had wandered. A week or so later we would enact the same ritual, her enjoyment of the game and our flirtation undiminished, her pleasure in our being together as unaffectedly apparent.

For years I used to dream of that lithe and sweat-coated body and its fragrant metamorphosis. Raked eyes that were slits of cobalt, towelling rubbed over legs faintly descried with dark hairs, bangles flashing from wrists the colour of smoke – as the months passed back at school it seemed incredible that it had once all been within reach.

Bengal Lancer

THE WORD 'BENGAL' had a fascination for me altogether disproportionate to the facts. When I wrote home I did not even have to put 'Bengal' on letters: Calcutta, India was quite sufficient. But the word itself – in whatever conjunction – conjured up for me physical and emotional associations of which I felt acutely deprived. What I had taken for granted as a child acquired a mysteriousness and romance the farther I was away from it.

The Bengal of my childhood was, in fact, cosy rather than mysterious: a tidy green world in which the smells and sounds of India were homely and not exotic. It was distance that opened up in my mind that larger Bengal of rice paddies and wheat under huge skies, of rivers curving metallic under palms, of tigers roaming the forests. My Bengal was a city, a family house on the edge of a river. It was encircled by green. The huge white dome and turrets of the Victoria Memorial loomed out of the bright haze on morning walks with the dogs, there was a temple at the end of the street issuing strange chanting and overpowering fragrances, but these were domestic sights, nothing out of the ordinary at all. It was only in those first annihilating months of homesickness that its strangeness, its terrifying remoteness from what I was now experiencing, and would have to go on experiencing, began to dawn on me. It was then that the very sight of the word Bengal began to induce an obsessiveness close to morbidity. It sprang out at me on bonfire nights from those fireworks, once used for signalling, called Bengal Lights; and it struck most from the cover of a book left casually on the billiard table of my prep school during my first term: *Bengal Lancer*.

Yeats-Brown's *Bengal Lancer* was first published in 1930, the year my parents left me at Belmont House, Wood Lane,

Falmouth, and returned to India without me. I remember asking the master to whom the book belonged if I could borrow it, hugging it all through the term as if somehow, like a wireless wave, it could link people across oceans.

I read it last thing at night, before lights out, all through those bleak weeks of loss. I read as slowly as I could. But re-reading the book now I cannot believe that under normal circumstances it would have meant much to me. Yeats-Brown's India was totally unlike anything I knew about.

The book begins with the author, aged nineteen, in a railway carriage with his two bulldogs: Brownstone, bought in Calcutta, Daisy ordered from the Army and Navy stores in London. He was on his way, a Bengal Lancer, to join the 17th Cavalry on the North-West Frontier.

That his dogs should be the subject, twenty-five years later than the experience, of his opening paragraph I found sympathetic. It was on dogs far more than on people that my mother lavished affection, and far from resenting this, it seemed to me sensible; a way of avoiding stifling physical intimacies of the kind I'd observed in other families. Dogs were a way out, an excuse to escape from desultory conversation. Sixty years after Yeats-Brown had his Daisy, I had my own: a bearded collie that lived to nearly seventeen and was as admirable a creature as any human being I have known.

Yeats-Brown's India was more or less exactly the one to which my father came, in different circumstances, as a young man. In fact, Yeats-Brown arrived five years earlier, full of anticipation of the exotic, an anticipation initially disappointed at his first posting in Bareilly, 'I had expected and imagined much, but not this sad, all-pervasive squalor. Where were the colours and contrasts I had found in books? Where were the Rajahs who ruled in splendour and those other Rajahs who drank potions of powdered pearls and woman's milk? Where the priests and nautch-girls, and idols whose bellies held rubies as big as pigeon's eggs? All I had seen was a tired people, mostly squatting on its heels and crouching over fires of cow-dung.' I don't imagine my father thought in those kind of terms at all.

Calcutta, in those pre-1914–18 war years, was still a place of immense opportunity. If business lacked the romantic image of the Army it certainly produced more money. The firm my father joined was called Villiers and Co. and in due course he came to specialize in coal. In 1926 he transferred to Shaw, Wallace, a firm founded in 1886 to act as agents for the tea gardens of R. G. Shaw and Company in Assam. Shaw, Wallace's other main activities were the import of piece goods from Manchester, the manufacture of fertilizers, flour, shipping and oil. In more recent years, under Indian management, they have diversified into computer services, liquor and chemicals. My father remained with them until his retirement at the end of 1942. By this time he had become Chairman, for the third year in succession, of the Indian Mining Association as well as leader of the European party in the Bengal Legislative Assembly. Throughout my childhood it was to the Shaw, Wallace offices at 4 Bankshall Street that I wrote, and where, in 1983, I lunched with the now wholly Indian Board of Directors and Chairman. In 1943 my father left for Bombay, to take up the Government appointment of Food Commissioner, his task to co-ordinate food supplies, at one of the worst moments of the war, for both the military and the civilian population.

My father had hardly got started with Villiers when war broke out. By then he had married my mother, in 1913, a second marriage for him, his first wife, Alice, having died of appendicitis shortly after they were married. My mother's family was at least fifth generation Anglo-Indian, on my grandfather's side; the first Fitzpatrick, John, entered the Madras Army as a Cadet in 1790.

My father returned from Mesopotamia in 1920, remaining on the Indian Army reserve for some years afterwards. He was not, like Yeats-Brown, a soldier by profession, his years abroad seeming to him merely interruption of business and family life. For Yeats-Brown his army service in India, the polo-playing and pig-sticking, led him, by way of imprisonment by the Turks, into the study of Indian philosophy. He became, in his way, an outsider, a penitent. My father had no scruples about the British presence in India. He saw in the East a way of redeeming the years of frugality and struggle on the Clyde, and his brothers, following his example, went even farther afield, to Hong Kong, China and the South Seas.

In the intense loneliness of my first year at school *Bengal Lancer* was a comfort. If my father's family was not a military one, at least my mother's had been. What cheered me up, in reading Yeats-Brown, was the realization that not only did my ancestry have romantic aspects, separation acquiring a compensating nobility in the process, but that not everyone, even in the Bengal Lancers, was a tough. Toughness, happily, did not seem a prerequisite of success, for certainly Yeats-Brown did not conform to my idea of toughness. He was short-sighted, bad at games and emotionally blighted, so he wrote; a failure at school, undistinguished at Sandhurst. But in India he blossomed. Smoking *charas* from a hookah with Pathan friends he imagined he could crawl through keyholes and step over the Himalayas.

It was with club life that I associated my father most, and on the second page of *Bengal Lancer* Yeats-Brown brought it back. 'I liked to finish my day at the club,' he wrote, 'in a world whose limits were known and where people answered my beck. An incandescent lamp coughed its light over shrivelled grass and dusty shrubbery; in its circle of illumination exiled heads were bent over English newspapers, their thoughts far away but close to mine. Outside, people prayed and plotted and mated and died on a scale unimaginable and uncomfortable. We English were a caste. White overlords or white monkeys – it was all the same. The Brahmins made a circle within which they cooked their food. So did we. We were a caste: pariahs to them, princes in our own estimation.'

I don't think, in my Cornish exile, that either of the alternative notions of 'white overlords or white monkeys' corresponded to my own impression, though one of a protected and privileged species I certainly felt myself to have been. I had no sense as a child that there was any feeling between British and Indian other than affection. There were hierarchies, just as there were everywhere else, presumably, and we were the rulers. But colour, in a racial context, never came into it. How could one fail to admire the 'colour' of most Indians? Surely they did not think of us as 'pariahs', or we consider ourselves a 'caste'?

'The Club' – leather, whisky, cigars, the cries of *Quoi Hai* and the ricochetting of billiard balls – became for me the Bengal Club, stretching from its ponderous white-porticoed front on Chowringhee to its courtyard flanked by flowering trees and lawns opening at the back on to Russell Street. Founded in 1827, the club not only occupied one of Macaulay's former houses but several adjacent mansions of similar opulence.

From here, often slightly unsteady after a vast succession of *burra pegs*, my father would return home for dinner. The smells of mulligatawny, of frying *bekti*, that most delicious of Indian fish, would drift up to mingle with the smell of Scotch as he opened my mosquito net to kiss me good-night. When I went back to India in 1936 I was old enough to dine at the Bengal Club with my father. I had made up for me within twenty-four hours of my arrival my first proper suit, a chalk-striped grey affair that I wore with suede shoes I could scarcely bear to take my eyes off.

Membership of the Bengal Club was the ultimate mark of arrival as a Burra Sahib. Its members, senior officials of the ICS, directors of the larger companies, the more eminent lawyers and surgeons, moved over its marble floors with the stateliness of those accustomed to being deferred to. Yeats-Brown remarks that the smell of crushed geraniums was always enough to summon up for him the Peshawar nights of his subaltern days. For me, back in England, I had only to see a leather armchair with a brass ashtray beside it to be transported to the verandah of the Bengal Club.

62

What most filtered through to me from Yeats-Brown –
however imperfectly I understood it – was the idea of an
alternative India, a place of secret, sensuous activities and
mysterious happenings far removed from the commercial
bustle familiar to me. Some of them related to pleasant grown-
up matters, of which I had as yet little inkling, others to
incidents of a kind I was aware of.

The matter of the King Cobra, for example. One of my
earliest memories was of sitting in the bath at the age of three or
four, with the taps running. The bearer, who was supervising
my washing, had gone out to the compound and in his brief
absence a cobra began to slither down from the pipes attached
to the water tank. Whenever I told the story afterwards I
described the cobra as coming out of one of the taps, but this
seems to me now unlikely.

The cobra, however, was there, swaying drunkenly in front of
me. I sat motionless, unable to move or cry out. A few moments
later the bearer, a bidi between his betel-stained lips, wandered
casually back. He was about to bend down to test the water
when he became aware of the cobra. For a moment he froze;
then appearing to melt out of the room he was gone, gliding
back seconds later with a large stick. This he suddenly cracked
down back-handed on the snake's head, causing it to slither like
a piece of hose on top of me. The bearer scooped its twitching
body out of the water to the compound and there it was hung up
on a branch as if to dry.

Throughout the whole of my childhood, and long after, I had
nightmares about snakes. Usually my father and I would be
walking at dusk in single file along one of those raised tracks
which you see all over India running between paddy fields. The
track is narrow and on either side below us, twisting and
slithering, snakes swarm, so that any slip or stumble would be
fatal.

I don't think the rest of my family had my horror of snakes.
My sister Daphne, who through marriage lived most of her life
in India, once told me she had never seen a single snake. For me

the horror has remained, although I too have never since seen a snake out in the open in India.

I doubt whether my parents, who showed little interest in the magical or other powers of saddhus, would have allowed one to venture inside the gates of 7/1 Burdwan Road, but reading Yeats-Brown's cobra story I wished they had. What happened to him was this. One afternoon his bearer Jagwant had come running in to the study of his Bareilly bungalow to report that a man was dying in the lane outside, having been bitten by a snake. On the recommendation of one of the crowd that had gathered, a saddhu, alleged to be able to bring the dead back to life, was summoned. An emaciated, ash-smeared figure soon arrived, but despite straddlings of the corpse, flute-playing and the chanting of mantras the man died and remained dead. The saddhu, however, declared that for ten rupees he would entice 'the Great One', the cobra, from his hiding place.

Yeats-Brown allowed the saddhu fifteen minutes, the time necessary for himself to change for polo. The saddhu entered the house and, sitting down, began to play soundlessly on his reed pipe. After several false alarms, and the subsequent removal of the dogs who were said to be hindering the process, the saddhu, now trembling, rose to his feet and pointed towards the bathroom. As Yeats-Brown approached a hamadryad hissed up on to its tail, its hood outspread.

The snake was disposed of and the money handed over. Before leaving, however, Yeats-Brown asked the saddhu if he could acquire his knowledge. The saddhu replied 'What does a great Sahib like your Honour want with such things? I learnt from my father and my father learnt from my grandfather. My father could pour water into his mouth and pass it directly through his bowels. My grandfather was waxed all over and buried alive for forty-three days. I can swallow five different coloured handkerchiefs and vomit them up in any order you wish, and I can lift a cannon-ball with my eyelids. If your Honour wishes to see these things I can come again . . .'

It was typical of Yeats-Brown that rather than dismiss the

saddhu as a mere 'beef-eating magician', as his bearer Jagwant, and certainly my father would have described him, he felt eager to learn from him. This rare openness to experience, of whatever kind, much impressed me. The British in India were not notable for their interest in religions, Indian or their own, or the paranormal, let alone witchcraft or any species of sorcery. This protected them from the bogus, of which there was no shortage, but it deprived them of any real insight into Indian thinking and behaviour. The curiosity, and gullibility, shown by westerners in the 1960s and 70s was a post-war phenomenon.

It was all the more remarkable therefore that a polo-playing, pig-sticking professional soldier should go out of his way to sit at the feet of wise men with the aim of reconciling the philosophies of East and West. Yeats-Brown questioned gurus, philosophers, scholars, even attending Mrs Besant's lectures whenever possible. He found her and her protégé, Krishnamurti, sympathetic but was disappointed in their friends. His main discovery was that in the East information is not lightly given, and that unlike Europeans, who are constantly trying to foist their ideas on others – Christianity, education, democracy – Hindus have no wish to convert. 'The Brahmins consider knowledge to be a dangerous tool, and the giving of it to the ignorant like giving a razor instead of a rattle to a baby.'

Not long after the publication of Yeats-Brown's book a film appeared with the title *Lives of a Bengal Lancer*. Gary Cooper and Franchot Tone were the stars but I don't think there was much resemblance between the gently meditative book it was supposed to be based on and the American-accented, sentimental and action-packed film.

Yeats-Brown was the first of those writers who were also men of action who attracted me to writing. When Yeats-Brown, who to my later dismay became a supporter of Mosley, wrote a sentence like 'Here were the plains of India, made for the pursuit of the pig; and beyond them, the holy cities and the mountains' he opened my eyes to a duality that was in my own nature. For as I grew up what I most wanted to reconcile was

65

not pig-sticking and holiness, but, not so very different, sport and poetry. The 'delectable landscape' of India which Yeats-Brown perceived between Benares and Agra through the windows of his leave train, was what in the end came to move me more than anything else, but I doubt whether, had I not been influenced by his own feeling for it, I would, so young, have respected the nature of that emotion.

Bengal Lancer is, like Kipling's *Kim*, that most affecting of all travel books about India, essentially a quest. I could not get on with the archaic language and strange preoccupations of *Kim* as a child, but its descriptions of the Grand Trunk Road set up reverberations that lasted. Yeats-Brown's descriptions of Benares, where the quest proper is begun, are equal to anything in Kipling, the repulsion no obstacle to acceptance: 'It is no good pretending the repulsion did not exist: Benares is an incarnation of the Hindu mind, full of shocks and surprises. You cannot view her through the eyes of the flesh, or if you do, you will want to shut them. Her real life burns in the Unconscious.'

The outbreak of war found Yeats-Brown on leave in Ireland. After a brief spell on the Western Front – his old regiment having remained in India – he found himself posted, without ever having seen an aeroplane, to Basra as an Observer of the Flying Corps in the Mesopotamian Flight. I have a photograph of my father, newly commissioned, in that same city of Sinbad in which Yeats-Brown disembarked. Between them and Baghdad are 12,000 Turks.

The honeymoon days of the first few months in Mesopotamia were abruptly shattered. The plane in which Yeats-Brown was flying crashed into a telegraph post on landing and he and his pilot were captured by Shammar Arabs. They were taken north to Mosul, to a fortress which, a war later, I was to fly over with a Fleet Air Arm colleague, recently become a pilot in the service of a sheik. 'So we passed out of the world of living men, into prison life.'

Prison, hospital, peace; then war again in Waziristan,

Lucknow as a major in command of his own squadron. 'I was jerked like a hooked fish from the waters of Yoga to the arid uplands of the North-West Frontier.'

I cannot remember how much of all this the film of *Bengal Lancer* dealt with. I doubt whether it concerned itself with its author's 'revolt against my ghost-like existence as an officer of vanished Bengal Lancers' and his sudden departure from the Army, one evening at the 'cow-dust hour'. The book ends with Yeats-Brown meditating in the Himalayas, awaiting the dawn after a night of prolonged discussion about the mysteries of love and devotion.

I was not converted by Yeats-Brown's mystical inclinations, but my attachment to his memoirs, born of homesickness rather than literary interest, has survived.

The India I was trying to re-discover drifted in and out of my life, through school, university, war and journalism, for the next thirty years. Sometimes I was acutely conscious of it, Calcutta suddenly *there* as I opened the envelope of a letter from my father – the endless cawing of crows, the smells of cowdung and horses, the cries of rickshaw wallahs – sometimes for months on end it was lost to me, as if under a Hooghly fog.

It was thirty years, after my winter visit of 1937, before I was to see Calcutta again. In the years since, it has once again, though almost unrecognizable in its pattern of life, come to seem home. All the houses I lived in as a child, though now mainly company houses or owned by Marwaris, still stand. Racing continues much as it always did, and the Calcutta Cricket Club, though no longer at Eden Gardens, flourishes.

Kalighat paintings, the diaries of Fanny Parks; Edward Lear's water-colours, F. Yeats-Brown's *Bengal Lancer*. These have little in common, it would seem. But they each, in their different ways and at different times, contributed to the idea of India that grew in me as I grew up.

Strangers' Child

BELMONT HOUSE, FALMOUTH, had only about twenty pupils, all of them day-boys except for myself. It was not a bad school, though I cannot imagine what made my parents pick on it out of thousands of others. I think my mother had the idea that the Cornish climate was suited to an Indian-born child.

At the age of seven I became one of the breed that Uncle Harry, kind, dying and put-upon, termed 'strangers' children' in Kipling's story 'Baa Baa, Black Sheep'. By the time I read that story the days of voluntary abandonment had been superceded by an unavoidable separation: war, and both my parents were dead.

In Kipling's story the boy Punch feels not only desolate but betrayed. The mother, leaving her children, prays 'Let strangers love my children and be as good to them as I should be, but let me preserve their love and their confidence for ever and ever.' I never felt betrayed in Punch's sense, since it was made clear to me that my frail stature was a result of the Calcutta climate and that had I remained in India I would not have lasted long. This was not in fact the case, for there are good schools in India in comparatively healthy places, such as Dehra Dun and Darjeeling. But they were not regarded as quite the thing. If my father had been allowed his way I would have been given a wholly Scottish education, Cargilfield and Fettes, which to him as a boy in Greenock, cleared out of the Highlands, must have seemed the heights of privilege. Fortunately my mother's views on climate prevailed.

Punch's mother's prayer was, as in my case, only half answered, as was inevitable. Strangers were always good to me, but in the proportion that I felt at home with them so did I feel less part of my own family. As a 'stranger's child' you may get affection, but you do not often get the physical expression of love that a child gets from its own parents. However kindly you are treated, you never lose the feeling of being a 'paying guest'. There may be no family quarrels to disturb you, but you learn to become anonymous. When the time came, the prospect of seeing my parents again, and having to own emotional allegiance to people I could scarcely remember, became increasingly embarrassing. Before long it was my parents who appeared to be strangers.

My mother took a cottage in the village of Mawnan Smith for my first holidays from Belmont and then returned to India. For the next three years I spent my holidays on a farm near Truro.

Some people take to farm life like ducks to water. My two sisters, eight and four years older, were never off horseback. I quickly got bored with riding and in any case my sisters soon departed, one to India to get married, the other to a school in France. Mr James, the farmer, had no teeth but gums that could crack walnuts. He always wore a black bowler on his bald head. He was reckoned a fine horseman and many ladies of the county came to him for riding lessons. The only advice he ever gave, or thought worth giving, were the words: 'Sit on your bum', which injunction caused the earnestly bobbing women to grip with their thighs and squeal delightedly.

'Jimmy' James died soon after I began to spend my holidays on his farm. His widow, a vast, splendid woman, one day slipped on the iron bootscraper by the back door and it took half the farm staff to heave her up. She made wonderful pasties, scones and fresh bread, and every afternoon great mounds of home-made splits and clotted cream were deposited on the long kitchen table. The smell from the bakery filled the whole house and her too.

Upstairs, in a room the door of which I never saw opened, a reputedly mad female relative existed. Sometimes one could hear incomprehensible ramblings and occasionally cries and a crash. It gave one a very creepy feeling going past the door but details were never provided. One day 'she' was no longer there.

The James family had two sons: Ralph, who was lame, with

69

one huge boot, and in consequence very heavy, and Billy, who had fair wavy hair and was a good all-round sportsman. There were also three daughters, aged between seventeen and twenty-five: Isa, the eldest, who went off to South America, Mary, known as 'Boysie,' dark and lively, and Nancy, tawny-haired, wide-mouthed, wild, who married a mushroom farmer. Some-times, when there was no other room for me, I was required to share a bed with Mary or Nancy, an experience which even at the age of seven I found inexplicably exciting. All three girls, in their different ways, were attractive and had numerous suitors, of whom I was inordinately jealous.

My three years at the farm were made memorable in an unpredictable way. I imagine my parents thought it would be a healthy life, but I don't remember involving myself in any aspect of the farm's activities, except as a spectator or when in need of company. On the other hand, every moment that Ralph and Billy could spare from their work was devoted to playing either football or cricket with me in the narrow courtyard at the back of the house.

In this area of about fifteen yards by three, bounded on one side by the scullery and kitchen and on the other by outhouses, Ralph and I would play against Billy. If it was soccer Ralph, being immobile and dependent on a stick, played back and I played forward. Since it was physically impossible to get past an opponent head on, the wall had to be used like a cushion in billiards. In this fashion, the wall operating as a colleague, we developed a 'push and run' style similar to that used by the Spurs under Arthur Rowe in their great triumphs of twenty years later. In the 1950s when I used to watch the Spurs regularly, the rapid exchange of passes between Burgess, Bailey and Medley, between Ramsey, Nicholson and Walters often reminded me of those courtyard games. After a whole holiday spent in this fashion it was scarcely surprising that school football seemed a crude and unimaginative game.

The value of courtyard cricket was that you were obliged to play straight, for otherwise the ball rebounded off the wall and hit you, or you hit the wall with your bat, or you broke the scullery window. There could not have been a better training ground for either game.

In the summer we would play, before and after supper, until it got dark, or Billy had to see to farm matters. It cannot, in retrospect, have been much fun for Billy, who when he could spare the time opened the innings for the Cornish Choughs, and on winter Saturdays played inside-left for Wadebridge. Ralph, however, had few distractions. All day long he patrolled the farm on an old mare, his legs almost touching the ground on either side. There must have been outside labour on the farm but I have only a vague memory of it.

Ralph was the ideal companion, kind, generous and good-natured, at the disposal of anyone who wanted him. If I learned nothing else on the farm I left it as well equipped a cricketer and footballer as a boy of ten could hope to be. In addition, the James girls played hockey for Cornwall, occasional matches being staged on farm land. So if I was not playing cricket or soccer I was practising hockey with skilful players.

Belmont House, which must have been a kind of pre-prep school, since I don't remember boys much older than myself, had, besides the headmaster, Capt. J. L. Thomas, only one resident assistant master, Mr Metcalf. Miss Crawford, who wore a thumbstall and smelled of chalk, came in every day to teach geography. The Thomases had a tomboyish daughter, Joyce.

Where the school used to be, Falmouth School of Art now stands and I used occasionally to address letters to Peter Redgrove there. Falmouth to us was simply a wide bay with sailing boats scattered against green headlands. The sea, though close, we only saw briefly on weekend walks, though at night we heard foghorns and the sirens of ships. Lessons must have taken place but nothing counted for me except the moment of release, the field below the house, centre of daylong dreaming and cruised by seagulls, at last accessible.

I shared none of the usual childhood and adolescent passions

– botanising, making model aeroplanes, carpentry – that absorbed the dayboys at Belmont, and games there, to my disappointment, were on a frivolous level. I was reduced to collecting stamps, but indoor life was no substitute for me and I missed Ralph and Billy dreadfully. It was a relief when after three years my parents came home on leave and removed me to a more grown-up school in Sussex.

PART II

First and Last Gods

Green Sussex fading into blue
with one gray glimpse of sea.
Alfred Tennyson

I was lucky that my arrival at St Andrews, East Grinstead, coincided with a revival of fortune for Sussex cricket. After the pre-Great War golden age of Ranjitsinhji and Fry, 'old' George Cox and Fred Tate, the Relfs and Joe Vine, Sussex went into comparative decline during the twenties. I came to St Andrews in the summer of 1932 and that year, under Duleepsinhji, Sussex were runners-up in the championship, as they were to be again in the next two years. When the term ended it looked as if Sussex might even win the championship for the first time in their history. I spent every moment I could during the holidays watching them play at Hove or Eastbourne, but sadly Duleep's health broke down at a crucial moment in August and without their best batsman Sussex could not quite manage it.

Duleep, all charm and elegance at the wicket, never played first-class cricket again. But my awareness of him, as an Indian playing for Sussex, the nephew of the legendary Ranji, seemed to narrow the great distance between Sussex and India.

Duleep's physical frailty – even before tuberculosis destroyed him he had suffered continuously with chest trouble, as had Ranji too – especially endeared him to me, since I was extremely small for my age and thin. When I had been given my football colours at Belmont the Headmaster, reading my name out, stopped in mid-sentence to query it with Mr Metcalf, as if incredulous that someone so minuscule could deserve them. I had a nasty moment several years later when, chosen to captain the Public Schools Under 15 XI at Lord's, I reported to the venerable Carleton Tufnell, organizer of the match. He opened

75

the door of his Westminster house, where I had been invited to spend the night before the match and be made familiar with my team, and stared blankly at me. On hearing my name – now given rather anxiously to him – he continued to stare, before finally relenting and admitting me with the words: 'I'd imagined someone much bigger than you. I hope you can manage it.'

That first summer of mine in Sussex, Duleep hit three successive hundreds, a feat he had exceeded the year previously when he hit four, the second of which was for England against New Zealand at the Oval. Every lunch time, newspapers were put on a table in the morning room at St Andrews and I could not concentrate on anything else until I knew how Sussex had done the day before. It is not much different even now.

To a boy of ten the Sussex team were gods, vulnerable but beyond criticism. Duleep was succeeded as captain in 1933 by R. S. G. Scott, an Oxford Blue who, like Duleep, died young, aged only forty-eight. Scott, who died in 1957, made no great impression on me, but after one season he gave way to Alan Melville, a South African and former Oxford captain. I was so impressed by the fact that Melville owned to no other initial but 'A', that as soon as I could I jettisoned my own other initial.

Alan Melville was my ideal of a certain type of cricketer: tall, willowy, handsome in a febrile, nervous sort of way. I see him with his right blazer cuff turned back, a cigarette between long, aesthete's fingers. At the wicket Melville was no less graceful than Duleep, with a classically upright and sideways-on stance. He was a marvellous player of fast bowling, alternating the most delicate late cuts with rippling drives and hooks. Melville returned to South Africa after only five seasons, but under his captaincy Sussex flourished. Back in South Africa, Melville was appointed captain of their Test side and he later achieved the extraordinary feat of four successive Test hundreds against England, one in South Africa in 1939 and the others in the first two Test matches at Trent Bridge and Lord's in 1947. He was by then a more restrained, less lyrical batsman than during his

76

Sussex days and I saw him now as an obdurate stumbling block to England rather than as the romantic hero of my youth.

I see the Sussex side of the 1930s more clearly than any since. Ted Bowley, who shared in the highest first-wicket partnership of 490 with John Langridge at Hove in 1933, was just about finished, so in my mind's eye the innings is opened by John Langridge and J. H. Parks.

Jim Parks was a neat, bird-like man, his head sunk into his shoulders so that he appeared to have no neck. He came from the Haywards Heath area, where I was to spend all my holidays from St Andrews and Haileybury, and he had the red face and voice of the typical countryman. Batting, he stood still as a scarecrow until the last second, whereupon he would hook or cut abruptly, as if a secret mechanism had been set off. In 1937 he had a miraculous season, swishing opposing bowlers all over the field from the moment he went in. He made eleven centuries that summer, scoring three thousand runs and taking a hundred wickets, something no one had ever done before or is likely to do again. Bowling, he was a slow-medium off-drifter, who cut the ball both ways and was hard to get away.

John Langridge, tall and loose-limbed, was never the prettiest of players, very square-on to the bowler and often boring. But just when he had sent even the most loyal Sussex supporter to sleep he would start to cut and pull and generally make hay. He was never easy to shift and as long as he was there Sussex were not beaten. He went through an obsessive ritual at the wicket, touching almost every part of his anatomy from his cap to his box while awaiting the ball. John Langridge was one of the best slip fielders in the world, pocketing the sharpest of chances so unobtrusively that it was impossible to tell he had caught them.

Sussex, quite apart from Ranji and Duleep, had always been a family team; Fred and Maurice Tate, George Cox, father and son, Jim and Harry Parks, the Gilligan and Oakes brothers, James and John Langridge, and later Richard, left-handed son of James. James Langridge, elder brother to John, was a

77

left-handed all-rounder of almost sleepy gracefulness. Nothing he ever did appeared hurried. He was a batsman and spin bowler of classic correctness, possessed of an effortless cover drive and, as a bowler, of loop and flight. He went in at No. 5 and if Sussex were in trouble Jim, calm and unruffled, usually got them out of it.

Jim Parks's brother, Harry, was as fair as Jim was glossily dark. Both Jim Parks and Jim Langridge played occasionally for England, and had it not been for the war John Langridge almost certainly would have done so. Harry, coming in at No. 6, had no aspirations beyond the county but he was a saver of lost causes, often batting with Jim Langridge, free and dashing in contrast to Langridge's silken repose. Harry was a magnificent fielder in the deep, and in practice games at school it was Harry's fielding and throwing from the boundary we tried to imitate, just as it was John Langridge's speed of reflex at slip.

The Sussex team during my first years at St Andrews had nine regulars, J. H. Parks, John Langridge, A. Melville, T. Cook, James Langridge, H. W. Parks, M. W. Tate, A. F. Wensley, and 'Tich' Cornford. The last two places usually went to one of the amateurs, R. G. Stainton or A. J. Holmes, and either Jim Cornford or the Fulham footballer Jim Hammond, both medium-fast bowlers.

Maurice Tate, sadly, was ending his days as a great bowler but his action remained as beautiful and economical as ever. 'Trunk' Heywood – so-called because of his large nose – the cricket master at St Andrews, wanted me to model myself on him. So I watched him whenever I could, practising off the same length of run, nine paces, and bowling with the same high-held left arm and pivot of hip. Jim Cornford was in the same mould as Tate though he lacked Maurice's strength and stamina.

After Alan Melville had departed, Sussex were skippered until the war by A. J. Holmes, who used to appear in the scorecards as Flight Lieutenant, later as Squadron Leader. I don't know if Holmes had ever been air-crew but he didn't look it. He was bulky, awkward of movement, with large feet pointing outwards. His hair was thin and parted in the middle and he had a ginger moustache. When he stooped to pick up a ball at mid-off you imagined the creak.

Holmes, who first played for Sussex the year I was born, was thirty-six when he took over the Sussex captaincy but his ungainliness made him look older. I don't know how he got the job, but although he occasionally thumped runs in hearty old-fashioned style he was a moderate performer. Worse, for me, he did not conform to the romantic image I cherished of Sussex amateurs.

Hugh Bartlett, who arrived out of the blue in 1938, certainly did, and this more than made up for Holmes's stodginess. By now, with Tate and Wensley gone, Sussex were finding it hard to bowl opponents out. They had acquired Jack Nye, a fair-haired giant of a country boy, who ran in almost from the sight-screen and banged the ball down from a great height, but he was usually more menacing in prospect than in reality.

There was, during my last years at St Andrews, no more entertaining batting side in the country. After John Langridge and Jim Parks came Charlie Oakes, a beautiful striker of the ball in a languid fashion, who tended to make 30 or 40 effortlessly and then get out. At No. 4 was George Cox, son of 'old' George, a contemporary of Ranji, who in his day had no equal as a cutter and driver through the covers. No one has ever played cricket more joyously than 'young' George and once he was properly set he made the lives of fast bowlers a misery. James Langridge came in at 5, to regulate the innings in whatever way was necessary, and then at No. 6 Bartlett emerged. For a few nerve-racking overs little contact was made, then Bartlett would middle one and the fun began. Soon the ball was skimming back over the bowler's head and to all parts of the boundary.

Bartlett, who had captained Cambridge in 1936, was a revelation. Tall, bronzed, and faintly Byronic of feature, he was a left-hander who hit with tremendous power off back and front

79

foot equally. There were no compromises about Bartlett's methods; in defence he played straight but his judgment of length was so early that defensive strokes were a last resort. Against the Australians that year of 1938 he made a hundred in 57 minutes, the fastest century of the season.

One felt with Bartlett that it could not last, but it did, for one whole glorious and unforgettable summer, and the best part of another one. Nothing could have been more thrilling during those two years than watching Bartlett send good bowling sailing into the trees. I discovered later how nervous Hugh was, chain-smoking from the start of the Sussex innings, but his nervousness could never have exceeded mine as I waited for him to bat. In the second of those years I got into the Hailey-bury XI and passionately though I wanted to succeed I minded even more that Bartlett should. No memory of the whole of the thirties is clearer to me than Bartlett's two innings in Sussex's win against Worcestershire during the Eastbourne week of 1939. In the first innings he had made 89 in 44 minutes, easily on course again for the fastest century of the season when he was caught by Charlie Palmer on the ropes at extra cover. In the second innings, when Sussex needed 200 to win in 95 minutes, Bartlett made 59 not out in half an hour. War was only weeks away but I went off home oblivious and as happy as a lark.

The last August of peace: sweat-stained shirts drying on the pavilion balcony, cleaned boots laid out crisp as meringues in the sun, bats the colour of cream propped against deck-chairs. In dressing rooms sweat, linseed, and embrocation mingle together, but outside everything seemed the height of stylishness. Jim Parks and Jim Langridge in their MCC blazers, dark blue with red and gold piping, were creatures apart, but no less wonderful to me were those others, John Langridge, Cox, Cook, Bert Wensley, Harry Parks, Charlie Oakes, Hugh Bartlett, whose every movement and expression were the stuff of my dreams. At Eastbourne cricket is played to a background of croquet and bowls, old Colonels and straight-backed memsa-hibs going unconcernedly about their daily ritual, indifferent to the pock of bat on ball and the marauding seagulls. The images of the game – a defensive stroke correctly made, the bat coming down in a lovely arc to meet the ball with the full face, the surgical delicacy of a late cut, the wafer-thin deflections of a glance, the defiance of a hook, the abandon of a slashed cover-drive – these became the stored poetry of my winters, predecessors to poetry itself.

In 1938–39 Hugh Bartlett went to South Africa with MCC but did not play in a Test. During the war he served as a glider pilot and returned to captain Sussex for three seasons. Sussex had no bowlers in those first post-war seasons and Bartlett had a difficult time of it. He himself had lost the recklessness of 1938 and no longer terrorized bowlers. The war had taken something from his eye and nerve and there were to be few of those soaring drives over the bowler's head that had lit up those last summers of the thirties. There were others who would return to Sussex cricket grounds mere shadows of their earlier selves.

St Andrews had once been the home of the South African millionaire, Sir Abe Bailey, and its cricket field had been used for practice by the South African Test team. The house was sprawling Scottish baronial, its lavish grounds on a plateau above a wooded valley. In winter its long corridors made it appallingly cold and I suffered agonies from chilblains. I stammered as well, the Fitzpatrick affliction. So, as a matter of fact, did the Headmaster, Kenneth Bull, who smoked like a chimney but had a fine tenor voice. He took an age in chapel to announce the hymns, his nicotine-stained fingers pressing on his temple as if in prayer.

K. R. Bull – 'Mr Kenneth' – was a dapper and squat Old Harrovian. He appeared in the most elegant tweed suits, set off by high-collared checked shirts and becoming club ties, his favourites being those of the Bluemantles and Band of Brothers. Sometimes he wore plus-fours, his shoes gleaming like conkers. He used to take First XI colours to Lord's for the university match, when we would stop at Croydon airport for refreshments on the way. On such occasions Mr Bull wore a grey flannel suit and his MCC tie and we shone in its reflection.

I don't think Kenneth Bull was very cultivated but he was a gutsy fellow who had won the MC during the 1914–18 war. He had, so he informed us, a tin plate in his stomach and during boxing would invite the smaller boys to hit him there as hard as they liked. I took a great interest in the masters' ties; indeed in all their clothes. Some, like Mr Tidmarsh, the music master, and Mr March, an amiable duffer, were a great disappointment, the same old stained flannel trousers and threadbare tweed jackets appearing term after term. Mr March was red-faced, wore thick, dark-rimmed specs and was renowned for his cunning at dealing with questions to which he had no clue as to the answer. 'Someone put that boy out of his misery,' he would say, addressing the class, 'surely *someone* knows the answer.' If no convincing suggestion was forthcoming he would briskly say: 'Right, look it up before you see me again, and make sure you remember it.'

Mrs Bull was elegant and much taller than her husband, with a pompadour hair style which added inches to the disparity. She and her adolescent daughter were once glimpsed sunbathing naked by the swimming pool, a long way off from the nearest observation post, but an event that caused speculation and excitement for weeks afterwards. In his farewell talk about sex to school-leavers Mr Bull would warn boys not to waste 'it', leaving one with the anxiety that if one did, 'it' might suddenly run out, a terrible prospect. He was rather vague in his description of sexual feeling, making it seem that it came upon one without warning, so that if there was no girl present the chance was lost. It was not clear how often the urge came or what happened if it did not come to the girl at the same time. What Mr Bull did emphasize, though, was that making love was the most wonderful feeling in the world, so that one was left hoping that occasionally the person, the place and the desire would coincide.

Walking at break one day in my first week at St Andrews a prefect called Vivian told me that I was 'wanted' down by the bushes. I set off in all innocence, only to be ambushed near the rhododendrons and set upon. Much more than the physical assault I minded that someone in authority had connived at it. That was the end of ready trust as far as I was concerned. Henceforth, when anyone said to me 'You're wanted', I knew it meant bad news.

Rectory Life and Stolen Silver

THE HAILEYBURY connection was well established at St Andrews, though the Harrow tendency was stronger. It was not, though, because of any persuasion from school that I went to Haileybury, even though my closest friend, Nigel Brooks, the school's crack rifle shot and boxer, was going there. Brooks in fact went to Haileybury a term later than me, and, as often happens when friends are in different houses, we scarcely spoke again. He had the romantic names of Nigel Aubrey Gaillard and ended up in the Indian Cavalry.

It might have been expected that my parents would have favoured Haileybury as the former East India College, but I don't think this was so. Having deposited me at St Andrews they returned to India, leaving me in the care of the Reverend J. L. Brack, Rector of Ardingly, a village ten miles to the south-west. I don't know where Mr Brack, who looked exactly like an advertisement for Three Nuns Tobacco – dog-collared, bald and jolly – went to school, but he sent both his sons, Noel and Christopher, to Haileybury. I liked them, so it seemed a good idea to follow in their footsteps. Clergymen's sons got in to Haileybury at reduced fees, a factor which might have tempted my father to take Holy Orders, though a more unlikely clergyman it would have been hard to imagine.

I was not the only boy at St Andrews farmed out to the Bracks. Dick Symes-Thompson, whose parents were coffee-farming in Kenya, and Peter Espeut, whose father was in Cable and Wireless and working in the Cape Verde Islands, came to Ardingly shortly after I did, and the three of us, except for when our parents were on leave, spent most holidays for the next eight years there. Dick went eventually to Harrow and Peter to Haileybury. I saw Peter at Haileybury even less than I saw Nigel Brooks, since he was neither in my house nor doing

Modern Languages. Peter went down as a Midshipman with the *Gloucestershire* in 1942.

The routine at Ardingly scarcely changed between 1932, when I spent my first holidays there, and 1942, when I left from Haywards Heath station to join the Navy. On Sundays we had a roast, and we ate this in one form or another, preceded by soup at dinner, for the rest of the week. Lunch was always cold meat, baked potato and salad, followed by cheese.

As long as we turned up at meals we were free to do as we pleased. There was a half-size billiard table in the hall, we all three had bicycles, and we all three loved cricket. During eight years thousands of games of billiards, including billiard fives, must have been played, until in the end, bombarded into insensibility, the cushions disintegrated.

The bicycles had a dual purpose; firstly, for transporting us to Ardingly Station, from where, twice a week, we took the train to Haywards Heath to go to the cinema, and secondly, for immensely complicated obstacle races along the paths that divided woods, rose gardens, lawns, vegetable patches, tennis court, shrubberies and graveyards.

Haywards Heath, then as now a station rather than a town, had two cinemas, both eventually made obsolete by TV. That meant four possible films a week, each film showing for three days. It was rare for more than two of these to provide enough counter-attraction to bicycle races and cricket, but in the winter we sometimes saw all four films. I bought records of Jack Hulbert singing 'Letting in the Sunshine', of Jack Buchanan singing 'Good Night, Vienna' and of Bobby Howes's song 'I don't know why the great Buonaparte, Took Josephine for a ride in his pony cart, But – You Give Me Ideas'. There was no sex in the offing at Ardingly Rectory and I don't remember a girl ever coming near the place. As a result, the film stars of the day, such as Jean Harlow, Madeleine Carroll, Carole Lombard, Myrna Loy, Barbara Stanwyck, appeared impossibly remote, as did the idea of Mr Bull's 'most wonderful feeling in the world'. Now and again a hefty Central European girl came to help out in the house and work in the kitchen, the Rector brightening visibly and laughing uproariously at her mere presence. But she was outside our domain.

Mr Brack was one of those old-style country parsons who was a 'character' in the Parish. Every day he set off in his battered trilby and ancient Morris to visit the elderly and sick, looking every inch the part and bringing comfort and good cheer. His response to almost everything was to laugh. I don't think he was particularly devout or knowledgeable in ecclesiastical matters, but he was a good, practical country priest. His sermons, even when he got them out of a book, were incredibly boring, and his monotonous delivery made it a near thing between himself and the congregation as to who would drop off first. The 'book' sermons he rattled through unconvincingly, as if it was only too plain to anyone with half an ear that they were not his own work. Sometimes he lost his place beyond recall or got muddled into another sermon, but his wife, being slightly deaf, continued to look up at him with rapt attention. Luckily, when he looked like pottering on for ever, their cairn terrier would suddenly wake up and begin to bark. That brought the sermon to an immediate end, even if it was in mid-sentence.

Mr Brack had played rugby for his college at Cambridge and the high point of his year was the University match at Twickenham, mentally prepared for weeks in advance. Mrs Brack accompanied him and they set off early on the day with rugs and thermos, sandwiches and beer. It was the outing of the year for the old Morris, too.

Few of Mr Bracks's parishioners were likely to be concerned with doctrinal matters and I imagine discussions of spiritual or emotional crisis would have embarrassed him. His approach was functional; a matter of doing errands, bringing eggs, fetching medicines, making jokes. Fears were to be laughed away. But if they refused to go, what then?

I never had a serious talk with Mr Brack and I don't think any of the other holiday boarders ever did either. He was an outdoor man, who wanted everything on a convivial plane, out in the open. Any idea of discussing sexual problems or religious doubts with him would have been inconceivable, an uncomfortable intrusion of awkward subjects into a polite relationship. His task was to make light of what was dark and to be of good cheer. When a butler-pantryman called Capel, who spent his spare time running round the lanes in filthy white shorts, ran off with all the silver one afternoon he simply roared with laughter.

It was Capel who initiated such discussions of sex as there were. One of the sturdy Yugoslavs so attractive to the Rector and twice Capel's size once sent him spinning into the pond when he attempted some unwanted familiarity. He emerged slimy and dripping but not in any way discountenanced. 'She's a fiery one,' he said to us admiringly, 'she's longing for it really.'

Whether she was or not Capel never got near enough to find out, at least as far as we knew. His patent-leather hair and sallow, conventionally handsome features, marred only by chipped, tobacco-stained teeth, stood him in better stead with the fresh-faced maids who came up from the village to help out. Capel would flatter and abuse them alternately, manoeuvring them at some stage of the day into deserted sculleries or ironing cupboards, from which they would emerge ruffled and bright-eyed, and Capel, at a suitable interval, ostentatiously non-chalant. 'You boys want to get in there,' he'd say, nodding in the direction of Violet or Ruby, now busying herself with shelling peas. 'You can't expect me to do all the work.'

A stout cook came in from the village, so Capel's main duties were cleaning the silver, for which he wore a green baize apron, and odd jobs about the place. Most evenings he sat in his apron doing his football pools coupon or studying the runners at various race-meetings. There was never a morning when, having ascertained the Reverend's whereabouts and made certain that Mrs Brack had observed him on the premises, he did not make off on his bike to the village to put on a bet. He was as confident of his tipping abilities as he was of his political judgment. 'That Mullosini, he's the fellow!' What impressed him, as a devotee of physical fitness, was the Duce's appearance of virility, his horse-riding and general strutting about, which he compared favourably to the likes of Baldwin and Chamberlain. For Hitler he had no use. 'Flabby chops,' he called him, and one day appeared with a false Hitler moustache, imitating one of his speeches to us in the kitchen until the unexpected arrival of Mrs Brack wiped both the speech and the moustache off his face.

A more unhealthy-looking man than the hollow-chested and spindly-legged Capel, who was probably in his mid-thirties, it would be hard to imagine. A chain-smoker of Woodbines, he coughed incessantly and when he appeared after lunch in his running attire he looked more fit for the mortuary than for country lanes. Taking a deep breath, he would grind out his fag-end with a dirty gym shoe and doggedly set off down Balcombe Hill, waving his arm aloft in farewell. His running vest bore the number 3 on it, for he had, so he informed us, belonged to an Athletic Club in London and been given time off from his job at a London club. He had left there, he confided, because he needed country air to keep in tip-top condition.

Capel, for some reason, had a neurotic fear of the churchyard. Returning from the pub late at night, he would skirt the tombstones as if afraid corpses would rise out of them. Sometimes we would encounter him stealing in through the back door, his face white and his hair plastered flat with sweat. 'Them bloody spooks give me the shits,' he'd say, reaching for the cooking brandy and taking a good swig.

No matter how hard Capel trained, and he appeared to run several miles every afternoon, he never lost the greenish, undersea tinge to his complexion. Smoking and beer presumably undid the benefit of the exercise.

He was scornful of cricket as a means of keeping fit, though he would field for us sometimes in between duties, baize apron to the fore and fag in hand. As he came up to bowl once, the ball shot out of the back of his hand and broke a greenhouse window on the other side of the hedge. Another time I hit the ball at him when he was fielding and in his haste to protect himself he threw the fag from his fingers. It landed somewhere between his trousers and his apron, unnoticed until a smell of smouldering began to drift across the lawn. Suddenly there was a squawk from Capel as pieces of burning ash began to ignite his pubic hair. He made no more active appearances after that, contenting himself with lying on the bank and blowing smoke-rings into the sky.

Although he gave no real indication of permanence – 'I like to keep moving,' he would remark sagely, 'keeps me young,' – it was a surprise to come back one holiday and find him gone.

The maids laughed about him. 'He'll be in the nick if they ever find him.' I don't think in fact much effort was made to track Capel down. He'd simply taken off one day on his run, having stacked his clothes and an apron full of silver somewhere outside. There were rumours, on inquiry, that Capel's need to move on was more practical than psychological, previous employers having had reason for complaint. He was reported later as having been seen heading for Ireland. I liked to think of him running along the fuchsia-hedged lanes of the west coast or squelching into bogs, the 3 on his back disappearing into the mist and his lank hair flopping. An old country house in Ireland, somewhere not too far from the Curragh, would have suited him fine, and made a nice setting for the silver.

The Rectory staff, which changed rapidly for some reason, consisted as a general rule of a cook, a pantryman, and a maid, with one or two jobbing gardeners. The Rectory, a large rambling building of red brick, adjoined the church, and on the far side the land sloped down to Balcombe valley. The road down West Hill to Balcombe Mill was so steep that if you bicycled down it without using brakes you would certainly crash.

Ardingly had a good football team, whose centre-forward,

Dean, was the terror of opposing defences. The ball shot from his head like a bullet and his elbows flattened the full backs as he soared between them. His fame in the village was only approached by that of Don Stride, who worked in the butcher's and sang solos in church. Don's voice was crude but powerful and he held on to the melody long after everyone else had relinquished it, setting up a kind of underswell. His red face and slicked-back, liquorice-coloured hair gave him the appearance of a bullfighter and when he came forward out of the choir stalls in his surplice to sing it was indeed as if he was about to engage a formidable adversary. Don's voice often quavered at the end of notes, but the sheer volume of it made up for technical shortcomings. He was not as controlled a tenor as Mr Bull, but he would have blasted him out of sight.

At the centre of Rectory life was Mrs Brack, then, I suppose, in her sixties and still going strong when I moved back to Sussex twenty-five years later. She was, for all of us, the mother substitute and we were fortunate to have someone so generally understanding and companionable. She must once have been beautiful and though now silvery-haired still had a gentleness of feature and sweetness of expression that were rarely misleading.

She went everywhere at a brisk trot, perpetually busy; ordering, mending, 'seeing to' something or other, writing letters. The Rural Dean would be out in the parish or sealed away behind his study door. The perpetual click-clack of billiard balls in the hall must have driven them both mad but they never complained.

Every afternoon Mrs Brack went 'for a run' with her two cairn terriers: Kinky, so-called because of his deformed tail, and Dougal. During the several holidays when I was the only boarder I used to accompany her. There were various alternative routes, down towards Balcombe Woods, through the farm or along the lane to the village, but whichever it was Mrs Brack set off at a sprightly lick. Whenever, years later, listening to race commentaries, either on the course or on TV, I heard the expression 'taking them along' or 'at the head of affairs' used of the leading horse, it would remind me of Mrs Brack, so spirited was the pace that she set.

These walks were not only good exercise, 'blowing the cobwebs away' but, without making a song and dance about it, made it possible to discuss 'Life'. I don't think I ever had specific problems, but I was often acutely homesick at St Andrews until my last year and Mrs Brack's cosy motherliness in the holidays and her letters to school, mainly about the dogs, meant a lot. I don't think she would have been understanding of any unconventional situation, or indeed have encouraged self-pity, but she was sympathetic and warm and that was what mattered.

The walk over, tea was taken in the drawing room: scones, jam, buns and cakes, and tea from a silver teapot. The Rector sometimes turned up for this, wolfing down what was available, and departing rapidly on some real or invented errand. He was a restless man and always gave the impression that, having had to listen to the woes of his parishioners all day, anything was preferable to more conversation.

After tea, Mrs Brack got out her needlework or sewing, occasionally going through the vast 'Stores' catalogue from the Army and Navy out of which she did much of her household ordering.

Sometimes there were grown-up 'boarders' around: Morag Harbord, for instance, throaty and tweeded, unmarried and in her forties. Morag smoked continually from a tortoise-shell holder and brought a cheerful touch of sophistication to the premises. There was no drink visible in normal circumstances, but I imagine Morag must have kept a supply in her room, for its effect was sometimes apparent. Presumably she had a place of her own somewhere, for although she spent months at a time at the Rectory she was by no means always there. Every morning she set off for Piltdown Golf Course, returning in time for dinner. I did not find her life mysterious then, but I do now.

Dean Butcher also flitted in from time to time, before leaving for the Sudan. He, like Martin Lindsay the explorer, had been 'one of us' a decade earlier and was just down from Cambridge. His room contained scientific equipment and reports of analyses of urine, which excited our curiosity. Dean was keen on a very pretty girl called Doreen Sutton, to do with Sutton Seeds, but though she came to the Rectory a few times I don't think their relationship survived his departure.

In due course after tea the grown-ups sloped off to their rooms. About seven o'clock Mrs Brack, having attended to her correspondence and perhaps fallen asleep in the process, went upstairs for her bath. She would emerge at half-past seven in some velvet concoction, a shawl over her shoulders, the embodiment of a sweet and gracious gentlewoman. Morag, if she were present, might have traded in her suede 'golfing' jacket and stout brogues for a dinner dress, and with the rest of us in tweed jackets and ties, hair neatly brushed, it was a presentable group that sat down after the Rector had mumbled grace.

It was Mr Brack's habit at lunch time to tap his extended fingers against each other and then, palms turned outwards, hold them up to the sun as it streamed in at him through the morning-room windows. Sometimes between conversations he would make a mewing kind of noise, not quite a hum, nor exactly tremulous, but obviously nervous in origin. This, accompanied by a slight trembling of the fingers, was conceivably a symptom of the stroke that half-paralysed him some years later. It was an upsetting experience, returning to Ardingly one holiday, to be confronted by an almost expressionless hulk beached on its back, which daily I would try and shave. No man had been more habitually jolly and hail-fellow-well-met than Mr Brack and it was heart-breaking to see him dull-eyed and speechless. No longer would he warm his hands at the morning sun, or laugh uproariously at the sexual provocativeness of a Czech serving wench.

Of the three Brack children, Heather had married a retired naval officer, Noel worked in the publishing house of Longmans, Green, of which he later became Managing Director, and Chris, the apple of his mother's eye, was off to Canada to teach.

Then in his early thirties, Noel was the archetypal elder son, considerate and responsible. He was good company, too, and his visits always bucked things up.

Chris was another matter. Whereas Noel was of medium height and unremarkable in appearance, though sensitive in feature, Chris looked like an old-fashioned movie star. Six foot-three, with dark wavy hair coming to a pronounced widow's peak, a thin Ronald Colman moustache, and wide shoulders, he had dreamy, slightly protuberant eyes, the dreaminess perhaps a legacy from sleeping sickness. He stared into space disconcertingly, often seemingly unaware he was being addressed.

He scarcely noticed us, unlike Noel, who interested himself as conscientiously as a godfather in our doings. Chris's time at Haileybury had been interrupted by a mysterious illness, but it had not prevented him from being a shining light in the 1925 XI. Unfortunately, there was some doubt about his bowling action, and he was no-balled at Lord's. Chris took an intimida-tingly long run and banged the ball down from a great height, but even when I saw him bowling years later in the Haywards Heath week his elbow seemed bent at the moment of delivery. He was, however, a handsome left-handed batsman who scored prolifically in club cricket when he could be bothered to play.

It was Chris's arrival on the scene, from some prep-schoolmastering job, that first brought home to us that, appear-ances to the contrary, we were not 'family'. No comparable fuss was made of Heather or Noel, whose visits if anything re-inforced our family status, but the news that Chris was about to descend sent Mrs Brack into a complete spin. She had no longer eyes or ears for anything but him and we boys were suddenly non-existent. This scarcely mattered when all three of us, or even two of us, were there, because we could take care of ourselves, but when I was there on my own this total transference of affection was wounding. I told myself that it was perfectly natural for Mrs Brack to concentrate on her own son and to devote herself exclusively to him when he came home, but nevertheless the atmosphere changed completely. No longer was I part of a privileged circle, independent yet loved, but outside it altogether; a mere paying boarder. It was not the superficial betrayal I had experienced at Vivian's hands at St Andrews, but something far more damaging. Hitherto, I had welcomed my freedom from the emotional constraints of family, or thought I had, secure in the uncomplicated affection of Mrs Brack. To discover this could be turned off like a tap was a bitter blow.

To be fair, I am quite sure that none of this was intentional on Mrs Brack's part; it was simply that whenever Chris was around she had no idea except to please him. All the light in her eyes and warmth of her voice went his way, and when she had reason to talk to us it was in a distant, dismissive tone quite unlike her normal one.

Whether Chris welcomed such exclusive attention there was no means of knowing. He was never at home at any one time for long and mostly he mooned about restlessly. One holiday there was a tremendous to-do because Chris had got a job teaching in Canada and had to be kitted out. Mrs Brack pored over her 'Stores' catalogue, in those days as thick a volume as *Who's Who*, her magnifying glass circling over the small print. Long before he was due to leave, anoraks, fur boots, checked woollen shirts, skis, and trapper's peaked caps had arrived and were duly tried on. Chris began to look more and more like a cigarette advertisement, preening himself as he looked this way and that in the mirror. Unfortunately, there was no means of knowing what his Canadian pupils thought of this dude bear hunter, but the Canadian episode was not apparently a great success, and the trapper's robes were replaced by RAF officer's uniform, ground staff duties, once war was declared.

The Rural Dean might well have felt put out by this access of frenzy where all had been calm before, but he merely laughed at

94

every sign of his wife's doting. Soon, of course, Chris was gone, if not to Canada, then to some other distant prep-school, and after a suitable period of mourning on Mrs Brack's part, former relationships were resumed.

One Easter term I returned from St Andrews in much pain, having twisted my leg at rugger. I discovered, a week after the injury occurred, that I still could not straighten my knee, but the school doctor said that once the swelling had subsided it would be perfectly all right and that I was not to fuss. When, after a week at Ardingly, there was no sign of improvement Mrs Brack called in her doctor. He, in turn, decided to call in a specialist from Brighton. The latter, a burly Scot, felt around for about ten seconds, grunted when I repeated what the school doctor had said, and advised an immediate operation. 'If we don't get this attended to right away, laddie, your leg will set and you'll be hobbling about for the rest of your days.'

Within forty-eight hours I was laid out in one of the spare bedrooms at the Rectory waiting for the anaesthetist. Later that day I was able to sit out on the lawn with my leg up. Chris was there at the time with a singer called Eve Maxwell-Lyte, a descendant of Henry Lyte the hymn writer. Together they performed duets at private concerts and one of my first memories after coming round was of Chris's admired tenor drifting through the drawing room windows singing 'Have you seen my Lady, With a Glor-y of golden Hair'.

The Worsley Summer

LEAVING ST ANDREWS for Haileybury meant immediate demotion from my position as captain of cricket and second head of school to nonentity. During my last summer at St Andrews, I had laid waste at such neighbouring prep schools as Ashdown House, Fonthill, Copthorne and Brambletye, regularly taking six or seven wickets for next to nothing, and then making the runs off my own bat. I had no illusions, though, about this success being transferred to a higher level, nor was I encouraged to have any by Trunk. Having failed to get in the Haileybury XI himself and having watched numerous prep school stars crash to earth after leaving he said no more to me than 'I've asked "Tiddler" Wennink to keep an eye open for you but it's up to you after that.' 'Tiddler' Wennink, a stalwart of the Haileybury XIs and XVs in both Chris Brack's and Trunk's day, was the master in charge of Colts cricket at Haileybury. Thin as a rake in his youth he was now distinctly portly, with a deep Teutonic voice. No sooner had I arrived than I was put into the special Under 15 net, under Wennink's deceptively baleful gaze.

It was not until the very end of my first term, however, that cricket did much for me. Then, as it was to do at Lee-on-Solent six years later, it saved my bacon.

The whole of that first term I was persecuted by a boy named Worsley, two terms my senior. I was the only new boy in my house, Le Bas, that summer, six having joined it the previous term and four the term before that. The result of this was that there were ten boys of the same year, and roughly the same age, as me, all senior, so that for the whole of my time at Haileybury I was below them in house seniority.

It is difficult looking back to define quite how Worsley made himself so unpleasant and my life such hell. The procedure at

96

Haileybury was that on arrival you shared a Dormitory Class-room, the DC, with about ten other boys. This was a small locker-furnished room adjoining the actual dormitory, this latter consisting of two facing rows of twenty-five or more open cubicles, separated by waist-high wooden partitions. House Prayers, for which the whole house assembled, took place in the DC every evening, the prefects trooping in last, followed by the Housemaster; in the case of Le Bas, it was J. B. D. Joce, trailing a scarf of scent behind him.

After a couple of terms, sometimes a year, you advanced to a Junior Common Room on the other side of the quad. By the time you were sixteen, depending on your work, you became eligible to share a study for four, and then for two. If you became a prefect or were in the sixth you ended up with a study of your own. These single studies consisted of a window seat under a barred window, a desk and a chair, but though their dimensions were those of a monk's cell, they were much prized.

Worsley was a small, fair-haired boy with an exceptionally dominating character. He was, I learned, the son of an Old Haileyburian and he had been born when his father was nearly sixty. Sometime during the previous winter Worsley had been operated on for mastoid and the bone behind his ears still bore the scars.

Having no one to share my situation with, I was especially vulnerable. Those one term senior to me had more or less paired off or formed protective alliances of some kind. Worsley, however, had no mate, so felt himself free to act as gadfly. My arrival was a godsend to him, for now there was someone not only junior to him who couldn't answer back but who was on his own.

I thought later what a good inquisitor Worsley would have made, how persistent an interrogator of recalcitrant prisoners. He did not believe in open confrontation, preferring to trip or flick ears, his own being sacrosanct owing to his mastoids. His basic method was to humiliate, to demean, following up verbal sarcasms by demands to do this or that, fetch his books, dust his

97

locker, taste his shoe polish to make sure it wasn't contaminated, sharpen his pencils, count his paper clips, petty delaying activities calculated to make one late or waste time. Often he would hide books and steal letters, reading them aloud and gloating over my discomfiture. He simply enjoyed seeing how far he could go, immune himself from retribution by weight of seniority and assumed moral support.

I used to dread returning to the DC after lessons, for there would be Worsley, scowling impatiently, waiting to impose some further senseless task, reluctance to perform which resulted in threats of unspecified brutalities and torments. There was nothing, in fact, very drastic that Worsley could have done, but his constant niggling and malice was something I was not used to, and though he was small he was wiry, and I was smaller still. What is more, he exuded malevolence. There was no moment of free time when I did not feel Worsley's spiteful eyes on me, his mind ticking over for some fresh act of cruelty.

None of the others took any part in Worsley's obsessive baiting, but they did not object either. Sometimes I would observe a glint of amusement through someone's spectacles, a voyeuristic pleasure, sometimes simple anticipation at what was going to happen. Mostly, though, they went their own indifferent ways. Worsley had thrown his measly weight about among them the previous term and they were relieved to be rid of him.

Peter Espeut had passed first into the school that year among non-scholars and I had passed second. We both of us, therefore, missed out several forms, he doing Classics in middle school, I Modern Languages. As a consequence of this I never had a single science lesson in my whole life, science not being a subject taught at St Andrews and only compulsory in the Lower School at Haileybury.

Lessons were a relief, for they freed me from Worsley. Another relief was that, after being initially roped in to the choir to sing 'London of Cities Thou art the Flower' the Master of Music, Henry Havergal, his jowls wobbling and covered in sweat as he perpetually was, dubbed me a growler, as I certainly was. I was able therefore to escape into the summer air and, as the evenings lengthened, to go to the nets. I tried to conceal my release from Worsley, in case he should come after me, but he soon discovered it. 'Where do you think you're going?' he would demand on those evenings. 'I've got things for you to do here.' But even I wasn't having that and though Worsley used often to twist my arm as I went out, causing me to drop pads and gloves, which he would then kick about as I tried to pick them up, I got away in the end.

Unfortunately, no one else in the Le Bas DC had any interest in cricket, so I had always to go down to the nets on my own and hope to find someone from another house. As often as not, Worsley would eventually appear, glaring threateningly and making remarks to a companion.

It was right at the end of term that matters came to a head. Every free moment I had was devoted to cricket practice and when I wasn't playing myself, I lay on the bank behind the 1st XI nets with my eyes glued on the bloods of the day: the dark, suave-looking Ronnie Childs, captain in his fourth year of the XI and with never a hair out of place; the willowy Norman Harrison, who was to make two centuries in the match against Uppingham a year later; 'Grundy' Hildick-Smith, a subsequent amateur squash rackets champion; Ronnie Jupp, from my own house, who played for the Lord's Schools and who became the Public Schools Rackets champion. Each, batting and bowling, had his own characteristics. Out of Worsley's clutches, the 1st XI nets seemed a rehearsal of paradise.

Apart from Jupp, Le Bas was not a cricket house. The prefects in my first term included the formidably-built and swarthy P. R. B. Mitchell, Captain of Rugger, Geoffrey Worden and Miles Pitts-Tucker, both in the XV. Mitchell, Worden and Evans, another prefect, were in the Tennis VI. In all but cricket Le Bas was a house to be reckoned with.

Since I was the most junior boy in the House I sat next to this glamorous and sophisticated group at all meals, the custom being for House prefects to sit at one end of the table, with the youngest boys in closest proximity. I don't think a single word was ever addressed to me, but it was enough to be in so privileged a position, party to such high-level gossip and discussion of world affairs.

Jupp had yet to come into his own as a cricketer and I would look with envy at other House tables; members of the XI and 2nd XI, the Colts and Under 15 games, scattered among them and none remotely accessible to me.

The inhabitants of the Le Bas DC were in the main bespectacled and sluggish, their energies devoted to avoiding exercise. To someone brought up like myself on *The Magnet* they seemed Bunterish rather than in the mould of Harry Wharton or Bob Cherry. Their pursuits, such as they were, tended to the homely, collecting caterpillars or doing matchbox tricks. Each term there was some new craze, which absorbed everyone's attention and then disappeared into oblivion.

In some curious fashion Le Bas, by means of a bye and a fluky victory on a terrible pitch, were going strong in the House Cricket Competition. Mitchell bowled erratically but at fearsome speed, terrifying the life out of opponents, and everyone managed to contribute something.

There must have been casualties in the team, injuries or measles, for on the day of the semi-finals I was belatedly sent for, more to make up the numbers, probably, than anything else. F. J. Seabrook, the master in charge of cricket, was an OH, who had himself been in Le Bas, and it must have been he, on the strength of Colts nets, who recommended me to Pitts-Tucker. Jim Seabrook was a fine left-handed batsman, despite wearing glasses, and dashing cover point. He taught geography to the lowest forms, the hallmark of a non-academic, but was a kind and understanding man, rarely seen without his cloth cap. He suffered badly from boils or piles and usually carried a cushion about with him. 'Down the line' he would admonish at the nets in his braying voice 'Play down the line' and that was how all imitations of him began and ended.

In true Magnet style I came in to bat at No. 11, thirty-five needed to win against the holders, Lawrence. Pitts-Tucker and I made all but three of them together in the highest partnership of the match. Since I had taken two wickets in the few overs I was allotted in the Lawrence innings I returned walking on air and to much applause, not least from members of the DC, dragooned on this occasion into watching. I became aware of Mitchell and various other 'bloods' looking at me as if they had never seen me before despite my presence at their elbows for every meal over the last three months.

That evening, perhaps prematurely, I received my house colours, and Worsley was twitching as he came back from reading the notice. Since I had only played once for the house I scarcely expected it, but there was now little of the term left and most of the team were leaving. More important to me than getting my colours was the complete change in attitude shown by the rest of the DC, Worsley excepted. For once, Worsley was the odd man out.

Aware of the shift in fortunes, Worsley made a fresh effort to impose his authority. He started up in his usual fashion, issuing facetious orders and making sarcastic remarks. He had not got very far, when Davies, a former henchman, suddenly turned on him. As he did so, there was a kind of spontaneous uprising among the others. Joke-books, caterpillar boxes, meccano, cards, microscopes – the normal centres of absorbed attention during baiting hours – were cast aside and someone called out 'Let's get Worsley.'

In no time, to Worsley's initial amazement and then impotent rage, he was seized and stripped. Flour was strewn over his skinny body, ink poured on him, and eggs broken over his face.

For ten minutes Worsley struggled vainly against these humiliations. No real hurt was done except to his dignity. When finally he was allowed to get up he was in tears.

For the remaining few days of term Worsley kept a healthy distance. Ignored by the others he avoided my eye, spending as little time among us as was possible.

All through those summer holidays I thought of Worsley. I had no confidence, knowing the ruthlessness and authority of his character, that after an eight-week convalescence his aggression and predatoriness would not be restored. What I dreaded most was that all the previous year's DC except him would move up to the JCR and that he would be left in charge. I found myself having nightmares as the autumn term approached, waking up in my bed at the Rectory covered in sweat. I envisaged Worsley's endless revenge-taking, his mastoid-scarred head bent over mine as he hissed orders.

It was with extreme anxiety but assumed nonchalance, therefore, that on the first day of term I forced myself to look at the house list. It was on the JCR names that I focused first, praying that I should find his there. No sign of it. My heart sank. I looked again to make sure, but there was no doubt. Reluctantly, and in total misery, I turned my gaze to the DC list. But there was no sign of Worsley's name there either, in fact my own name was at the top. What had happened? Some typing error must have taken place, for the whole of the previous term's DC had been moved up *en bloc*, except for me. In the DC there was now my name, followed by those of new boys.

I began to suspect I was having hallucinations, brought on by dread. Then I heard someone call out behind me. 'Heard the news? Worsley's dead. Knocked off his bicycle during the hols.'

That evening, at prayers, Mr Joce, announcing Worsley's death, put on as solemn a voice as he could manage. I felt his pop-eyes alight fractionally on me before he swept out, leaving as usual a wake of lavender water. The ex-members of the DC fidgeted in some embarrassment. 'Bad luck about poor old Worsley,' someone said afterwards to muttered agreement, and that was that. The subject was gladly dropped. No one ever mentioned him again.

Housemasters and Others

I IMAGINE events at junior level passed J. B. D. Joce by. He was, by nature, a bored and idle man, who viewed life with amused detachment. Wilfrid Blunt, who taught art at the time, got into trouble for introducing modern paintings to the boys and went to consult Joce, a fellow bachelor, about what he should do. 'Just sit back, Blunt,' Joce advised, 'and draw your salary.'

Joce's appearance never ceased to fascinate me, resembling as he did a well-known Hollywood-French actor of the time called Adolphe Menjou. His grey wings of hair were brushed back from a central V., a matching moustache drooped beneath a thin nose and protuberant eyes, and he held himself well. He dressed elegantly, sniffed spasmodically in a faintly disdainful manner, and walked with his head thrown back. He seemed to me the height of sophistication, with his aftershave and pomaded hair, his silk handkerchiefs and polished brogues, his air of fatigued imperturbability.

It was his habit when addressing boys to smile, as if there was something infinitely absurd about their mere presence. 'Wah, my poor fellow,' he would drawl.

There were various rumours about Jibbidy J., the most touted being that he was in some way responsible for the arrest of Trotsky. He had joined Haileybury as a junior master from Cambridge as far back as 1914, but he must have joined up soon afterwards, for he spent most of the war as a Lieutenant in the RNVR. In some mysterious fashion he holed up in Mexico, but the facts were as obscure as in the case of another adventurer in Mexico, the novelist B. Traven, author of *The Death Ship* and *The Treasure of the Sierra Madre*. It would have been just like Joce to have known him.

By the time I arrived in Le Bas, Joce had already been

housemaster for fifteen years, any incipient enthusiasm long since passed. It was put about that he was involved with the Brighton Gang, some flashy southcoast crooks then notorious, and certainly he spent his holidays in Brighton, it was presumed in casinos and bars.

What Joce wanted more than anything was a quiet life. As schoolmasters go he was delightfully free of moralizing and conventional hypocrisy. On the rare occasions he felt obliged to pass on adverse criticism, publicly to the house, or privately, or even relay a school notice at prayers, he did so with an immense show of reluctance, rolling his eyes heavenward. He was, I discovered, much liked by his prefects, to whom I imagine he behaved with the utmost civility. To a boy newly arrived in his house he seemed remote and inaccessible. It may be that he knew more than he let on, but had learned when not to interfere. Unfortunately, just at the time when I might have got to know him better, he gave the House up, though he carried on teaching. He retired to Brighton eventually, though I think the Gang had long since split up or been put inside.

Joce taught French and German, and at one stage he taught me. His lessons were leisurely affairs in which it was hard to keep awake. 'Translate a passage, my poor fellow,' he would drawl, and then put his hands over his eyes. When sufficient time had elapsed he would interrupt, 'Wah, that's enough, someone else try a bit.' Thus did we progress through Goethe and Schiller, Lessing and Kleist.

Joce drew the line at boys putting their feet up. 'Wah, my poor fellow,' he called out on one occasion to Peter Vansittart, 'I saw a bloke shot for doing that.' Hodgkinson, another member of our German set, much appreciated Joce, who used to start lessons by saying 'Wah, my poor Hodgkinson, have a good rest, you look washed out.' Hodgkinson had the blankest of expressions and did in fact look as if he'd been put through a mangle. He got no such respite when Kitley, a healthy, puritanical type, took us for German. 'Stop fiddling, Hodgkinson, you make me physically sick,' he called out once when

Hodgkinson was absentmindedly playing with his balls. Poor Hodgkinson, as amiable as he was dozy, went down with the *Cossack* as an Ordinary Signalman, aged twenty. For all his faults he deserved better than to come under the command of the vain Captain Vian. It was Vian, when an Admiral, who during a freezing service on deck broke off in mid-address to admonish a wretched, sick sailor, hauled out of his hammock on Vian's orders, for coughing. 'For goodness say, man, control yourself. It's not only an insult to God, it's an insult to me.'

There were relatively few masters with whom I came into close contact. My form master was W. A. Tregenza, a Cornishman and a decent dull dog. He interested me mainly because he had slicked-down hair and features much like those of Herbert Sutcliffe, then, with Hobbs, England's opening batsman. Tregenza's French sounded Cornish, his voice being totally without variations of tone. His monotony of voice was nevertheless deceptive, for in his quiet way he was often amusing, though less tolerant of those who wished to sleep during his lessons. Hodgkinson in particular used to nod off during readings of Lamartine or de Vigny, only for Tregenza to stop short in what he was saying and stare at him. Eventually, in the unnatural silence, Hodgkinson would come to, opening his eyes in immense surprise when he realized the whole form was gazing at him.

The Master during my whole time at Haileybury was Canon E. F. Bonhote. I suppose during my four years I must have spoken to him but I can't remember it. He was known as The Boot, whether as a contraction of his name or because of his bootlike countenance no one seemed to know. The Boot, with his long jaw and cadaverous features thrust out, stalked the quad as if permanently on the trail of impurity. There was no shortage of that about, but it is doubtful whether the Boot had enough feeling for life to sniff it out. Hampden Jackson, a brilliant teacher of history, described Bonhote in a letter to Wilfrid Blunt, absent in Florence at the time, as 'a prison chaplain by birth . . . his spiritual name is Parker – after Nosey of that ilk, not after Sir Hyde.'

Bonhote's impact on Haileybury was negligible. As far as most of the other masters were concerned, they existed – unless you happened to be taught by them – as mere nicknames, of whom it was impossible to believe they had a private life.

The Science and Maths masters never came my way, so I was able to observe them as inhabitants of another planet. Art classes were conducted by Wilfrid Blunt. Blunt, immensely tall, with a long head, elongated still further by ridged pompadour hair, wore arty ties and was immediately recognizable as a different species to most of his colleagues. He had a golden, soaring voice, more beautiful than either Mr Bull's or Chris Brack's to my untutored ear, and was greatly in evidence at concerts, having given song recitals at the Wigmore Hall the previous year. He was Anthony Blunt's brother. It was assumed that he and the newly appointed lady nutritionist were courting at one time, but she suddenly married H. D. Hake, a housemaster whose hoarse voice gave rise to the rumour that he had only one ball, the other having suffered fatal injury in a rackets court. The lady nutritionist disappeared off with Hake to Australia, where he had been appointed Headmaster of The King's School, Parramatta.

H. D. Hake was a C.B. Fry-like figure in attainment, immensely thin and erect in bearing. He had himself been Head of the School at Haileybury, in the cricket XI for five years, three of them as captain, as well as in the rackets pair for four years. He got hockey and rackets blues at Cambridge, and occasionally played cricket for Hampshire. All this suggested heroic stature but Hake kept himself very much to himself. Possibly ideas of matrimony and emigration were occupying his thoughts at the time of my arrival, because he made no appearances on the cricket field, either on Big Side or with Colts, or in the rackets court.

Blunt gave no signs of rejection at the flight of Hake with the pink-faced and milky nutritionist, though his own simultaneous departure led to conjectures of emotional distress. It turned out, from Blunt's published autobiography, *Married to a Single Life*, that his tastes were in any case quite different.

Had Blunt stayed longer at Haileybury my feeling for painting might have been advanced by a decade. But probably not; there are times when one is susceptible and others when nothing on earth could arouse one's interest. Blunt cared even less about cricket than I did about pottery, which was his speciality in those days.

Most rumours current at Haileybury, though patently false, had long histories. The man in charge of White City, the school lavatories, was known as God; his past was supposed to have encompassed high rank in the Foreign Office, Oxford Blues, and military fame before disgrace befell him and he took up his present post. In some versions he was an Old Haileyburian fallen on hard times.

Certain masters had nicknames that bore no observable relation to their habits or personalities. 'Randy' Rees, for example, had a demure, mouse-like appearance and manner, totally at odds with any idea of sexuality. He was given to emitting a curious, yellowish fluid into his handkerchief at odd moments, a legacy, it was reported, of having been gassed in the Great War. It was difficult to imagine Rees commanding men, so negligible did he seem, but he had served as a Lieutenant in the Royal Field Artillery in France. No doubt he did not throw up for fun. Rees was consistently given a hard time, as it apparently never occurred to anyone that he was a man deserving of respect and sympathy, not a valid object of derision.

The name 'Horsey', as applied to G. R. Smith, had more merit, since Smith was much given to wearing breeches and was frequently to be observed on horse-back. He, too, had suffered appallingly in the war, his burns as a 2nd Lieutenant in the Royal Flying Corps having necessitated skin grafts over most of his face, giving him a simultaneous old-young appearance.

Curiously, Lionel Gough, who taught English, escaped ridicule, for he affected the most obvious and flamboyant red wig. He departed the term after I arrived to become a priest, but religion followed extreme right- and left-wing politics into oblivion. When Wilfrid Blunt met him years later he was surprised to find him not only married but obsessed with hunting.

Caleb Gordon Whitefield, Housemaster of Bartle Frere, huffed and wheezed; no doubt the result of hideous experiences in Flanders, where he was mentioned in despatches. Whitefield was not loved outside his house, and possibly not in it either, for he had a Uriah-Heepish manner and no charm.

I wish I had known Joce better and that I had realized he was still alive and living in Brighton when I went to live on the northern slopes of the South Downs in 1955. He died, in fact, soon afterwards, but one might have got from him a more realistic and mature view of those who taught us than we were ever likely to have had ourselves. On the other hand Joce himself was so detached and aloof, even from his own colleagues, that he might simply have reinforced one's own prejudices.

I believe Joce was Portuguese Jewish in origin; certainly he seemed European rather than British. The only other Joce I ever came across was a surgeon in Adelaide who removed my appendix.

It was rare to see Joce in company. Nearly always he was alone, strolling gently along, novel in hand and humming to himself, the familiar trail of scent following him. 'Wah, my poor friend,' he would say if he came across any member of his house, nodding genially, and passing on. His usual clothes were a tweed jacket and matching waistcoat, presumably of some suit whose trousers he had abandoned in favour of grey flannels.

Joce retired from Le Bas at the end of the 1938 summer term, A. T. A. Wallace succeeding him. Wallace could hardly have been more different; a scientist, athletic and purposeful in appearance, an obvious and clean-limbed enemy of slackness.

Under Joce the House had more or less run itself, his prefects being either scholars or in the XI or XV. Wallace inherited a house whose luminaries had all gone. Instead of the grave and talented Pitts-Tucker we had a Head of House who stood at the entrance of his cubicle and rotated his cock like a propeller, grinning at his skill.

I thought Wallace and I would get on badly and that he would see in me a decadence and self-indulgence at odds with the more spartan regime he was bent on encouraging. For example, there was the matter of the Corps, in which Wallace had become a leading light. Quite how it came about I can't remember but I was the only boy in the whole school who on neither medical nor moral grounds was not a member of the OTC. In theory, membership of the Corps was voluntary but every boy, unless a confessed pacifist or suffering from some physical disability, was expected to join. I suppose Joce never pressed the point and I had simply opted out. As a result I was spared the tedium of parades and field days, the polishing of boots and cleaning of webbing that occupied and irritated others. Oddly enough, no one appeared to resent my freedom from these chores, merely expressing envy. Had I the faintest notion then of what lay ahead of me I might have thought again, but as it turned out, even four years in the Corps at Haileybury would not have saved me from sea-service as a rating in the Navy.

While everyone else was parading I played squash or rackets. Only John Drinkall, who later won four post-war blues at Cambridge, and Alan Fairbairn, both Amateur Champions after leaving, could beat me at squash, but though Ronnie Jupp and I won the House rackets in Wallace's first term as House-master, I was never in quite the same class as a rackets player as Jupp, Drinkall or Alan Fairbairn.

Wallace, surprisingly, seemed kindly disposed towards me. He raised the matter of the Corps once but did not pursue it when I showed no enthusiasm. The reverse of hail-fellow-well-met, he nevertheless showed an unexpected tact and sensitivity in his dealings with everyone. At the same time, in his strong silent way, shoulders braced and pipe in square jaw, he made one want to please him.

Before long Wallace and I were playing squash regularly every week and the fact that I could beat him, just, made our relationship happily competitive. He was genuinely proud for the House when I got into the XI and though no cricketer himself, he watched whenever possible.

During my last term Wallace was obliged to cane me, an embarrassment for both of us, since I had to be briefly de-prefected as well. Every Ascension Day there was a school holiday during which boys were supposed to roam the surrounding countryside, Wormley Woods or Epping Forest. What was expressly forbidden was the use of public transport or visits to towns or cinemas. A friend and I decided to go to Wimbledon where some kind of exhibition or possibly Davis Cup match was being played. On our way back, observing us plodding up the Avenue, The Boot gave us a lift. He asked politely how we had spent our day and we provided a detailed account of a healthy day's rambling looking for butterflies, picnicking, fishing. He appeared approving of us and we parted happily, probably the only time we had spoken during the previous year.

Next morning Wallace sent for us. He did not seem annoyed but simply pointed to a photograph on the back page of *The Times* showing a section of the crowd at Wimbledon. In the centre of the picture, identifiable beyond dispute, were Lennox-Simpson and myself, cigarettes in hand.

'I understand from the Master,' Wallace said, 'that you misled him about your activities yesterday. He is very displeased that you should have deceived him. He expects me to punish you accordingly. I have no option therefore but to de-prefect both of you for a month and to beat you.'

He turned away. 'I'll take you one at a time. Lennox-Simpson, you first. Ross, please wait outside.'

I closed the door behind me and hung about in the passage.

There was a sound of swishing. A minute or two later Lennox-Simpson emerged. 'Your turn,' he said, making a feeble, faintly tearful attempt to smile.

I went in and took my coat off, making to bend down over the two chairs that had been put out in the study back to back. Wallace was in his shirt sleeves. We looked at each other. 'I'm sorry,' he said briefly.

Friendship was no impediment to duty and the six strokes came down like lashes, hurting more than I had believed possible. Wallace was panting by the end. I got awkwardly to my feet and reached for my jacket. Wallace held out his hand. I tried not to show that there were tears in my eyes and was surprised to find that there were tears in his eyes, too. It made no difference to our relationship, but it still seemed unnecessarily demeaning. After a couple of days the pain wore off, Lennox-Simpson's and my bruises were duly applauded when next we appeared naked, and life went on much as before.

Wallace left the same term as I did, in August 1940. I went up in October to St John's College, Oxford, and he went into the Army. In 1943, as a Major on the Army-Air Co-operation Staff, he received the Military Cross. He was shot down and killed on a flying sortie in North Africa shortly afterwards.

As it happened, had Wallace survived, he would not have had the same house to return to. The term after we left Le Bas was closed and turned into a Hospital Ward. It re-opened two years later under the name of Kipling. There seemed some irony in that.

The Golden Apples

Some there are who get on the wrong track
Early on, victims of nannies or parents at odds
With each other or myopia or fatness,
Butterfingers spending their lives going back,
Plunging the darkness for pieces of suffering.
These remember only misery and scorn, the curt nods
Of masters responsive to more appetizing pupils,
The feeling of being failures and feeling
Failure to be irrevocable, their own and God's,
Who had made them eccentric, ugly or comic.
But, later, from lessening oblivion, humiliation, distil
Subtle essences, no need to be popular;
Tortures of childhood are made into *objets d'art*.
These fatten at High Table, turn novelist or critic.

Others, however, restless in unsexy beds, assistants
At private or public schools, obscure servants
Of trade in a crumbling empire, dream of the distance
Time has put between them and their prospects
So certain once as they moved with confidence,
Taking the Greeks as text and pretext,
Through enviable teams and prizes, romantic friendships
That grew less interesting, like their scholarship.
The features, too, have hardened, grown coarse
Where once scrawled lines of nose and lip
Were tender. Shrinking each year, these must force
Themselves back to the orchard where the golden apple
Falls and their friends wear puzzled faces,
And those they barely noticed, lagging in all the races,
Are the ones they have to grapple.

Success, My Dears

Adsis, Musa, canentibus,
Laeta voce canentibus,
Longos clara per annos
Haileyburia floreat

As a school, Haileybury in the middle and late Thirties was a place to which no anti-elitist could properly take exception. There was little money about, most boys being the sons of naval or army officers, or of clergymen. A few had Indian or colonial connections of some kind, there was a sprinkling of Indian princelings. I never had the impression that any of my contemporaries were more than just comfortably off. It was somehow in keeping that the first Haileyburian to become Prime Minister was Mr C. R. Attlee, and that he should be Labour.

If it was a school without extremes of wealth or social pretensions Haileybury was nevertheless conscious of its place in the scheme of things. This constituted producing high-ranking officers in the Armed Forces, senior civil servants, doctors, lawyers, colonial administrators. At one time, shortly before the end of the war, three out of the top five RAF commands were held by Haileyburians, as were three out of the top six Army commands a decade earlier; Lord Oaksey was the Presiding Judge at the Nuremberg trials, and apart from Attlee as Prime Minister there were two other Haileyburians in the Cabinet.

The term I went to Haileybury, Hitler, having withdrawn Germany three years earlier from the League of Nations, re-occupied the Rhineland. By the time I got into the XI, an event more relevant to me then than anything happening in the outside world, Germany had marched into Austria, claimed the Sudetenland and taken possession of the rest of Czechoslovakia. A month after I was to make my first appearance for Haileybury against Cheltenham at Lord's – in fact rain prevented a ball being bowled – we were at war. The Munich agreement, made so complacently and innocently by Chamberlain, had been proved to be what its detractors had claimed, a shoddy piece of paper.

Looking back, it seems extraordinary that all this should have meant so little. But outside the History VIth and those coming under the influence of Hampden Jackson and his successor, in the winter of 1938, Martin Wight, there was scarcely any intrusion of political feeling into our self-contained world. Although Haileybury after the war was probably more powerfully represented in the Labour party with Attlee, Christopher Mayhew and Geoffrey de Freitas than any other school, the atmosphere during my time was scarcely one to encourage independence of thought. Political science and 'current affairs' were subjects outside the normal curriculum and, as such, periods of comparative rest. Words like 'bourgeois' were sometimes bandied about as expressions of mockery and directed at businessmen in general, but in the main such of my generation as survived learned, if not at Haileybury, then in the Forces, to keep their heads down over matters that did not, they felt, concern them.

In 1932 W. H. Auden had published *The Orators* in which he had dedicated a poem to the Captain of the Sedbergh School XV

> Success my dears – Ah!
> Rounding the curve of the drive
> Standing up, waving, cheering from car,
>   The time of their life:
> The fags are flushed, would die at their heroes' feet;
> Quick, someone, tug at that handle, get
> At them shouting, shoulder them high, who won by
>   their pluck and their dare.

'My dears' would scarcely have seemed a suitable address in a poem to the Captain of the Haileybury XV, and indeed 'camp' of any kind was rare at Haileybury. Of the two most obvious 'camp' figures, one became a High Church Anglican priest, much loved in a poor parish, and the other a distinguished actor in Australia. Haileybury produced a fair crop of actors – Hugh Williams, Frank Vosper, Robert Flemyng, Stephen Haggard, among others – and the school play meant more in the life of the school than anything done by way of art or literature. Rex Whistler, killed in the Normandy landings, was the only painter of note to come from Haileybury, though he soon escaped to the Slade, and such talent as was shown in the school literary magazine, *Extra*, seemed not to have survived leaving. Needless to say, *Extra*, in my eyes, seemed as remote an expression of taste as the pages of the *Yellow Book*.

The kind of preoccupations described by Cyril Connolly as being common to his Eton generation found no place in the lives of anyone I knew.

That Haileybury was essentially philistine, though perhaps no more than most other public schools, is beyond argument. Art was regarded as an eccentricity, its practitioners deviants of some kind and unlikely to come to any good. I doubt whether any public school encouraged a general interest in painting or poetry, and Haileybury, despite the efforts of Wilfrid Blunt, was no exception. As far as I was concerned the French and German romantics, required reading in any case, provided all the aesthetic nourishment I needed. Even Tregenza's gloomy Cornish delivery could not quite ruin the sonorities of Lamartine's

> Souvent sur la montagne, à l'ombre du vieux chêne,
> Au coucher du soleil, tristement je m'assieds;
> Je promène au hasard mes regards sur la plaine,
> Dont le tableau changeant se déroule à mes pieds.

Lamartine's *L'Isolement*, *Le Lac* and *Le Souvenir* I came to know by heart; his volume *Méditations*, published in 1820, the same year as Géricault showed his *Radeau de la Méduse*, was to me the epitome of romantic feeling. Lamartine's career – revolutionary, diplomat, traveller – seemed suitable for a poet and his succession of love affairs went some way for me towards making the idea of a poet respectable. It was not a concept, though, that related to the present. Contemporaries of Delacroix and Ingres, the French romantic poets practised an exotic art whose heroes tended to be killed in battle and whose heroines to die young. The *Nuits* poems of de Musset, their violent feelings expressed in the most serene and classical language, the haunting music of de Vigny and Verlaine, were of precisely the kind to make an effect on an impressionable but totally unintellectual sensibility. The passion of their love-affairs, their ability – in the cases of Lamartine and de Vigny – to conform and shine in political and military life, their handsome uniformed appearance, made them seem of more heroic cut than their English contemporaries. The French in general, despite their sententiousness and solemnity, exerted more of a hold on my imagination then than Byron and Shelley, for it was sound rather than sense that attracted me. As examples, however – in the wake of Eliot, Pound and Auden – for the writing of English poetry, they were disastrous. Soon enough I learned to separate the life from the works but such discernment as I acquired fatally damaged my infatuation with the French Romantics.

In the chapter of *Enemies of Promise*, published in 1938, called 'The Mandarin Dialect' Cyril Connolly concerned himself with definitions of style. His own instinct was to defend style against those who would argue that the best writers have no style; that, in Samuel Butler's words 'the best writing, like the best-dressed man, is sober, subdued and inconspicuous.'

'Style,' Connolly asserted, 'is not a manner of writing, it is a relationship; the relation in art between form and content.' He went on to state that the vocabulary of a writer is his currency 'but it is a paper currency and its value depends on the reserve of mind and heart which back it.'

Enemies of Promise was begun fifteen years after Connolly left Eton. Most of his schoolboyish preoccupations – with his own

character or lack of it, his vanity, idleness and worldliness –
remained with him to the end, but they served him well both in
this book and in others, for his introspectiveness enabled him to
assess and query the habits, values and disciplines of school life
in a way few manage.

Such self-awareness was not common at Haileybury. But
Connolly's interest in style revived in myself echoes of a similar
preoccupation. The dandyism and mandarin manners that
affected me, however, were not to do with literature but
behaviour, and, more strictly, with behaviour in sport.

However much school life worked against aesthetic appreciation a craving, perhaps sub-conscious, for beauty in expression of one kind or another existed in most boys. For myself it
took the form of observing the heroes of my adolescence in
terms of how they dressed and their mannerisms on the field of
play. Effortlessness and elegance were the ideal; a style that,
however apparently affected, yet appeared natural and unconscious.

Many of the leading amateur cricketers of the time – D. R.
Jardine, lately captain of England during the Bodyline tour of
Australia, Errol Holmes, captain of Surrey, Freddie Brown and
Alan Melville, for example – were rarely to be seen without a
knotted handkerchief or silk muffler round their necks. Needless to say, when my turn came and I considered myself
sufficiently secure for it not to appear ludicrous, I followed suit.
Another apparent foible was the turning back of the right blazer
cuff. Dandies, as Connolly rightly stated, are perfectionists and
most perfectionists in the playing of games have more than a
touch of the dandy in them.

The result is a fastidiousness in dress and a scrupulous
concern with technique. The development of a style in prose
and poetry and the perfecting of a stroke at cricket or rackets
have much in common. They are the result of a desire for
excellence, for the gesture that contrives an exact equivalent,
and which can be achieved only by self-discipline and practice.

Watching Walter Hammond make a cover drive or Alan

Melville a leg-glance, or, nearer home, Ronnie Jupp kill the ball at rackets, was an aesthetic experience but one to which at that stage I could attach no label. Every good batsman had his own unmistakable way of going about things, even when letting the ball go by outside the off stump, bat raised in a gesture of indifference or contempt, the line of the body as expressive in its way as that of a dancer.

That art and literature dealt at a deeper level of aesthetics than sport was something of which I may have been aware, but whatever lip service I paid to the idea, for myself the proposition that sport was poetry in action was more potent. However much I resisted the attraction of the poetry of poetry I was susceptible enough to it in other guises.

It astonished me later, when I came to it, to find Auden in one of the Odes in *The Orators* writing such lines as:

> Symondson – praise him at once! –
> Our right-wing three-quarter back
> Sergy, bulwark of every defence,
>   Mainspring of attack:
> When aligned like a squadron of bombers they flew downfield
> And over and over again we yelled
> 'Let the ball out to Sergy'. They did, he scored, and we dance.

because although the campness is uncomfortably evident, it came as a revelation that such a subject could be used in the 1930s for poetry. Auden, no less than Connolly, was immune to the aesthetic excitements of sport, that same excitement that Montherlant found in the body itself rather than in what it did. But watching a centre three-quarter cutting through on Big Side or Norman Harrison in the nets on Pavilion, I knew differently. The shiver down the spine that lines of poetry such as Housman's

> Into my heart an air that kills
> From yon far country blows:
> What are those blue remembered hills,
> What spires, what farms are those?

or passages of music produced was, in my case, more likely to be caused by the classic action of a bowler or the reaction of a batsman timing the ball so late the impact seemed feather-light and caressive, invisible almost in proportion to the effect. Such feelings, for me, were first steps in the evolution of a sensibility slow to come to terms with itself.

I had thought that the phrase 'Heart of the heartless world' belonged uniquely to the beautiful poem 'To Margot Heinemann' written by John Cornford shortly before he was killed in Spain.

> Heart of the heartless world,
> Dear heart, the thought of you
> Is the pain at my side,
> The shadow that chills my view.
>
> The wind rises in the evening
> Reminds them that autumn is near.
> I am afraid to lose you,
> I am afraid of my fear

One holiday at Ardingly, reading *The Orators*, I came across this:

> Heart of the heartless world
> Whose pulse we count upon;
> Alive, the live on which you have called
>   Both pro and con,
> Good to a gillie, to an elver times out of mind
> Tender to work – shy and games – shy kind
> Does he think? Not as kind as all that; he shall find
>   One fine day he is sold.

Auden called *The Orators* 'an English study' and indeed, with its Address for a Prize Day and Odes to school footballers and schoolmasters, it could hardly be more English in its preoccupations. I found it pretty impossible to make head or tail of much of it, but what was exciting was the realization that school as such could be made the material for poetry. Auden's jokeyness and irreverence of tone summoned up a whole new way of considering The Boot and Tregenza. The opening address ends: 'Draw up a list of rotters and slackers, of proscribed persons under headings like this. Committees for municipal or racial improvement – the headmaster. Disbelievers in the occult – the school chaplain. The bogusly cheerful – the games master. The really disgusted – the teacher of modern languages. 'All these have got to die without issue. Unless my memory fails me there's a stoke hole under the floor of this hall, the Black Hole we called it in my day. New boys were always put in it. Ah, I see I am right. Well look to it. Quick, guard that door, stop that man. Good. Now boys bustle them, ready, steady – go.'

Such a way of writing, the pedagogic facetious style used for anarchic purposes, was a valuable corrective to large doses of Racine and Victor Hugo.

A Photograph of Hammond

Even at 1/500th you can't freeze him,
Make his image quite static.
He remains more mobile than diagrammatic.

Take compass, protractor. However
You dismantle him, the parts
Remain true, suggest velocity.

Leonardo would have made him fly,
This batsman so revving with power
He seems airborne.

Like some prototype birdman
Straining at silk moorings, he conveys
Ambiguity, both imprisonment and release.

Never mind the earthbound heaviness
Of hip, of shoulders, his cover-drive
Evokes airiness, an effortless take-off.

A study in anatomy, circa 1930. Anonymous.
But there, nonchalantly stuffed
In his pocket, that blue handkerchief signs it.

Cricket at Brighton

At night the Front like coloured barley-sugar; but now,
Soft blue, all soda, the air goes flat over flower-beds,
Blue railings and beaches. Below, half-painted boats, bow
Up, settle in sand, names like Moss-Rose and Dolphin
Drying in a breeze that flicks at the ribs of the tide.
The chalk coastline folds up its wings of Beachy Head
And Worthing, fluttering white over water like brides.
Regency squares, the Pavilion, oysters and mussels and gin.

Piers like wading confectionery, esplanades of striped tulip.
Cricket began here yesterday, the air heavy, suitable
For medium-paced bowlers. Deck-chairs, though, mostly were
                                                         vacant,
Faces white over startling green. Later, trains will decant
People with baskets, litter and opinions, the seaside's staple
Ingredients. To-day Langridge pushes the ball for unfussed
Singles; ladies clap from check rugs, talk to retired colonels.
On tomato-red verandahs the scoring rate is discussed.

Sussex *v.* Lancashire, the air birded and green after rain,
Dew on syringa and cherry. Seaward the water
Is satin, pale emerald, fretted with lace at the edges,
The whole sky rinsed easy like nerves after pain.
May here is childhood, lost somewhere between and never
Recovered, but again moved nearer, as a lever
Turned on the pier flickers the Past into pictures.
A time of immediacy, optimism, without stricture.

Postcards and bathing-machines and old prints.
Something comes back, the inkling, the momentary hint
Of what we had wanted to be, though differently now,
For the conditions are different and what we had wanted
We wanted as we were then, without conscience, unhaunted,
And given the chance must refuse to want it again.
Only, occasionally, we escape, we return where we were:
Watching cricket at Brighton, Tate bowling through sea-scented
    air.

On an Engraving of
Alfred Mynn Esq (1852)

Grasped like a twig in his enormous hands,
The crude bat is a measure, as now his expanding
Frame places him in Time – a Victorian,
Whose engraved features yellow while a band
Plays in the distance, and a gulf of pleasure
Yawns. Now, as we watch his careful,
Studied posture, we imagine the bowler rolling up his sleeve.

Beneath the solemn black-quiffed forehead
The eyes, like cameras, study us – developments
Of their passive gaze; and what is said
Nobody knows, as all we see is part
Of our costumed Past – the stomach bellying like a sail,

Pale-blue sash, and narrow, faded flannels.
And what is hidden is the art
That made his name a byword in a social age,
The brilliant speed and swinging flight
No portrait can suggest, words recreate or disparage.

Test Match at Lord's

Bailey bowling, McLean cuts him late for one.
I walk from the Long Room into slanting sun.
Two ancients halt as Statham starts his run.
Then, elbows linked, but straight as sailors
On a tilting deck, they move. One, square-shouldered as a tailor's
Model, leans over, whispering in the other's ear:
'Go easy. Steps here. This end bowling.'
Turning, I watch Barnes guide Rhodes into fresher air,
As if to continue an innings, though Rhodes may only play by ear.

123

Stanley Matthews

Not often *con brio*, but *andante, andante*,
    horseless, though jockey-like and jaunty,
Straddling the touchline, live margin
    not out of the game, nor quite in,
Made by him green and magnetic, stroller
Indifferent as a cat dissembling, rolling
A little as on deck, till the mouse, the ball,
    slides palely to him,
And shyly, almost with deprecatory cough, he is off.

Head of a Perugino, with faint flare
Of the nostrils, as though Lipizzaner-like,
    he sniffed at the air,
Finding it good beneath him, he draws
Defenders towards him, the ball a bait
They refuse like a poisoned chocolate,
    retreating, till he slows his gait
To a walk, inviting the tackle, inciting it.

At last, unrefusable, dangling the ball at the instep
He is charged – and stiffening so slowly
It is rarely perceptible, he executes with a squirm
Of the hips, a twist more suggestive than apparent,
    that lazily disdainful move *toreros* term
      a Veronica – it's enough.
Only emptiness following him, pursuing some scent
Of his own, he weaves in towards,
    not away from, fresh tacklers,
Who, turning about to gain time, are by him
    harried, pursued not pursuers.

Now gathers speed, nursing the ball as he cruises,
Eyes judging distance, noting the gaps, the spaces
Vital for colleagues to move to, slowing a trace,
As from Vivaldi to Dibdin, pausing,
        and leisurely, leisurely, swings
To the left upright his centre, on hips
His hands, observing the goalkeeper spring,
        heads rising vainly to the ball's curve
Just as it's plucked from them; and dispassionately
Back to his mark he trots, whistling through closed lips.

Trim as a yacht, with similar lightness
        – of keel, of reaction to surface – with salt air
Tanned, this incomparable player, in decline fair
                to look at, nor in decline either,
Improving like wine with age, has come far –
        born to one, a barber, who boxed
Not with such filial magnificence, but well.
'The greatest of all time,' *meraviglioso*, Matthews –
        Stoke City, Blackpool and England.
Expressionless enchanter, weaving as on strings
Conceptual patterns to a private music, heard
Only by him, to whose slowly emerging theme
He rehearses steps, soloist in compulsions of a dream.

Racehorses at Gulfstream

Turning for home, at last off the bridle,
They seem as they lengthen their strides

Almost to falter. Beneath them, green thickens,
Goes drowsy, as though a film

Were being slowed, the frame frozen.
They have for a second the air

Of somnambulists, moving loosely
In envelopes of water. An uphill element

Is against them. They break free,
And their actions, recovering, turn languorous,

Muscles slithering in quarters
Transparent under sweat, their veins swollen.

Palmettos and flags become fixed blurs,
And towing in their slipstreams long shadows

They dent distance as it dwindles,
Air, earth conniving, eyes limitless.

Stallion and Teaser

For him, who is above preliminaries,
It is no more than the seigneurial
Raising of hooves round a mane,
A brief thrusting. He strolls off,
Lordly as the sun, indifferent now
To the mare, her bride's eyes dying.
But for that other, amiable,
Grey around the lip, who never
Quite made it, civilities
Of courtship are what he must settle for –
Eyes hazy with love-light, the nuzzle
Of arched necks, legs quivering
As if caressed by cool breezes. She bridles,
Looses her urine. And removed from her,
Pawing stubble in the distance,
He must comfort himself with a suitor's
Dwindling euphoria, remembering
Her shiver, sweat drying on his skin.

Watching Benaud Bowl

Leg-spinners pose problems much like love,
Requiring commitment, the taking of a chance.
Half-way deludes; the bold advance.

Right back, there's time to watch
Developments, though maybe too late.
It's not spectacular, but can conciliate.

Instinctively romantics move towards,
Preventing complexities by their embrace,
Batsman and lover embarked as overlords.

A Cricketer in Retirement

For George Cox

The marine and the regency, sea frets,
And somewhere the Downs backing a station
Like a Victorian conservatory. I come upon
A scorecard yellow as old flannels and suddenly
I see him, smilingly prowling the covers
In soft shoes, shirt rolled to the forearm,
Light as a yacht swaying at its moorings,
Receptive to breezes. An element
Of silk, of ease, with none of the old dutiful
Sense of the regiment, the parade-ground
Posture that gave even the best of them the air of retainers.
Instead, a kind of compassion linking top hats
With turnips, the traditional turning to devilry.
One apart, yet part all the same,
Of that familiar pattern of families,
Parkses and Langridges, Tates and Oakes and Gilligans,
Griffiths and Busses, Sussex is rich in,
The soft air phrased by their fickleness.

Never one for half-measures, as generous
With ducks as half-centuries, he seemed
To calculate extravagance, waywardly spendthrift
With the cold calculators, Yorkshire, the Australians,
Hove and the Saffrons ablaze with his fireworks,
Dad wincing in his grave. With others,
Less challenging, he was often vulnerable,
Giving his wicket to those who were glad of it,
Indulgently negligent against parachuting spinners.
Now there are no scorecards, just pulled hamstrings
In village cricket and instead of fancy-free
Strokes in festival arenas the soothing
Of successors. The forearms make gardens,
And the journeys have lengthened, a sunset
Of orchards and vineyards, where reclining in a bath
Of imperial proportions he observes a wife
As delicate with pastry as he was at the wicket.

World Cup

It is, after all, a kind
Of music, an elaborating of themes
That swell and subside, which
In the converting of open spaces
Take on a clean edge.
    A throw, a chip,
A flick, Wilson to Charlton,
To Moore, to Hunt, to Greaves –
The diagonals cross, green space is charmed.

A precise movement, balletic in ordained
Agility, with the players as if magnetised
Moving into places seemingly allotted them
– They seem from above to be pushed like counters,
And only the fluffed pass, the momentary
Crudity disconcerting as a clerical oath,
Destroys the illusion. A goal restores it.

Arms raised like gladiators, they embrace.
Human emotions swamp them, childishly even
For such protagonists of perfection.
     And involved in this mixture
Of the fallible and the dreamy,
The percussive and the lilting, they demonstrate
How art exists on many levels, spirit
And matter close-knit as strangling lianas.

Death of a Trainer

In Memory of Alan Oughton

Among fellow jockeys bandy and small
He was straight as a board and tall,
So long to the knees
He could pick up and squeeze
Novices and rogues round all sorts of courses.
Neither bred to the sea nor horses,
The son of a Pompey tailor,
He walked with brisk roll of a sailor,
Tilted, as by saddle or quarter deck,
A curve from hipbone to neck.

Falls caught up with him, of the kind habitual
To riders over sticks, but he seemed at last
Safe in his Findon stables, at his disposal
A handful of jumpers not especially fast
Nor clever, but amenable to discipline
And patience, ridden out on a skyline
Of downland and sea, in lime dawn
Or half darkness, clouds torn
By gales blistering the channel,
Mist thickening beechwoods to flannel.

Busy as a ship, smelling of hay
And leather, of mash and linseed,
The yard seemed that ideal harbour
In which work has the essence of play,
Day-long, night-long, obedient to need,
The summer's sweetness, winter's bleak labour.
But season following season, winner
Following winner, so did pain circle,
Eyes grow strained and the thin body thinner,
Until there was only the long hell.

What I still see is a skeletal guy
Half imagined, half real, between races at Fontwell,
Saddle under one arm, threading his way
Through the weighing room, or wiping jellied eel
From his lips, sawdust running out of him
As he drops in the distance, each limb
Jerky as if on a string, patch
Over one eye, trilby dead straight,
And a gelding quickening to snatch
Up the verdict, just leaving it too late.

Crusoe

As a present for captaining an unbeaten XI at St Andrews, Trunk Heywood had given me a copy of R. C. Robertson-Glasgow's *The Brighter Side of Cricket*. During my time at Haileybury this was my bedside book more often than any other, though latterly the problem arose of how to reconcile such an interest with the writings of Auden and Connolly, and such political commentators as G. E. R. Gedye and F. A. Voight, newly emergent on my horizon. I had neither the confidence nor wit quite to realize that these things were not mutually exclusive. I did not think it likely that there would be others in thrall equally to Auden and to cricket. Poetry and cricket, perhaps, but poetry of another sort. Nothing at Haileybury or at Oxford suggested to the contrary, so I was obliged to live out two secret, or perhaps more precisely, submerged lives.

Robertson-Glasgow remained, nevertheless, an important influence, for he, even more than Bernard Darwin and Neville Cardus, the two sporting mandarins of the twenties and thirties, taught me that the writing of good prose depended on the quality of mind brought to bear rather than on the subject. Robertson-Glasgow was, in the first instance, a classical scholar; his prose no less supple and elegant than, for example, Cyril Connolly's. It was simply focused on different things. The problem with Robertson-Glasgow, as at that time it seemed with Wodehouse, was that he could never quite bring himself to be serious about anything. Again, I imagined Robertson-Glasgow to be as naturally reactionary as Wodehouse and Sapper, thus ruling himself out of being taken seriously as a writer on grounds of both levity and political frivolousness.

And yet, and yet; I had only to open *The Brighter Side of Cricket* to be both moved and enchanted; moved by the beauty of the writing and the sense of transience that underlay it; enchanted by the magical evocation of English summers, cricket grounds and cricketers. Robertson-Glasgow managed to be funny and lyrical at the same time and moreover he wrote as an Oxford Blue and a county cricketer. My developing literary snobbishness might oblige me to regard Robertson-Glasgow's forms of writing with detachment, but if he could not hold the appeal of 'real' poets with cricketing backgrounds – Sassoon and Blunden for example – he struck chords that they could not. For if they were poets who played at cricket he was a cricketer who did more than play at writing.

When I met Crusoe, as he was called, I realized he was a different creature altogether from the elegant and stylish figures of my adolescent imagination. All the style had gone into the writing. He was a large, bald man, with a deafening laugh. He talked non-stop and he had a disconcerting habit of thrusting his face right up close and then weaving away. I played against him at Oxford when he was in his forties and he could still make the ball nip off the pitch at a lively pace. He had a high rollicking action, the inswinger his staple ball, but he could get it to straighten and sometimes veer the other way.

A notable cricketer at Charterhouse, Crusoe played four times for Oxford against Cambridge between 1920 and 1923, his contemporaries in those matches including four England captains – Arthur Gilligan, Percy Chapman, Douglas Jardine and Gubby Allen – and another half-dozen of Test standard. For some odd reason, although he took 146 wickets for Oxford all told, he managed only two in his four games at Lord's. Nevertheless, he once took nine for 38 for Somerset against Middlesex and was good enough to play for the Gentlemen against the Players. His term as a regular county cricketer, though, was no more than the span of his residence at Oxford. He went on playing for some years in the holidays, but as he remarked in his autobiography *46 Not Out* 'Till now I had been a practising cricketer. Afterwards, I was but an intervener.'

What I did not know in those days was that Crusoe was a

manic-depressive who had more than once tried to take his own life. Sadly, he was in the end to succeed, by which time I had taken his old job at the *Observer*. He simply got up in the Press Box one afternoon, put on his old battered trilby and raincoat, and announced he was calling it a day. He went back to his house on the Thames and never came to a first-class cricket match again.

Crusoe was as difficult to stop in full flow of talk as either Cardus or Fry, and he was noisier than either. He made the pavilion literally shake with his roars and there was no gain-saying his conviviality, though if you were feeling frail it was alarming. Underneath the raconteur and joker there was, nevertheless, a man of considerateness and charm, also of a gravity that seldom got into his writing.

Crusoe was against hypocrisy: 'I have never regarded cricket as a branch of religion,' he wrote. 'I have never believed that cricket can hold Empires together or that cricketers chosen to represent their country in distant parts should be told, year after year, that they are Ambassadors . . . The air of holy pomp started from the main temple at Lord's, and it breathed over the Press like a miasma. *"Procul, O Procul Este, Profani!"* We are not as other men. Sometimes I look back at reports of games in which I took part and I have thought "What has become of that earthy striving, that comic, tragic thing which was our match of cricket?"'

Such remarks did not always make for friends in high places, where the 'comic, tragic thing' was given dimensions and status beyond its nature. But it was what Crusoe wrote about with grace and good humour, a humour which did not desert him in Test Matches, in some respects to his disadvantage. Whereas Cardus, in Crusoe's own phrase, was 'master of the rhapsodical style', without equal on the great moments and the great cricketers, Crusoe wrote about Test Matches as if they took place in the Parks at Oxford, which he no doubt wished they did. He could, and did, write marvellously about the great players of the day, but his heart was with Oxford and Somerset.

Reading him you felt he got as much enjoyment out of the blacksmith slogging and the curate taking one on the shins as out of a cover drive by Hammond or a hook by Sutcliffe. Perhaps it was because he himself twice took Sutcliffe's wicket, once bowling him in a sea-mist at Scarborough, and so felt no false deference.

Crusoe was essentially a miniaturist, his natural length seven to eight hundred words. He was a master of compression, able in the space allotted – under the generic title of *Sporting Prints* – to capture the essence of a player's technique and character, his background and style. The hundreds of cricket *Prints* he composed, ranging from such as Tom Hayward and Archie Maclaren up to Cyril Walters and Alf Gover, have the concise-ness of poems, the evocativeness of watercolours. Some of the subjects were before his time, some after, but the vast majority he had the advantage of having played with or against.

However, *The Brighter Side of Cricket* was not to do with the great except in parenthesis. Rather, it was an attempt to reflect on an addiction to cricket in its various manifestations, from childhood on. He wrote about the game not as a self-contained affair of tactics and statistics but as part of the world – possibly the brightest part – we inherit, as we do youth, family, school. 'In the kaleidoscope of infancy,' he wrote, 'such things as goblins in the dark corners of the nursery at twilight, a sour-edged Eton collar, coloured Easter eggs, or the back of the vicar's head in the Creed, are worthy rivals to cricket. But all of them, cricket as well, are fugitive . . .'

It was in character that Crusoe should describe the ideal form of spectatorship as stopping by some village green 'where cricket was played before America was one nation' and interest was devoid of anxiety. He wrote about such things as nets, fielding practice, family cricket in the garden, village rivalries, affectionate towards the clumsy and comic, but managing to suggest by a phrase or two that from the same material of cow-shots and dropped catches came the extravagant inven-tions of Macartney and the lazy sweetness of Ranji.

For most boys the concept of beauty takes getting used to. What Crusoe achieved in a passage like the one above or in his paragraph on the Parks at Oxford 'the smell of the trees in Parks Road, and soon the urchins at cricket under the trees, irrelevant perambulators, and Tom Hayward, reluctantly retrieving *coups de vache* from the longer and wetter grass' was the verbalization of feelings we all had but had no name for. In 'The One-Way Critic' the narrator turns on a myopic moaner complaining that cricket is not what it was

> 'The state of cricket goes from bad to worse;
> Where are the bowlers of my boyhood's prime?
> Where are the batsmen of the pristine years?
> Where are the fieldsmen of the former time?'

and after lambasting him for the 'strangling fugue of senile jeremiads' turns back to the match:

> I ceas'd; and turn'd to Larwood's bounding run,
> And Woolley's rapier flashing in the sun.

The tone is light, the language unexceptional, but I learned from Crusoe, whose own style derived from a classical education and a romantic temperament, something precious. I was scarcely aware of it except as an intimation of *tristesse*; the understanding that little separates laughter from tears, and that what we feel most deeply is sometimes best expressed lightly.

There is something of Dickens and of Surtees in Crusoe's appreciation of character, and he taught one to use one's eyes. To write well about a player you have to dismantle his technique and then put it together again, at the same time remaining receptive to the elusive gesture, the half-glimpsed shadow across the features or the eyes that is the man himself. Crusoe did all of this, gently, wittily, courteously. There was no malice in him.

In 'Long Vacation', as in many other pieces, he wrote not of the lofty immortals whom one could only ever hope to admire

135

from a distance but of experiences, with luck, already part of, or just ahead of one. 'Work, such as it was, is over. The mind is disburdened of the hideous complexities of that tortuous Teuton, Immanuel Kant. By the Porter's Lodge I meet my tutor, who has done his best. He is off to try out the wines of France and the architecture of Italy. Parting makes him polite; and he hopes, hesitating for the phrase, that we shall meet with the requisite measure of success at Lord's. As to us, we go off to Brighton, to try out the bowling of Maurice Tate, to fish from rowing-boats, and to shoot in the underground rifle-range on the Pier.'

Some sort of comparable future was envisageable, if only just. As the autumn term of 1939 was about to start – and I had laid in a stock of coloured pullovers, my newly-earned privilege as a member of the XI – the Soviet Union invaded Poland from the east, the Germans completing the conquest of the country by the end of the month. The winter of the 'phoney war' was only brightened by the courageous resistance of the Finns under Field-Marshal Mannerheim to the Soviet occupation.

Fire-watching began but otherwise we were not much affected. I was at Ardingly in April when the Germans invaded Norway and Denmark and the summer term had only been going a week when the Germans began pouring through Holland and Belgium. The Maginot line, stretching from the Swiss to the Belgian border and fondly imagined impregnable, was outflanked within a week. In the last few days of May what was left of the British force in France, about 300,000 men, was taken off the beaches of Dunkirk by such vessels – from warships to pleasure steamers and fishing boats – as could make the journey.

That summer, first stunned, then increasingly incredulous that no invasion of England seemed imminent following the surrender of France, we lived from day to day. I took six wickets against Bedford and had five simple slip catches dropped off my first three overs against Eton. As hopes rose that we might see the summer term out without interruption after all, so

136

did cricket take on more meaning. Alec Sheldon and Alan Fairbairn hit fifty after fifty and Bill Purkiss, week after week, bowled his inswingers with professional accuracy. Against an OH side captained by Jim Seabrook and including Ronnie Jupp, whom I had caught for 98, Bill took six wickets in the first innings and I five in the second. Jimmy Burridge, with whom I was to play both cricket and squash for Oxford a year later, made 141 against us, and Peter Vansittart, a bowler of some pace but dubious action, took one wicket.

The sun blazed down all through June and July, and at the end of term we went to Lord's to play Marlborough. The match ended in a close-fought draw, in which I took seven wickets, there was never a cloud in the sky, and after being run out for 0 in the first innings I made 33 not out in the second. Alec Sheldon, with whom I had a long partnership, batted wonderfully on the last afternoon. Sadly, I was never to see him again.

There was a Public Schools fortnight at Richmond in August and Bill Purkiss and I bowled together with the new ball in most of the matches. There were air-raid warnings and fire-drills, but for all that it seemed a month of miraculous contentment, too good to last. Nor did it, for, though little did we know it, the best for both of us, as far as cricket was concerned, was almost over.

I look out through the iron bars of my single-study window at Pavilion for the last time, which is also the last time for anyone from Le Bas house; lawns, wooden seats on the banks sloping down to the playing area, and beyond that the second XI pitches, the pitches for house matches, Colts games and those amorphous entertainments in which the ball whizzes dangerously from one game to another and the participants, scarcely players, occupy themselves by thinking about anything rather than the game in hand: butterflies, Mr Cox's 'gateaus' in the grubber, railway engines, illicit smoking in Goldings Wood, some idealized profile that somewhere caught their attention. If I turn slightly to the left, Day Lewis's *The Nabara* on my lap as I lie along the window seat, I see the line of trees – repository of sixes hit from the Grubber end – that separates Pavilion from XX acre. Beyond, to the north and east, the woods thicken and curve, a succession of greens and blues misting into low hills.

For four years the architecture of the place, legacy of the old East India College – Wilkins's Ionic portico seen from the old London to Hertford coach road through the chestnuts of The Avenue; the great, disproportionately soaring dome of the Romanesque chapel, on the south side of which the lovely façade of Terrace looks out over Big Side: the immaculate lawns of the Quad beside which daily we made the walk from Le Bas through the Lodge and into the classrooms – all this had been taken for granted. I scarcely ever looked at any of it, it was simply there. Wilfrid Blunt, in his book *The Haileybury Buildings*, describes Wilkins – architect of the National Gallery, of University College, Gower Street, and many buildings at Cambridge – as not great in the sense that Hawksmoor and Wren were great, but 'dignified, with a never-failing sense of proportion . . . He was a man of sensibility and culture, and he built for gentlemen.'

Though dreadful things were done to Wilkins's Haileybury in the last years of the nineteenth century, enough remained to a schoolboy's untutored eye to provide a sense of order and style, of space and tradition. What might have appeared barrack-like and institutional was softened by creeper, flowers, shrubs and trees. On all sides green encircled and flooded.

Farrow, the grizzled old Le Bas toby, his slops done for the day, disappears up the road to the College Arms. Soon, too, Bert Wensley, with his great koala eyes and nose, sets off home, trilby modestly raked. How admirable and tactful he was as a coach, and how good to have had a bowler rather than a batsman, able at will to dent anyone's complacency by uprooting their middle stump with scarcely detectable change of action.

The Germans, in their preparation for Operation *Sealion*, the occupation of Britain, had already started bombing ships in the channel and air-bases in southern England. The great aerial dogfights between Spitfires and Messerschmitts, by the end of which the Luftwaffe had lost over 1500 planes and all ideas of invasion had to be abandoned, were only weeks off. But now, as dusk gave way to dark, where what had once been hundreds of lighted windows glittering like liners, there was only night. The blindfold of blackout returned Haileybury to an invisible clearing in the woods.

I make one last circuit, past the San where as a new guv'nor I was startled to see the lopsidedly-smiling school doctor, OH vintage 1886, suddenly emerge from his surgery to call out 'Sistah! Sistah! a piece of lint for a penis about this size' holding first finger and thumb to illustrate an object about the width of a pencil. Cutting down towards XX acre I circle the squash and rackets courts, where over four years I must have spent thousands of hours of sweating pleasure. Whatever had happened to depress one, nothing ever seemed so bad after an afternoon on those courts and a hot bath. Arthur Whetton, the rackets professional, is still around, re-stringing a racket and chatting to Slingsby, the games-shop manager from next door. Both soon left to join the RAF and both, as members of bomber squadrons, were killed, Arthur in the raid on Nürnberg.

Squash rackets is about angles and touch; rackets about quickness of reaction and strength. In both games tactics and length are as important as variety of stroke. It is almost impossible to 'kill' a ball in squash, which puts a premium on retrieving and stamina. In rackets the harder ball whistles round the court and the severe hitter can, by cut and timing, leave his opponent stranded. In these courts I really became aware for the first time of aesthetic pleasure in sport, the last-second masking of a drop shot, the gauging of a lob so that it flopped into the corner like a shot partridge, the clean hit that clung to the side walls and died.

Past XX acre, along Pavilion, the bare patches in the nets like skidmarks, and up the steps into the room lined by panels bearing the names of Haileybury XIs since the days of the

Mutiny. Of those who entered the school in the years 1905–12 and who were of an age to go to the war, one in three was killed. What would be our luck this time?

Big Side is on my right now, the columns of Terrace the colour of moonlight. Perhaps some bemused German pilot might mistake Blomfield's monstrous dome perched over Wilkins's façade for St Paul's and let go his bombs, scuttling thankfully off to safety? There were those who would bless him.

The Bradby, hideous Victorian monstrosity and dark as a dungeon, calculated to demolish rather than stimulate any feelings for art or for music, would be another ideal target. Alongside it, the gymnasium, with its odious smell of ropes, vaulting horses and boxing gloves, all of which I abandoned after a single attendance, gleams balefully. This is all foreign territory, with the never-visited laboratories and carpentry shops, and on the other side of the lane the Armoury, presided over by Sergeant Majors Chantler and Hiscock. Were these the same two, 'Groisy' Hair and 'Groisy' Whiskers – the one with black hair gleaming like liquorice and surely dyed, the other with waxed, ivory-coloured moustache-ends as sharp as bayonets – who conducted PT and gym, or another pair altogether?

Just visible in the dark lies the redbrick hulk of the Grubber, to the unprejudiced eye squat and ugly, but a treasury of ham rolls and cup-cakes, of sausages, eggs, and baked beans, of cherries and strawberries in season. Mr Cox, in charge, has the air of a man serving in Fortnum and Mason, faintly deferential in manner but infinitely superior in voice. 'Gateau, Sir?', he would enquire loftily of an inky and diminutive youth pointing above the counter to a French Cream Sandwich.

Beyond the Grubber the swimming pool emits its familiar whiff of chlorine, and then, in fields and lanes and farm buildings, in copses and outhouses, the known world of adolescence comes to an end.

Back in my study I return to Day Lewis, carried around and

read off and on in buses going to cricket matches, on Sunday afternoons on the banks of Pavilion, during Tregenza's lessons and after fried eggs and baked beans on weekday evenings: most especially the long poem *The Nabara*, an account of the attack on the Spanish Government trawler *Nabara* by the rebel cruiser *Canarias*. Day Lewis was never my most favoured poet but the dramatic narrative of this one-sided engagement acquired a lasting fascination for me.

> For two hours more they fought, while *Nabara* beneath their feet
> Was turned to a heap of smouldering scrap-iron. Once again
> The flames they had checked a while broke out. When the forward
> gun
> Was hit, they turned about
> Bringing the after gun to bear. They fought in pain
> And the instant knowledge of death: but the waters filling their
> riven
> Ship could not quench the love that fired them. As each man fell
> To the deck, his body took fire as if death made visible
> That burning spirit. For two more hours they fought, and at seven
> They fired their last shell.
> Of her officers all but one were dead. Of her engineers
> All but one were dead. Of the fifty-two that had sailed
> In her, all were dead but fourteen – and each of these half killed
> With wounds. And the night-dew fell in a hush of ashen tears,
> And *Nabara*'s tongue was stilled.

I found it marvellously heroic, and as poetry affecting, the exploits of these 'men of the basque country, the Mar Cantabrico', for whom 'Freedom is more than a word, more than the base coinage of statesmen.' It also seemed quite academic, reading it in my safe study; literature, and really nothing to do with me at all.

Oxford

OXFORD WAS IN A STATE of mutilation; an extension of the Ministry of Food and Agriculture, the place swarming with civil servants carrying gas-masks. Undergraduates were there on loan, unless unfit for National Service or Conscientious Objectors, these latter not safe indefinitely either. Since no one else expected to be there long – 'Come in, No. 3, your time is up' – there was a feeling of unreality and dislocation.

There were compensations; no exaggerated enmities between hearties and aesthetes (which now was I?), no sense that one was at the start of a three-year slog the results of which would determine the rest of one's life. By the time I arrived in October 1940 the last of the German daylight bomber attacks had been savagely repulsed, fifty-six German aircraft being destroyed in a single day. No one knew it at the time, but that was the end of all ideas of *Sealion*, the Germans having lost over 2500 planes.

During the whole of my time at Oxford, October 1940–March 1942, England seemed remotely moored, a long way from the real action. Mussolini – Capel's 'Mullosini' – had declared war on the Allies, in June, and before long British troops had been driven out of Somaliland, taking their revenge under Wavell in Libya. The Germans invaded Greece and soon after Christmas the Allies attacked the Italians in Eritrea, forcing them out of Africa by the summer. Then, a week before we were due to play Cambridge at Lord's, the Germans put Operation Barbarossa – the 'crushing of Soviet Russia in a quick campaign before the end of the war against England' – into action. By December 1941 German troops were in the suburbs of Moscow, millions of Russian civilians having been deported as slaves to Germany or murdered. Nine months later the Germans were finally halted at Stalingrad; the Russian convoys, of the reality of which I was blissfully ignorant, had already begun to operate. Exactly six months before I sailed in *Onslow* for Murmansk, PQ 17 had departed on its disastrous voyage, an unforgivable Admiralty blunder having resulted in the withdrawal of the cruiser and destroyer escort and the scattering of the now defenceless merchantmen. Twenty-one of the thirty-four ships that set out were sunk by either aircraft or U-boats within five days. The next convoy to leave for Russia was to be my own.

There was virtually no good news from any battle front during the eighteen months at Oxford in which I played squash rackets every single day of the winter and cricket several days a week in the summer. U-boat packs were causing havoc in the Atlantic, the convoys, with minimum escorts, at their mercy. Over a thousand Allied ships went down in a single year.

The Navy, however, was not short of crews for the ships that were in commission, so what I had expected to be a year, a mere whiff of an Oxford deprived of character and eccentricity, turned into five terms. I cannot say that, towards the end, I had much heart for work.

I think it must have been Tregenza's idea that I should try for St John's, I assumed because he himself had been there. But it turned out that he hadn't. When I arrived for an interview I discovered that it was a college with a beautiful garden, that Robert Graves had been there, and that the ghost of Archbishop Laud could on occasion be seen stalking the Library at night.

St John's may not be one of the more fashionable of Oxford colleges, but it is one of the most agreeable, modest in scale and without pretensions. Few of its undergraduate members had much money, hardly any came from the more exclusive public schools.

I shared rooms my first term with Ronnie Wheatley, deceptively solemn in appearance, ex-Edinburgh Academy and also doing Modern Languages. His father was a picture dealer and

143

when I was stationed at Rosyth and idiotically acquired a neurotic Bedlington, his mother looked after it for me. Unfortunately, the animal was knocked over trying to follow the tram taking me back on board and had to be put down. After Army service Ronnie became a military historian, writing, as it happened, the official history of Operation *Sealion*.

Although Ronnie and I had little ostensibly in common outside our work, we got on well. We needed to, since we shared a sleeping area the size of a ship's cabin. Every morning a red-faced, brawny youth, assistant to the scout, noisily banged the ends of our beds up and down until we got up. There was no running water and the washbasins, lavatories and baths were in the next quad. Chamber pots were standard issue. The lack of central heating was never quite compensated for by an open fireplace in the large, panelled room in which we worked, for fuel was rationed and it could only be used for a few hours in the day.

In retrospect, the years 1940–42 might seem to have constituted a dazzling period in the literary life of the college, but this was far from apparent at the time. Philip Larkin arrived the same term as I to read English, and Kingsley Amis two terms later, to be followed by John Wain. None of them, however, was, in terms of literary talent, noticeably precocious. The *Cherwell*, at that time the main literary magazine, was in the hands of Sidney Keyes and Michael Meyer, and I don't think any of us contributed to it significantly, if at all.

There was no doubt, though, who, of us all, appeared the most sophisticated, best-read, widely connected and gifted. Bruce Montgomery, a choral scholar from Merchant Taylors, with whom Ronnie and I shared tutorials that year, may have been slightly older than us, but he was light years ahead in experience. Not only did he have a well-known actress as a girl friend – no boast, for she was produced for us on her visits to Oxford, when not touring in a play or filming – but he had himself written plays, a critical work on Romanticism, and essays on Wyndham Lewis, Montherlant and John Dickson

Carr, his three favourite writers. None of these had been published but they existed as bound typescripts and seemed, in their range of reference, brilliant beyond belief.

In appearance Bruce was pale and slim, with quizzical, rather rubbery features and neatly combed, marmalade-coloured hair. He walked with a stick, a slight lameness which was the legacy of childhood polio, and he smoked from a holder. His familiarity with writers, painters, and musicians I had never heard of, made me reluctant to expose my own ignorance in his presence, but he was always wryly polite, sympathetic, and generous in the communication of his own enthusiasms. He had little use for contemporary poetry, the result probably of an excess of Wyndham Lewis, but about all else his knowledge appeared encyclopaedic and his taste reliable.

If one had been obliged then to forecast in which direction Bruce's talents would finally be realized I suppose one would have gone for the theatre. There was always the danger that such precocity – in painting, in composing music, both choral and popular, as well as in writing – might fizzle out and that, once out in the real world, Bruce, with his cane, bow-tie and cigarette holder, might seem to symbolize a particular kind of Oxford dilettante. There was no knowing, too, in relation to prevailing taste, which as far as I was concerned was governed by Faber & Faber – Eliot, Auden, MacNeice, Spender – and the *New Statesman*, whether Bruce's faintly reactionary cynicism might not work fatally against him.

One need not have worried, even though the plays came to nothing and the critical works were never published. For, after taking his degree and embarking on a brief period of school-mastering, Bruce contrived to combine the writing of highly successful detective stories with the composing of film and choral music. He wanted, I think, more than anything to create some form of drama in which music had the same relevance as Weill's music to Brecht's text, but though he made several attempts at finding an equivalent idiom for his various talents they never fused. In the end he had to settle for a double identity, Bruce Montgomery, composer, Edmund Crispin, crime-writer. I don't know how highly regarded his more serious music was, but he was never short of commissions for film work and for years his crime novels, in their canary Gollancz jackets, made almost annual raids on the bookstalls.

The first of these, *The Case of the Gilded Fly*, was published in February 1944 and immediately went into several impressions. Its hero is Gervase Fen, Professor of English Language and Literature at the University of Oxford. Bruce's description of Fen so accurately applied to W. G. Moore, our Tutor, that it was impossible not to see one as the other. 'At no time a patient man . . . he shuffled his feet and agitated his long lanky body. His cheerful, ruddy, clean-shaven face grew even ruddier than usual: his dark hair, sedulously plastered down with water, broke out into disaffected fragments towards the crown.'

It was Moore's custom when starting a tutorial to give his ancient turnip of a watch – already laid out on the table – a few preliminary windings. We became so fascinated by this apparently pointless ritual – V. S. Pritchett, when Literary Editor of the *New Statesman*, once described Philip Toynbee as the kind of reviewer who had to 'wipe his feet on the doormat first' before getting down to business, and Moore's attentions to his watch were presumably of similarly nervous origin – that we experimented one day by winding it up first. Moore began his usual polite enquiries about what form our discussion of Corneille or Molière should take, distractedly attempting to wind the watch at the same time. It eventually dawned on him that he was having no success with the latter and after pausing to give it his undivided attention and shake it vigorously, he put it down with an expression of mingled disbelief and disgust.

A copy of *The Case of the Gilded Fly*, which is set in Oxford and concerns the deaths by violence of three people within a single week, reached me in *Badger*, just before setting out on a night patrol. Inside was a letter in Bruce's handwriting, addressed from Shrewsbury where he was teaching. 'Here's the piece of nonsense. I won't go into lengthy apologies for all the bad bits

146

(there are many). Luckily, it's sold well and I've nearly finished another.' He talks of working on a play for the Oxford Playhouse – 'a rather bawdy comedy about schoolmasters'; about the ambivalence of his feelings about teaching, and his efforts to make time to write: 'Like Trollope I've taken to getting up early and writing for two hours before breakfast. But I always feel so ill that the light-hearted spirit of comedy comes slowly . . . There has been a succession of girls, none of them interesting. Women have never inspired my work so all this amatory activity has done nothing but hold it up.'

The letter finished with a reference to Larkin. 'Philip has finished his novel. I think it's good in its own way, and he's writing some admirable poetry.'

The casual reference to girls made me, in my chaste *Badger* cabin, envious. I became curious, too, to find out what sort of poetry Philip, in that earlier time a disciple of Yeats, was writing that earned Bruce's not easily awarded approval. From *Badger*, St John's and Moore's watch seemed a long way off but it was good news to learn of things stirring among my contemporaries, an alarming number of whom were already dead. Nine years later Kingsley Amis was to publish *Lucky Jim* and to dedicate it to Philip Larkin.

The first poem in Philip's *The North Ship*, initially published by the bizarre Fortune Press twenty-one years before Faber got round to it, was in fact dedicated to Bruce Montgomery. It is not easy to detect the earthy and direct tone of Larkin's maturity in these romantic early poems written in the shadow of Auden and Dylan Thomas as well as of Yeats, for, as Philip remarked in his introduction to the Faber edition, 'I find in the poems not one abandoned self but several . . . this search for a style was merely one aspect of a general immaturity.' Lucky the poet who can come to an individual style with such apparent confidence so soon afterwards and over the next twenty years produce, as Philip did with such thrift and lack of haste, so many of the most haunting poems of the time. The shortest poem in *The North Ship* seemed to me always the most suggestive

147

of future possibilities; perhaps I liked it best because of its flavour of the French romantics:

> This is the first thing
> I have understood:
> Time is the echo of an axe
> Within a wood.

I don't think Philip and Bruce became friends until towards the end of their time together at Oxford, by when they must have been the only two survivors of our original group. Philip's eyesight and possibly stammer, which was very bad in those days, must have made him also unfit for the Services, but separated as they were by having lodgings in different parts of Oxford, by reading different subjects and by Bruce's taste for hotel bars rather than pubs, their paths rarely crossed during my time there. But, totally at variance though their tastes initially were, they undoubtedly stimulated each other.

Bruce, after Shrewsbury, returned to Brixham where his parents had lived. Surprisingly he appeared to have little taste for London and metropolitan life and, as the years went by, in contrast to the wordly and cosmopolitan face he had appeared to present on first acquaintance, increasingly enacted, on his rare London visits, the part of country bumpkin.

Bruce had his measure of success, but his health, never good, steadily deteriorated under a punishing alcoholic routine. It soon became plain that he was unlikely to make old bones. Nor did he; his liver gave out at a sadly early age.

In 1940, scholar's gown flapping and cane tapping as he hurried under my window to the Lodge and thence to the Randolph or the Playhouse bar, Bruce was just the right person to put the Oxford of the time into perspective. He, if anyone, had to regard work as something other than time-filling, but he managed to convey, with a faint air of surprise that anyone could think otherwise, that academic study was the merest scaffolding for serious intellectual and aesthetic adventure. It was indeed hard to think of him working at all, for he made work – whether conducting the choir, playing the organ, or reading Molière – a gay, exhilarating activity, to be taken at once immensely seriously and not seriously at all. The real business of the day was discussion, preferably whisky in hand, and in congenial and impersonal enough surroundings for the free and rapid exchange of ideas. This social freedom, however, had to be earned, being either a preliminary or a postscript to the struggle with oneself.

The early years of the war were a golden period for the Oxford Playhouse. Not only was there Pamela Brown, whose voice sent shivers up my spine, and with whom I assumed the whole university was as much in love as I, but among the female leads, Rosalie Crutchley, sister of Eddie, with whom I was to play at Lord's and who was the most classically correct batsman at Oxford, and Sigrid Landstad, a Hedy Lamarr type who specialized in steamy colonial roles in plays such as *White Cargo*. The older women's parts were taken by Nora Nicholson and Winifred Evans, who seemed to have been there for ever.

The leading men were John Byron, an engaging, bouncy actor, and, in older parts, Julian D'Albie. Peter Ashmore, who had been in the original production of Auden and Isherwood's *The Ascent of F6*, thereby assuming in my eyes legendary status, played a variety of character parts, managing to be both funny and moving. At some stage a balding, enthusiastic actor called Peter Copley, whom I envisage as permanently wearing gym shoes, joined the company and to my horror Pamela Brown, who had a slight polio-induced limp of the Bruce Montgomery type, married him almost immediately. After the war Pamela Brown was in numerous West End successes and films, but for some reason I could no longer bear to see her. At Oxford, as Hedda and as Nina in *The Seagull*, as well as in numerous forgettable comedies, her frail and elusive beauty and heart-break voice made my weekly visit to The Playhouse more of an event than any theatrical experience since. I can't remember whether she was in *Mrs Warren's Profession* but on my last night in Oxford I gave a party in my rooms, afterwards taking everyone to the theatre to see Shaw's play. Unfortunately I had drunk so much that I had to come out half-way through to be sick in the street and the commissionaire refused to let me back in. My guests therefore remained inside, blissfully oblivious of my whereabouts, while I slunk back to St John's to pass quietly out.

In my staircase at St John's was Peter Oldham, an organ scholar of Heathcliffian appearance, and Edward du Cann, neither his urbanity nor bloodhoundish expression so marked in those days. But though we were all on amiable terms it was only with Bruce that I remained friends on going down. I am not sure, too, that it wasn't with Bruce that I first met up again with Philip and Kingsley after the war. By the time Kingsley was settled into college I was in digs, so that, though I knew him by sight as a crony and fellow jazz-addict of Philip's, he was mostly a name to me, of local fame as a mimic and creator of amazingly realistic sound effects.

Sometime during the summer term I was elected to Vincent's, the Oxford equivalent of the Hawks club at Cambridge, its members drawn largely from past Blues and present members of University teams. You could drop in for egg sandwiches and sausages and drink beer out of tankards. Desmond Eagar, who had played for Oxford and Gloucestershire before the war, was stationed nearby and occasionally lunched; my first contact on a social level with someone who had actually played county cricket. It seemed an amazing privilege. Jim Seabrook and Bert Wensley had been something different, the relationship of master to pupil.

At the end of the summer, after Lord's, I returned to Oxford since I had nowhere else to go. Ardingly Rectory was no longer a home for me, because Mr Brack had died and a new Rector had taken over. For nearly two months I was virtually on my own, eating Heinz's Sandwich Spread on brown bread every day for lunch and usually going to an Indian restaurant, before it got into trouble for serving either cat food or cat, I forget which, for a cheap curry in the evening. In the afternoons I lay by the river making my first attempts at writing poetry, pale imitations of Eliot and MacNeice. Each day produced a new poem, some days several, and for a week or two they seemed to me promising. After that I couldn't bear to look at them, and they followed one another into the waste-paper basket.

I had failed at Lord's; Cambridge gave us a good beating. Otherwise I had a reasonable summer, making runs and taking wickets against Harrow and Malvern, Sandhurst and Oxfordshire, and against the British Empire XI hitting Tom Goddard, the huge and leather-handed Gloucestershire and England offspinner, for 18 in an over, including a six into the river.

Sadly, the Parks, with its magical-like grouping of trees and eloquent ghosts, had not been used since the war started, so our cricket was played on various college grounds. Just before Lord's I went up to Barwell to play for Northamptonshire, going in first with Mike Cassy, a colleague in the Oxford XI, against Leicestershire and making top score of 19 in a rout at the hands of the very useful H. A. Smith. Northamptonshire, with nine of their pre-war regulars, were bundled out for 57 on a wet pitch. V. W. C. Jupp, who had played for Sussex and England in Ranji's day before joining Northamptonshire and was now a stout fifty, captained us. Other stars of the last pre-war season playing that day were Jackie Timms, who got a 'pair', and Bill Merritt, the New Zealand Test leg-spinner, for Northamptonshire, and C. S. Dempster and L. G. Berry, Leicestershire's regular opening pair, as well as the better part of their 1939 side. If this was what playing county cricket was like then I liked the idea of it.

It is not hard for me to remember all this, for these were the last matches I played in the hope that cricket might hold a more than casual future for me. When I look back now on that late summer it is without premonition. By August cricket had given way to poetry – MacNeice's *Plant and Phantom* 'Time was away and somewhere else'; Spender's *The Still Centre* and Eliot's *Burnt Coker*; Auden's *Another Time* – and I imagined that no pleasures in cricket could ever match these, whether I ever managed to write a publishable poem or not.

My cricket bat stands in the corner, the colour of milky coffee. On my bedroom door a teddy-bear coat bought for £7, the property of an actor, hangs under a dark blue scarf. An Authentic square lies across the back of a chair, alongside another in the red and yellow stripes on black of St John's. They are what will survive of the summer, unlike the abandoned poems: symbols of belonging in a world of gas-masks.

Will Moore's shiny red face always looked cruelly sore from shaving. A lock of hair fell across his forehead and his blue eyes popped. He strode about the quad on his immensely long cicada-like legs, never without an engagement of one kind or another. Besides teaching, lecturing, and college matters, there were Civil Defence obligations, papers to be prepared, books underway on Molière and Corneille.

Not a patient man, he was nonetheless a patient tutor, unsparing in his attempts to seem genuinely interested in our callow views. Compared with Tregenza he was dynamic. He was also modest, funny and caustic, though never at our expense. He retained a certain wide-eyed innocence, guilelessly casting himself in the role of unworldly academic.

From time to time we were invited to Sunday tea. Mrs Moore was even more rosy-cheeked than her husband. They and their three children seemed a remarkably harmonious family, Joy Moore being as intellectually shrewd and unpretentious as her husband. Long after I had gone down Will continued to write encouraging and gossipy letters to me, the envelopes with their college crest momentarily transforming the bleakest of mess-decks. Enid Starkie, then lecturing on Baudelaire, lent me a copy of Rimbaud's *Une Saison en Enfer* before I left, and her increasingly irate demands for its return followed me from ship to ship, the book itself long since charred beyond recognition in the first flames of *Onslow*. Sometimes her letter and Will's arrived on board the same day, one soothing and sympathetic, the other like an angry hornet from the Inland Revenue.

In the autumn the university began to fill up again. I moved to digs in Holywell, my rooms cold and cheerless, my landlady, Mrs Dore, appropriately deaf as a door post. When I had money, I bought poetry from Blackwell's, each Faber volume costing six shillings. It was now obvious that I should not be around long enough to take any form of degree, so I took two 'sections' – wartime equivalents of Part I – in French and in German, failing in German language, which I put down to years of dozing in front of Joce and Tregenza.

In a Turl Street sports shop there was a University Squash Rackets 'ladder', the top five names on which would play against Cambridge. Any challenge from below had to be met within a week. By the time of the university match I had installed myself at No. 2, and there I played, getting beaten in Cambridge by John Bridger, who acquired five Blues before, in appreciation perhaps, taking Holy Orders.

When not accepting challenges I played against various dons. Will Moore was not a bad player but J. C. Masterman of Christ Church was a much better one. Masterman, genial and extrovert, handsome and grey-haired, was then about fifty. He used to turn up at the court in a camel-hair coat, often departing after the game on mysterious errands to London. I assumed he was involved in senior Intelligence work of some kind. Later on he became Provost of Worcester, but always to me suggested a sporting rather than an academic figure.

Masterman held a certain romantic glamour, for not only had he published two novels – *An Oxford Tragedy* and *Fate Cannot Harm Me*, as well as a study of Marshal Ney – but he was a remarkable all-round athlete. Interned in Germany through-out the 1914–18 war, having already got an athletics Blue for Oxford, he emerged to play hockey and lawn tennis for England, and to tour Canada with MCC. J. C. Masterman was one of those men whose natural charm and abilities involved him in all sorts of public service, chairman of this and that

153

committee, adviser to institutions, governor of public schools, in due course Vice-Chancellor of Oxford.

On the squash court he was an opponent of energy, skill and virtuosity, fitter if anything than I was. He appeared to be without deviousness; the kind of distinguished all-rounder who would dignify any school Speech Day.

I suppose Masterman was more administrator than scholar, but he was *considerable*, in whatever he did. Yet my admiration for him created certain conflicts in my mind. I could see, for example, that he was closer in style and tastes to someone like Siegfried Sassoon or Robertson-Glasgow – typically English, and glad to be – than to the novelists and poets of the Thirties who – despite the absence from our shores of Auden and Isherwood – now owned most of my allegiance.

It seems absurd that one should have worried so much about where one belonged, when the chances of belonging anywhere for long were so slight. Yet if, at the age of nineteen, one has a need for heroes, the problem was, which ones?

There was, I knew, going to be little in common between ostensibly Left-Wing poets who had never voluntarily played a game in their lives and those scholar athletes who could fit comfortably into any category of conventional society. Sassoon and Blunden, as once Rupert Brooke, fulfilled one kind of need, but their later poetry seemed archaic and dull compared to Auden. Someone like Masterman, cloaked in mystery and glittering with achievement, would, probably, despite his Firsts and Fellowships, turn out to be anti-modern poetry, anti-aesthete, anti-left-wing.

The conflicts between being one sort of person or another eventually resolved themselves. I forgot that my ideals had once been A. J. Raffles, amateur cracksman and cricketer – at least the initials were the same – The Saint and Bulldog Drummond, and even more so their originators. Faintly puritan, contemptuous of all Europeans, especially Jews and Germans, despising of the black races, these idealistic and opportunist patriots, forerunners of James Bond, now seemed fascistic anachronisms. Their resourcefulness and courage, their cool style and debonair appearance, once so appealing to me, began to be offset by their chauvinism and ultra right-wing values. In the end, when I said goodbye to Oxford, it was with the poems of Louis MacNeice in my pocket.

Cricket at Oxford

Pedalling between lectures, spokes throwing off
Sun like Catherine Wheels, the damp grass
Bestowing its sweetness from a long way off –
Perhaps the Australians were playing
On a May morning, family saloons
Swaying down the Broad en route
For the Parks, the whole city –
It seemed to me then – going about
In a daze, who won the toss,
Who's batting? And arrived,
Breathless from the Taylorian, pockets stuffed
With indecipherable notes on Baudelaire
Les diverses beautés qui parent ta jeunesse
And Rimbaud, it was to exchange
A *fin de siècle* poetry for the more immediate
Mesmeric magic of the scorecard –
Macindoe, Lomas, and hazier behind them
Indelible syllables of those lingering others,
Walford, De Saram, Bosanquet, Pataudi.
All day we would marvel at technique
Exercised, it seemed, for its own sake,
The extending of a tradition, as might
Language be refined: an innings
By McCabe packed with epigrams,
Bradman ruthless as if sacking a city.
'Pick, pack, pock, puck', Joyce's
'Drops of water in a fountain
Falling softly in the brimming bowl.'

Language and stroke play, the honey
Of the bats against trees
Whose green might have been arranged
By Poussin or Claude, grouped just so –
That park-music, connived at
And returned to how often for solace –
A refrain running through the years,
Faintly discernible, whatever the distance.

Variety Girls, Oxford

Sheila, Gloria, Billie, Noreen:
Going through the same routine,
Staring at the crumbling faience
Bright-eyed as we try to dance.

Saucy, playful, wicked minxes,
Expressionless in our art as Sphinxes,
We always get the bottom billing,
Flesh is weak but spirit willing.

One month called The Flirty Floozies,
Footlights on the latest bruises,
Next time known as Goodtime Girls,
Giggling under hennaed curls.

Each with slightly different charms,
Goodish legs *or* breasts *or* arms,
Beauties we have never been –
Sheila, Gloria, Billie, Noreen.

One thing no one ever could
Say is that we're any good,
Sandwiched in between scene-changes,
Kicking well within our ranges.

Yet we have our proper station,
A stable kind of reputation,
Opening shows but never nude,
Finale girls who'd think it rude

Undressing before the epicene:
Sheila, Gloria, Billie, Noreen.
Performing pets and comics alter
We alone can never falter,

With mottled thighs and dusty knees
Getting through our 1-2-3's.
This week we're the Nightlife Nifties
Symbols of the Nineteen-Fifties.

But only the oldest patrons guess
What the programme doesn't confess,
That we were once The Nightclub Naughties
A decade before the Forties.

PART III

JW51B

'WE'LL GET SOMEONE to relieve you when we can,' the First Lieutenant said, rather unconvincingly, 'but for the moment I'm afraid you're on your own.' The steel door, 'X', sealing off the for'ard part of the ship from the rest, clanged shut behind him. I was truly alone. The 'strangers' child' appeared to have reached a point of no return. My number was CJX 357590 and I was a Chatham rating. Scarcely anyone on board knew who I was or what I was supposed to be doing.

I adjusted my mask, wiped the eyepieces with my gloves and looked around. Spray from a huge hole in the port side was spurting in all directions, as if someone was siphoning it. The noise from the raised safety-valve overhead was deafening, a concerted hiss of steam sharpened to the level of torture. For'ard, above the magazine, a bonfire raged, its area of flame checked by the freezing swill at its base.

I directed the hose in my hands towards the heat, a pathetically inadequate gesture in relation to the volume of sea swirling only yards away. I was waist-deep in water and each time I moved I stumbled on one of the bodies that rolled like sodden hammocks beneath me. Somewhere under my feet two whole gun crews, wiped out in their entirety, began to pile up with the increasing list of the ship. Occasionally a face washed through the surface, all expression sponged away from its features.

Five minutes before, I had been standing uselessly by the pom-pom amidships watching the fire from *Hipper*'s eight-inch guns. Eight shells had burst minutes earlier in the sea just ahead of us. Four more salvos landed either just short or just over. It could only be a matter of time, however violently we altered course or at what speed.

Our own guns, firing constantly, were lifting the ship out of the water and it was only a single, piercing scream that made it plain that we ourselves had been hit.

For a week out of Iceland I had been searching vainly on my RL85 VHF interceptor for German signals, either aircraft or surface ships, but the weather had been too bad, and nothing had been close enough to pick up. Now, with the set out of action like almost everything else in the W/T office, I was waiting miserably on deck for something to do. A splinter had ripped across my face, stunning me, and four out of the six on watch beside me had received either direct hits or disabling blows. They had gone with scarcely a cry. It was there that the New Zealand No. 1, Lieutenant King, found me. 'If you're spare you can lend a hand for'ard,' he said. 'Most of 'A' and 'B' Guns are dead and the forward Fire and Repair party are non-existent. There are fires everywhere. It's a shambles.'

I followed King into the flat outside the W/T office. Hoses were being unrolled and fed for'ard. 'Here's a mask,' he said. 'Try and get as close to the fires as you can. I'm afraid we'll have to shut you in.'

The flames had been spreading so fast – from the cordite charges in the magazine below 'B' gun, from the blazing Petty Officers' Mess and No. 1 boiler room – that the steel-plated 'X' and 'Y' doors and hatches separating the forward part of the ship from the rest were being put to. If the magazine blew up, the main body of the ship could still be saved.

The shutting of the steel doors seemed the final act. In a ship littered with the dead and dying, at the mercy of a vastly superior German force, the chances of anyone checking to see whether a solitary ordinary seaman was still left alive behind 'X' and 'Y' doors were remote.

It seemed, in any case, more than likely I should have been blown sky-high long before there was any chance of finding out. Gusts of acrid smoke hung like a collar round my throat and in the battle between fire and water fire was winning.

The ship began to take on an even steeper list, and I could only train the hose by hanging on to a bulkhead. There were no lights, but in the glare from the advancing flames the hair of the drowned drifted like seaweed.

I began to wonder, making fancy patterns into the flames with my hose, how long this farce was worth continuing. One of the first shells to hit us had struck the funnel, the boiler casing in No. 1 boiler room being blown open as a consequence. At about the same time all the gunnery fire control circuits had been put out of action, making it impossible for the radar operators to calculate the ranges.

The cold was such that shells had become iced over and stuck in the breeches of the guns. The CPO's and ERA's messes were on fire and the smoke from them made the Sick Bay, already filled with wounded, uninhabitable.

The smell of morphia, antiseptic and burning paint that I had brought with me from the messdeck gradually washed off as the sea slopped up to my armpits. There seemed no way out for us, merely the ignominious situation of waiting to be polished off. The more accurate the German gunnery the less time we would have to wait.

Earlier that day I had been reading Richard Hillary's *The Last Enemy* which had been published not long before we sailed. In the prologue to the book, where he is describing baling out after his Spitfire had been hit, Hillary quotes Verlaine: '*J'ai voulu mourir à la guerre. La mort n'a pas voulu de moi.*' Only a few months earlier I, too, had been at Oxford reading Verlaine. If Death wanted me, I thought, he was not likely to get many better chances.

More than once in what seemed like the next hour, though it was scarcely half that, I had the feeling that I had been forgotten and that the ship had been abandoned. Several times, as we lurched and I fell sideways, I had to lever myself upright on someone's body. I began to wonder in my solitariness whether there might still be someone around me with some life in him, and whom I could resuscitate into companionship. But the bodies were so heavy, their several sodden layers of clothing making them double their weight, that I soon gave up my attempts to raise them. I knew few of their names, but I started to carry on a kind of lunatic dialogue as if they were my oldest friends.

The shudder and throb of the deck, detectable like a faint heartbeat under the hissing of steam, roar of flame, and swirling of water, suggested we were still manoeuvrable and making headway. But how was this possible, when an hour earlier I had seen through my binoculars the gunnery officers on *Hipper* giving orders to fire and their salvos dropping all round us?

I began to have the illusion that I had entered a strange limbo, a kind of ante-room to death, accessible only to those whose fate had already been sealed. Would it be simpler just to lie down in the seawater with my unknown messmates and get it over and done with? Minutes went by, the buckling and blistered bulkheads crackling in the flames. What was happening?

Soon after I had gone on watch at 0800 in *Onslow* a signal in morse had been flashed from *Obdurate* that two destroyers had been sighted south of the convoy. We had been wondering if the Russians would come out to meet us, but since they rarely bothered to communicate or reply to signals no one could be quite sure. *Obdurate* was requested to investigate.

For three quarters of an hour there was no development. Darkness had scarcely lifted and almost all that was visible were the 'not under control' lights of a tanker at the tail of the convoy.

I went out on deck but no sooner had I begun to breathe the snow-flecked air than short, sharp volleys of flame snorted across the horizon. Almost simultaneously the action station alarms – shrill, staccato rings – went off.

By the time I was back in the W/T office we had begun to keel over, swinging hard to port and picking up speed. My opposite number – we worked watch and watch about – was searching the frequencies for any R/T signal in German but the set remained obstinately uncommunicative. A few months earlier the codes used between German surface ships, U-boats and aircraft had been broken down and there had been notable successes since, particularly in the interception of E-boat traffic off the East coast. Now, maddeningly, we could get nothing. Perhaps, as the range closed, we would be luckier.

From the bridge the Captain's voice came down the voice pipe: 'Make to destroyers: *Join Me.*' We had in attendance three other Fleet class destroyers, *Obedient*, *Obdurate* and *Orwell*, but before they could take close order, *Obdurate* sent another signal giving the bearing of three unknown destroyers.

Although we could see nothing of what was going on, we could hear each one of Captain (D)'s signals as they were passed down the voice pipe, as well as his orders to the navigator.

It was soon plain that other ships were in the vicinity, for sighting reports came flooding in. We made an enemy report on Fleet Wave, full power, of 'one unknown, bearing 325, range 8 miles, course 140°'. Signals were sent successively to Scapa (for the Admiralty), to Senior British Naval Officer, Murmansk, and to Senior Officer, Force R (the cruiser escort of a home-ward-bound convoy recently sailed from Murmansk and de-tailed to provide long-range cover for us also), giving our position, and then, urgently, the signal 'One Cruiser bearing 340°.'

Out of the snow, almost directly ahead and closing fast, the long vulpine shape of the heavy cruiser *Admiral Hipper* had suddenly materialized. We could hear orders coming from the Director to the TS, 'All Guns Broadside', 'All Guns load, load, load'.

Within minutes *Onslow* had opened fire, the ship shuddering and recoiling as each salvo spat into the darkness. A report came in that *Achates*, laying a smoke-screen between the enemy and the convoy, had been set on fire.

We had been firing at extreme range and at a speed of 30 knots, but the threat of our torpedoes was now enough to make *Hipper* turn away. She had, it transpired, fired three separate salvos at ourselves and *Orwell*, but we had dodged them. As she turned a report came in from the cruiser *Sheffield* of Force R: 'Am approaching you on a course of 170°.'

There was no knowing how far off Force R was or how soon they would appear, supposing in such appalling visibility they could ever find us.

In the wireless office there was a faint sense of anti-climax. Was this all that was going to happen? The enemy were apparently steaming out of sight in one direction with the convoy headed safely in the other. This was a desirable result, but it remained vaguely unsatisfying.

The adrenalin released by news of the *Hipper* and her three accompanying destroyers – capable of demolishing our complete escort while staying comfortably out of our range – and then by the heartening sound of our own guns, began to subside. It was still barely light and there was nothing to be seen from the bridge except sea and snow.

It had been Captain (D)'s tactic in *Onslow* to keep ourselves between the *Hipper* and the convoy, but unknown to us the pocket battleship *Lützow* was approaching from the south.

Meanwhile, any illusions of security in *Onslow* were soon given a nasty jolt. Although in the wireless office we had been receiving a first-hand running commentary on the situation, it was one-sided and tactical. We had little idea of how many ships were attacking us or where they were. On the bridge, with visibility negligible, they were little better off. The difference was that they could see the enemy's gun flashes whereas all we could hear were our own guns.

The brief lull was ended by the sight of the *Hipper*, her three destroyers astern of her, turning about and steaming at full speed towards us. What had been a thin shape on the horizon, a mere intensification of the darkness, was transformed within minutes into menace. Throwing huge seas off her bows *Hipper* began to eat up the distance between us.

Turning on a parallel course we opened fire, the *Hipper*'s own guns spraying the sea between us and *Orwell* astern of us.

166

I took another turn on deck, the wireless office so congested that the one of us not on the set was better out of the way. As I walked aft to peer out in the half-light we slewed violently, repeated flashes of gunfire stabbing the horizon on our port beam. *Hipper* had altered her range and bearing, and now shell after shell was pitching just ahead of us.

I squeezed back into the office, just in time to hear the navigator's voice ordering sharp alterations of course and the reports drifting up from the radar operator: 'Salvo coming towards, going left, going right, coming towards'.

Hardly had the last words been uttered than the ship seemed to heave up out of the water, rock wildly and then plunge.

At each salvo we had altered course towards the *Hipper*, giving her less to aim at and narrowing the distance. Five salvos had in consequence overshot the mark. The first shell of the sixth exploded a few yards behind the bridge against the side of the funnel.

As jets of steam poured screaming out of the holes splinters tore across the radar offices and into the bridge. The two radar operators and one of the bridge look-outs were killed instantaneously. The Captain was wounded, blood pouring from an eye.

We knew nothing of this, hearing only the navigator's 'Port ten' as he aimed to dodge out of further trouble. The helm had barely begun to respond when a second shell hit, seeming to break us in two.

Within seconds flames and smoke had engulfed most of the forward part of the ship. We had been hit twice between the wheelhouse and the two for'ard 4.7s, the second salvo killing the two gun crews, wiping out the fire and repair parties, and the ammunition supply party next to 'B' gun.

It was this second blow that cut the electric leads, putting all except Fleet Wave W/T out of action, and making the RL85 useless. Either the Germans had maintained R/T silence or the conditions and range had been against us, for we never picked up a syllable on any channel.

It was now that we heard the Captain give the order to turn away, hard to starboard, reduce speed and make smoke. The flames and smoke gushing into the semi-dark made the last item seem faintly superfluous.

Behind us, those on the bridge of *Orwell* had the impression *Onslow* might have blown up. They, too, made smoke to screen us. *Hipper*, having appeared to have disposed of *Onslow*, now turned her attention to *Orwell*, salvo after salvo straddling her but making no direct hit.

For some reason, perhaps apprehensive of a torpedo attack out of the smoke, *Hipper* suddenly turned away.

The next half hour in *Onslow* was chaos, but a chaos retrieved with extraordinary skill and calm. No one knew how many had been killed, merely that the whole area forward of the funnel, and including the crew messes on three levels, was on fire.

The magazine, containing all the cordite charges and likely to explode, was immediately flooded and all the doors and hatches forward closed.

A Leading Seaman was stationed amidships to prevent anyone going into the forward messes, but he was roughly pushed aside by an Engineer officer who insisted on going down through a shell hole to see if anyone was alive.

The hoses were hauled out and everyone available was pressed into action, forming a human chain with buckets or helping to keep the hoses free.

It was while I was involved in this, watching the *Hipper*'s gunfire – huge smoke roses lined with flame – and wondering if the next salvo would finish us off, that King appeared on deck and asked me to take over from him.

Release came just when, for about the tenth time, I had decided to give myself one minute more of what seemed futile action. The din was so fearful that I never even heard the steel doors being pushed back, merely saw the First Lieutenant's face peer like a ghost through the smoke. 'I think you've been in here long enough,' he said. 'You'd better come out.'

I stumbled after him, scarcely able to credit what seemed like a miracle. 'We're not out of the wood yet by a long way,' King said, 'but we're rejoining the convoy. You might give a hand with the baling.'

Lines had formed in the flat outside the galleys and buckets were being passed from hand to hand. For the next hour, while the bodies of the dead and the badly wounded were carried past us out of the falling water, I became part of the human chain.

It was bitterly cold and the only light was from the still blazing fires.

I returned to the W/T office to inspect the debris. The operator on duty was tapping out in morse the signals: *Have been hit forward and in the engine-room. Am retiring on convoy making smoke-screen*, followed by: *Forward magazine flooded. Fire in forward boiler room. Am proceeding to southward of convoy.*

Although our W/T and asdics were still not functioning, a jury aerial had been rigged to enable us to communicate on Fleet Wave.

From time to time reports came in from activity to the west of us. Soon after we had rejoined the convoy, proceeding to the head of it at about half-speed, the two cruisers of Force R had sighted the *Hipper*, now joined by the pocket battleship *Lützow*, and three destroyers.

Steaming in at thirty knots from the darker northern horizon they took the German ships, outlined against the perceptibly lighter southern sky, completely by surprise. While *Hipper* was directing her attention at the smoke-laying *Achates* and considering how to re-establish contact with the convoy, the cruisers *Sheffield* and *Jamaica* closed unchallenged to a range of four miles. With her fifth salvo *Sheffield* hit the *Hipper* amidships and shortly after *Jamaica* struck her three times more, starting fires.

The destroyers round *Hipper* now laid a thick smoke-screen, obliterating her. Minutes later one of them, the *Friedrich Eckholdt*, steaming out of the smoke, found herself right in the path of *Sheffield*. She had no chance.

169

These details we picked up, bit by bit, and when I went back on deck flashes of gunfire were still flickering to the west. Unknown to us, the *Lützow*, the whole convoy at her mercy, had passed, a mere two miles off, across its bows without firing a shot.

If we, in our variously enclosed units, had often little idea of what was going on, those on the bridge of the major ships were hardly any better off. Much of the time they could see nothing, the sounds and glow of gunfire were all they had to go on. Even when vessels were picked up by radar, or were dimly visible through gaps in smoke, mist and snow, it was often only when challenged by light that friend was distinguished from foe, and then it could be too late.

Luckily for us, it was the Germans who were more uncertain of identification and despite, perhaps because of, their greater numbers and power, more aware of their vulnerability. Left to themselves, the destruction of the whole convoy of fourteen merchantmen would have been a formality. It was only by trying to drive the *Hipper* away from the convoy and threatening her with a torpedo attack that there was going to be any future for any of us, however slight.

News now came in that *Achates*, so valiantly laying her smoke-screen back and forth across the tail of the convoy, had gone down.

The horizon was still being illuminated by gun flashes, like a distant firework display with approaching thunder. Signals came in that both the *Hipper* and *Lützow* had reappeared on the port quarter of the convoy and had opened fire. The convoy made a second emergency turn away from the action and soon we could hear the guns of *Obdurate*, *Obedient* and *Orwell*, who had been steering a parallel course, blazing at the enemy.

The *Hipper* turned away into the darkness and our destroyers, only *Obdurate* among them receiving slight damage, swung back towards us.

It seemed, briefly, that we might get far enough away for darkness to fall before the Germans chose to re-engage. But although we had the illusion that we were heading away from the action, there was no certainty that we were not steering into an ambush.

In fact, astern of us, *Sheffield* and *Jamaica* were engaged in a running battle with the *Hipper* and *Lützow*. Although it was only mid-day – two hours since *Hipper* had hit us – what little light there had been had already disappeared. After fierce exchanges of gunfire the Germans withdrew to the west, Force R returning to shadow the homeward-bound convoy which it had still to sight.

We were still hard at work baling when a terrific explosion was heard in the distance. This turned out to be the death-throes of *Friedrich Eckholdt*, left apparently sinking two hours earlier.

It was difficult to keep a foothold in the semi-darkness, for not only were we listing badly, taking in water from the shell holes on the port side, but we were down by the bows too; a sad and undignified position for so beautiful a ship.

During the late afternoon forward compartments were flooded on the starboard side to balance the seas we were taking to port. Gradually we straightened up, the bows lifting correspondingly.

We had a break for double tots of rum and hot soup, and then another, two hours later, when the ship's company was assembled on deck, we stopped engines, and the dead were slid over the side in their canvas shrouds.

Soon afterwards, with the glass falling and our prospects of staying afloat in heavy seas negligible, we detached ourselves from the convoy, to whom we were now useless. We were still able, extraordinarily, to make nearly twenty knots, though every so often we rolled alarmingly, hanging as if we could never right ourselves.

Signals of the position, course and speed of the convoy were made to the Admiralty and we flashed our own farewells to *Obedient*, taking over from us as senior escort, and the remaining destroyers. We slipped off alone into the darkness, hoping that in the twelve hours it would take us to reach Kola we met nothing disagreeable.

The wounded lay under heavy blankets in the wardroom, the sweet smell of ether drifting over to where those of us not on watch dossed down in the passage outside.

There was no sign yet of the bad weather forecast to be moving south, and apart from a long swell the sea was smoother than at any time since we had sailed.

The Captain, heavily sedated, had scarcely been seen by anyone except the surgeon and his own steward since he had reluctantly been helped off the bridge at the height of the action.

It was an odd sensation lying in the semi-darkness, with only the glow from a hurricane lamp lighting the rows of bodies. From time to time someone stirred or groaned, otherwise the silence was broken only by the steady hum of the engines and the swish of the sea against the side.

We came alongside Vaenga Pier at noon, the surrounding hills covered in snow. The Captain and the other wounded were taken off in ambulances, the remainder trying to make the ship habitable so as to avoid having to sleep ashore in freezing huts with no water or lavatories. The forward messes were unusable and melting snow dripped everywhere. Mostly we slept on the wardroom floor.

For some days, while a group of surly Russian engineers, the only English-speaking one among them being a dazzling but equally unsmiling blonde, made up their minds about where and how repairs should be carried out, we worked among the twisted steel and burnt wood sorting things out. In the evenings, bundled up in layers of clothing so that we looked like bears, we waddled along the jetty to what passed for a canteen, a simple hut with wooden benches and crates of beer stacked behind a trellis table. From time to time Russians amused themselves taking pot shots at us as we stumbled back on board.

At intervals we could hear the thump of bombs and sporadic anti-aircraft fire. The Luftwaffe had a training base for pilots just across the border in Finland and at various times during the day and night they would practise their trade by flying the short distance up river and dropping their bombs. Some fell on Vaenga, some on Murmansk, but luckily none on us, since we had nothing to fire back with.

In due course our convoy, JW51B, arrived safely at Vaenga, and almost immediately we ourselves shifted berth to Rosta, a better-equipped port nearer Murmansk.

It was plain now that *Onslow* would be out of action for some weeks and I began to worry about my own future. At Rosta the news came in that the skipper, Captain R. St. V. Sherbrooke, half-blind and in hospital, had been awarded the VC for, in the words of Admiral of the Fleet Lord Tovey, 'one of the finest examples in either of the two World Wars of how to handle destroyers in action with heavier forces'.

The crew was assembled on deck to hear the announcement, after which we spliced the mainbrace. With a third of those who had sailed from Iceland in *Onslow* dead or badly wounded, celebrations below decks were faintly ironic.

The repercussions of the German failure to damage the convoy, despite their vastly superior forces and the advantages of proximity to their base and surprise, were immediate. Hitler, outraged, sent for Grand Admiral Raeder, not only sacking him but ordering the paying off of all the big ships. Within weeks the battleships *Gneisenau*, *Schleswig-Holstein*, *Tirpitz*, the cruisers *Leipzig*, *Hipper*, *Köln*, *Prinz Eugen*, *Nürnberg*, and *Emden*, the pocket battleships *Admiral Scheer* and *Lützow*, were taken out of service. The German High Seas Fleet never sailed again. Henceforth, it was to be a U-boat war.

All this, of course, emerged much later. Meanwhile, at Rosta, I received instructions to join *HMS Harrier*, the senior minesweeper in the escort of the homeward-bound convoy RA52.

RA52 sailed on 29 January 1943, *Onslow*, still badly battered and with only half her original crew on board, accompanying us for the first three days. No longer the flotilla leader, she seemed like a ghost ship, spectral and unsubstantial against the similar-coloured ocean. It was hard to credit that a month ago, in the same position of 73° 42' North, 32° 30' East, I had been a member of her crew, sailing unsuspectingly into the battle of her life. It seemed an act of betrayal, and vaguely disloyal, not to be sailing home in her now, but she was shortly to be detached to proceed on her own to Scapa for repairs while I was required for other things.

The next time I was to see her was alongside in the naval dockyard at Bombay where, sold to the Indian navy after the war, she bore the new name of *Tipu Sultan*.

Sherbrooke had already returned to England in *Obedient*, to begin a series of operations on his face. His left eye was removed and also a splinter close to the brain.

RA52 proceeded at 8 knots. *Harrier* was astern of the convoy, one of her tasks being to pick up survivors if anything was sunk. There was not long to wait. About noon, on a peaceful-looking, bright morning two days out, an Asdic contact was reported at extreme range on our starboard bow. Shortly afterwards, looking out from the fo'c'sle, I saw the track of a torpedo passing from right to left some two hundred yards ahead of us.

It seemed to be crawling, at the end of its tether, but it was making straight for the last vessel, a cumbersome American Liberty ship, on the port column of the convoy.

They had seen it, but agonizingly slow to respond to the helm were half-way through a hard turn to starboard when the torpedo hit. Within minutes of the explosion her bows began to lift and in slow motion she slid backwards into the sea.

It was like watching a film being played back at half-speed. One moment there was this stately procession of ships, keeping orderly, two-column station, smoke uncurling from each funnel, the next, one of them was quietly slithering out of sight.

So deliberate did it all seem, almost rehearsed, that it was difficult to connect it with reality. As we made to approach her, keeping a wary eye open for a second torpedo following in the wake of the first, we could see men struggling to lower the lifeboats. Others were trying to keep their feet, grasping at anything as the deck became vertical.

Several boats got away, those left on board either going down with the ship or jumping into the sea, swimming desperately to escape the suction round her screws. The last to jump was a fat cook, emerging from the galley with a chicken in each hand.

Destroyers wheeled round at high speed, bows taking water as they combed the starboard horizon. Contact was lost with the U-boat, which must have dived to safety and a patient wait on the sea-bed. Curiously, though there were frequent reports of U-boats and aircraft in the area, no further attack was made on us.

Meanwhile we took the survivors from the Liberty ship including the cook and his two bedraggled friends, on board, cold, frightened and most of them vowing never to make another trip. They cheered up after rum and hot soup, but these were civilian crews and once back home they were free to come and go as they pleased. Not many, I think, chose to sail this way again.

Once more I was supernumerary to the ship's complement, a 'bird of passage', sleeping on the floor of the Paymaster's cabin and spending the days bringing the Confidential Books up to date and deciphering coded signals. *Harrier* had been on patrol duty in the Arctic for several months, not only taking convoys up the Kola Inlet, but escorting them on to Archangel. The crew were in a much jumpier state than anything I had experienced in *Onslow*, and it was obviously high time they were on their way home.

Once back in Scapa I made my farewells and went off on leave. Two weeks later I was recalled to the old 'V and W' class destroyer, of 1914 vintage, *HMS Vivien*, her re-fit now completed, in which I had first gone to sea. For the next 18 months I sailed with her, escorting convoys from Rosyth to Sheerness and back, once a week in either direction. For two nights going south and two nights going north we were closed up at action stations as we passed through 'E-Boat alley' off the Suffolk coast. At last I had a home. Unlike in *Onslow*, I knew everyone and they knew me.

JW51B had begun for me, on 20 December 1942, with a telegram ordering me to report to the depot ship *Dunluce Castle* at Scapa Flow. I had joined *Vivien* a month earlier, having spent the previous six weeks at a house in Wimbledon mastering recently deciphered German codes. Hauled out of whatever branch of the service we were in – I had come from *Daedalus*, the Fleet Air Arm base at Lee-on-Solent – because of a knowledge of German, a dozen of us spent several hours a day with earphones on listening to intercepted or dummy conversations between German aircraft, surface ships and U-boats. We were known as 'Headache' operators, our receiving set an RL85.

My own knowledge of German was scanty, to say the least, in any case more to do with literature than life. I had never been to Germany nor conducted anything but the sketchiest of conversations in German. Joce and Tregenza had never spoken German to us, even if they had been capable of doing so. Nor for that matter had Will Moore. Nevertheless, so limited was the vocabulary involved, I was confident after my intensive course that I could interpret any set of signals we might pick up. I came to know the language and the voices coming through my earphones better than anyone else's in the world and when eventually I picked up my first real E-boat exchange it sounded exactly as it had done in Wimbledon.

Vivien, as it happened, was due in for a month's re-fit and I had done no more than two trips, sick as a dog both ways, before both watches were sent on leave.

It was from this leave that I was recalled. Originally it was *Vivien*'s senior 'Headache' operator, a German-speaking exile, who was nominated, but on learning that Arctic clothing was going to be required he managed to persuade the Admiralty department concerned, NID9, that he was allergic to wool. He was therefore excused and I was sent in his place. He later distinguished himself in MTBs and was decorated.

Dunluce Castle, which I reached via Thurso after a beautiful journey by train through the Grampians and North-West Highlands, was a dump. The ship's company, like most of those in depot ships and similar cushy numbers, had dug themselves in, fearful of getting a draft to a sea-going ship and resentful of those who interrupted their peace and quiet. The messdecks were alive with rats and cockroaches, and if there was any virtue to the place it was that it developed in one a healthy desire to get out as quickly as possible.

My turn came soon enough. I was to join the flotilla leader *Onslow*, already in the destroyer anchorage across the water, until further notice.

A launch came over next evening to pick me up. The buzz on board was that we were to pick up a convoy in Iceland and take it to Russia. The Russian convoys had been stopped for some time owing to heavy casualties but now, with daylight reduced to an hour or two in the Arctic as well as increasing pressure from Stalin, they were rumoured to be starting up again.

I was given a billet of two yards on top of the lockers in one of the seamen's messes; there were no spare lockers to store my clothes nor room to sling my hammock. I was the only new rating to join the ship and it was impossible not to feel out of it. *Onslow* had been many months, off and on, in the Arctic, and most of the crew were not slow to express their disgust at being required to return there. The fact that I was joining them 'for special duties' did nothing to lessen their apprehension about what lay ahead.

We sailed almost immediately for the anchorage at Loch Ewe, a seven-hour race to the south-west, the foam from our bows cascading over the bridge and the ship keeling over each time we altered course. The turquoise-blue RL85 seemed in good order, but there was nothing to pick up and it was enough for the time being to try and avoid being sick.

At Loch Ewe the convoy and escort conference took place and then the fourteen merchantmen – nine American, four British, one Panamanian – slid out in line ahead into the North Minch. They were not a pretty sight, rusty and down to their hulls, and looking more suited for the breaking-up yard than a winter journey to Russia and back. Between them they carried

200 tanks, 120 aircraft (fighters and bombers), 23,000 gallons of fuel and aviation spirit, and 2,000 vehicles. The fastest among them might manage twelve knots; the slowest, with a lot of huffing and puffing, barely nine.

We ourselves would pick them up a few hours sailing time north-east of Iceland, making our own way to Seidisfiord to join *Obedient, Oribi, Orwell* and *Obdurate* who were already there.

The passage to Iceland, made at the fastest possible speed, was a nightmare. A southerly gale, Force 12, had sprung up and time and again, as we crashed into the trough between huge waves, the ship shuddered as if her back were broken. The decks ran from bow to stern, the weight of water threatening to sink us. Amazingly we staggered upright, cutting through swirling scoops of grey-green foam before plunging again. Lifelines were rigged on the upper deck and it was impossible to walk or even stand without hanging on to them.

The Captain was anxious to get to Seidisfiord so as to have the maximum time with the other 'O' class destroyer captains. The weather was worsening hourly, and *Bulldog* and *Achates*, who got the brunt of it, were forced to heave-to. *Bulldog* in fact had to turn back and return to Scapa for repairs, missing the convoy. *Achates*, although damaged, was able to continue, sadly for her as it turned out.

Not until, thirty-six hours later, we turned into Seidisfiord did the buffeting and soaking stop. Even so, the wind tore down between the steep sides of the fiord making it almost as uncomfortable at anchor.

It was strange to be somewhere where there was no blackout. The riding lights of the destroyers at anchor, the masthead lights of the tanker *Scottish American* from which next day we were to fill up with oil, and the reflections on water of the quayside buildings would have made a romantic scene had it not been for the biting wind. Snow lay so thickly everywhere that the wooden houses on the lower slopes of the fiord were distinguishable only by their lights.

Next day, 23 December, *Achates*, looking bedraggled, turned up and, shortly afterwards, the escort captains came separately on board *Onslow*. The fiord, with snow glistening under a low sun, turned from angostura pink to apricot in late afternoon.

After supper I went ashore. There was a solitary Red Cross canteen on the jetty and a few shops, one of which sold silk stockings, virtually unobtainable in England. The Germans had infiltrated Iceland before the war, setting up signal stations from which later they were able to report the movements of convoys to lurking U-boats. The girls who worked in these shops were known to lead the sailors on, making dates which the sailors eventually had to break. Thus they knew when a convoy was due out. Their other tactic was to say they were temporarily out of stockings, but that if they knew the last possible time for collection they would try and get some in. More than one ship was torpedoed within minutes of reaching open sea. The girls operating these rackets appeared to be chosen for their looks and length of leg, pirouetting on steps as they reached for the top shelf and revealing to frustrated sailors enticing glimpses of bare thigh.

We sailed shortly before midnight on Christmas Eve. The Captain, whom most of the crew had never spoken to – since he had only recently joined – and knew only as a handsome, white-haired man of quiet voice and reserved manner, addressed the ship's company over the tannoy. After regrets about the better ways in which Christmas might have been spent and promising a real Christmas dinner when we reached Murmansk, he gave a brief account of the convoy's size and disposition, and of the role of the escorts. He ended up: 'I wish you all luck. We have a fair chance of getting through without being spotted. In any case we shall be covered by the cruisers of Force R for the last part of the journey, when we come closest to the German bases in Norway and are most likely to be attacked. At most there will be three hours of daylight.'

In the messes his speech, the exact words of which I could repeat thirty years later, was greeted with silence, punctuated by oaths. Griffiths, a black seaman, pretended to go off his rocker. 'Let me get off this bastard. Jesus Christ, I'll never get another bit. O Christ, let me off this sod.' Luckily, there was no time to hang about. No sooner had Sherbrooke finished speaking than special sea-duty men were ordered to their stations and the routine for preparing for sea got under way.

By midnight, we were clear of the boom and in open sea, soon rolling and pitching. Lower deck was cleared as we moved out through the minefield at the entrance to the fiord, our sister ships in line astern and the haze of light over Seidisfiord sinking below the horizon.

I spent the rest of that first night in the W/T office, making sure the set was receiving on all channels. It was routine procedure, for with a range of no more than twenty miles interceptions were unlikely. The possibility increased when, before dawn, signals were received reporting the proximity of a U-boat and the probable sighting of the convoy by a patrolling German aircraft.

Our first task now was to find the convoy, the five destroyers fanning out into line abreast three miles apart. It was during the afternoon watch that it came into sight, some miles off course but the four columns of ships keeping reasonable station under the protection of their Hunt class destroyer escort.

Once we had relieved them the Hunts peeled off in turn and made their way home to Scapa. The serious part of the journey had begun.

The next four days, while we were at maximum distance from the German air bases, the crews remained at cruising stations, four hours on, eight hours off. Sub-Lieutenant Midgely, the other 'Headache' operator, and I had, however, to work watch and watch, four hours on, four hours off, during the hours of darkness. Off duty, I tried to get some rest on the lockers, but the fug and discomfort were such that I spent as much time on deck as possible. We were now in the Arctic Circle and the temperatures were well below zero.

The convoy stretched out behind us, meticulously arranged pieces that reminded me of the games of Dover Patrol we played at my preparatory school. Every so often, according to a pre-arranged zig-zag, we altered course, taking the convoy with us.

Visibility was mostly poor, the ships mere intensifications of grey, detectable by the lip of foam at each bow. From time to time *Onslow* went down the convoy at speed, checking station-keeping and remonstrating with those making too much smoke, before returning to our position at the head and reducing to nine knots. *Orwell* and *Oribi* protected the port flank of the convoy, *Obedient* and *Obdurate* the starboard. Two trawlers and a corvette brought up the rear, on hand should there be survivors to be picked up.

If we had been sighted there was no immediate reaction. Although every hour was an hour nearer to Murmansk it also brought us closer to any ambush.

The fourth day out, by which time lack of sleep had produced an air of total unreality, we ran into a gale. On deck, with a howling wind and gusts of snow, it was almost impossible to see or to stand. Ships slid out of sight behind huge waves and then reared up at all angles. It had been exhausting enough going at twenty-five knots in high seas up to Iceland, but at eight knots, in a slow, slewing roll, with the wind on the beam, it was far worse.

By next morning the ship was as encased in frozen snow as if it had been left in an ice-box. It had also become dangerously top-heavy. Guns had constantly to be trained to prevent them icing up but even so, when the time came, half of them would prove to be unusable.

From all-night watch I went to crash out on the lockers, scarcely able to recognize the rest of the mess, virtual strangers in any case, as they came in muffled and dripping like huskies, only their eyes visible. From the second day onwards I was too seasick to eat, unable to get anything down to bring up. The smell of vomit everywhere mixed with that of wet duffle coat, stewing tea, seaboot stockings and burning toast. For years afterwards I was not even able to look at tea or eat toast.

The lucky ones could be sick robustly, eat and be sick again, feeling better in the process. Others, like myself, staggered to the heads retching drily and bringing up only the sour lining of the stomach. To keep upright for even a few minutes needed a major effort of will.

Before going into the W/T office to take over at the RL85, I used to go out on deck for fresh air. That was better, even though all you could see were cliffs of grey sea surging towards you or sidling away, the icy spray cutting at your face.

The horizon was the thinnest line between sea and sky. The convoy, coming in and out of focus, seemed almost stationary, the escorts nudging stragglers into place like sheepdogs.

It was too cold to stay out for more than a few minutes at a time, and easy to get washed overboard, for the pitching and rolling were unpredictable. Often when it seemed the roll was completed and the ship would start to right itself it rolled still farther, the screws rattling out of the water and the mast almost horizontal. Then it seemed the slightest wave would turn us over.

We always came round eventually, plunging with guncrack force into gaping hollows and taking creaming sheets over the bows. This process was infinitely preferable experienced on deck, where you could at least see what was happening, rather than in an airless office or mess, cooped up and at the mercy of sudden slithers, crashing crockery and swinging hammocks.

By the night of the 29th, our fifth day out, the pipes had frozen and there was no water. Off watch we took it in turns to hold our mouths open under the taps for single drops.

After Up Spirits and the rum issue I began at last to keep some food down, passing out immediately afterwards on the lockers and waking with a terrible thirst. I developed an obsessive longing for tinned peaches, fantasizing endlessly about them to an extent that even obliterated sexual imagining, the usual antidote to present misery.

There was no slackening of the gale. Hourly it increased,

forcing two merchantmen, whose deck cargo had shifted, to heave-to, and another four to become detached. Worse, from our point of view, *Oribi* lost contact during the night because of gyro failure and was of no further use.

When, at last, the storm began to let up it became apparent that five of the convoy were adrift. Although the wind had dropped from gale force it had left a sprawling swell almost as uncomfortable. Instead of crashing into space we corkscrewed and slid.

For the first time since we had sailed the weather did not seem the main enemy. The three previous days keeping going and upright had been the extent of most people's ambitions. Now, approaching the danger zone, not only had the convoy to be restored to some kind of order, but battle preparations to be made.

It was during the night of the 29th, in almost nil visibility, that we missed ramming *Orwell* on a zig-zag by a few feet. The Captain was not on the bridge at the time, the difference in his case between a VC and an Admiralty enquiry being a matter of seconds. The next morning was spent chipping away the suit of ice that had rendered our natural lines unrecognizable.

During the afternoon two of the missing merchantmen turned up, but *Oribi*, a trawler and two merchantmen remained unaccounted for.

At dusk we started up 'Headache' for what would probably be forty-eight hours non-stop searching. Sometime before midnight *Obdurate* flashed that a U-boat had been sighted and that she was preparing to ram. Immediately we went to Action Stations.

In fact U-354 had already fired torpedoes at the convoy but missed. Attacked by *Obdurate* it dived immediately. *Obedient* joined in, firing depth-charges, but without visible result.

The speed and course of the convoy were plainly no longer a secret. Almost certainly, the German air bases in Norway had been alerted, and equally certainly the group of ships lurking in Altenfiord – battleships, cruisers, destroyers – had steam up and were preparing to intercept as we rounded North Cape. It was simply a question of when.

In the W/T office successive signals from Murmansk reported the presence of destroyers and U-boats ahead of us. Surprisingly, the night passed peacefully, there was silence on all frequencies, and at 0800 the watch changed. Forty-five minutes later, cloud and sea tilting into each other to form a grey screen, the first contact was made between the three prowling German destroyers and the convoy. At 0915 the Germans opened fire and, seconds later, we ourselves went to Action Stations. The Battle of the Barents Sea had begun.

From time to time *Onslow* drifted into and out of my notice, generally in Admiralty Fleet Orders or in signals. After several months in dock she was made seaworthy again and became one of the escorts of JW55B to Murmansk a year later. In a peripheral skirmish the battle cruiser *Scharnhorst* was sunk off North Cape on its way to attack the convoy. This time *Onslow* was not directly involved. By now she had a new captain and virtually a new crew, and it was hard to feel quite the same about her.

JW51B

A Convoy

From the Supplement to the London Gazette, 17 October 1950: 'The conduct of all officers and men of the escort and covering forces throughout this successful action against greatly superior forces was in accordance with the traditions of the service. That an enemy force of at least one pocket battleship, one heavy cruiser and six destroyers, with all the advantages of surprise and concentration, should be held off for four hours by five destroyers and driven from the area by two 6-inch cruisers, without any loss to the convoy, is most creditable and satisfactory.'

The sea, phlegm-coloured, bone-white, fuming.

And Moulson waddled crabwise to his Action Station
And Smith wrote home on thin, ruled paper
And Wilson read Spicy Stories in his hammock,
And Reeder, McGregor, Wood and 'Blood' Reid
Played Uckers on the tea-wet, tilting table.
Bulkheads sweated, steel shuddered, silence grew.
A cockroach plopped, fat as a plum, on Dyson's lip.

A week out of Iceland, nosing the Barents Sea,
And guns were trained hourly to prevent freezing.
Snow on the ladders and life-lines, Jesus Christ
In the person of Torpedoman Jones, bearded
And tense as a Da Vinci, suffering from shell-shock.
A dropped spoon jumped him to Heaven.

Escort of six destroyers, the convoy fourteen merchantmen,
Carrying tanks, stores, artillery, Murmansk-bound.
Onslow, Obedient, Obdurate, Orwell, Achates,
And sailing from Scapa in a Force 12 gale,
Bulldog, damaged, turned back, *Achates*
Sprang her foremast, and *Oribi,* with gyro failure,
Lost touch, making her own way up.

Destroyers were the same again in ice,
Raked silhouettes in crusted overcoats that cramped
On guns and bridge. The look-outs stamped.
And into messes water seeped.

December the 24th, oiling at Seidis: and Watch Ashore
Went ashore, walking the pink inlet
In search of canned beer, silk stockings, and a bit
Of what you fancy, which was not there.
White muzzles of the fiord, hills of sphagnum.
And the trawlers like foals nuzzling the oiler.

CO's at conference, and anchors dragging,
While Masters spoke up for their limitations
And Captain (D) cajoled them to keep station,
Knowing the obstinacy of their independence,
How they liked to make the most
Of it – how it got them lost.
Charts were studied, and the screening diagrams
For *Circe*, *Ledbury* and *Chiddingfold*,
Whose job was to round up stragglers, laid down.
In the NAAFI Butcher and Bredon to keep warm
Danced with each other a mock hornpipe, and a sour
Putty-faced girl stood staring with a plate of cakes.

At 2300, when at home trees were being
Laden with presents and last year's Father Christmas
Was buttoning his duffle and seeing
Beyond the mineswept channel that one face
Warm on a pillow that trailed
Hair through dreams of reunion, they sailed,
Line abreast and making thirteen knots,
Visibility three miles, to O, the appointed spot.
Meeting the convoy at which place,
Circe and her sisters left them.
And on their own, into a head sea now,
Waves like tissue paper on every bow,
Erratically they pitched on a course of 320,
Yawing and rolling plenty.

Hammocks swinging as the sea swings,
   Creaking and straining and sly.
      One bright eye
Perpetually open, a smoky fever
Of dream in the lamp's shadowing rings.
   Some dreams are for ever.

And Tanzie Lee dreamed of St Anthony's choir,
And Ellis of the Jig and Tool ads in the *Argus*,
And Bennett of Pusser's Stores and what he could win,
And Totman of Tottenham Hotspur in the good days,
And the Buffer of feeling a woman in various ways.

The Log Book written on a tilting desk,
Records a position at noon on the 26th
Of 68° 23′ North, 6° 32′ West,
And the welcome sight of a Catalina.
Winds freshened, and at gale force
The convoy to 071° altered course,
And the big ships, their Marines
With more flannel than a Pusser's blanket,
Swung at familiar moorings.

Regular as a metronome,
The arc of roll, rolling them away,
      Away from home,
Though home is where you make it,
On a hard locker and a blanket,
As the bulging hammocks sway
And the darkness turns to grey,
      The grey of day.

On the twenty-ninth the trawler *Vizalma* hove to,
A merchantman shifted her cargo, speed was reduced
To six knots, and course again altered.
The convoy, neat once, faltered
In formation. 21, unable to keep her
Station, hove-to. *Bramble*, a minesweeper,
Was sent to search for three
That were missing. *Oribi* was absent.

We have a good chance, the Captain
(D) had said, of getting through,
Days being so short, and the crew
In the messes on Christmas Eve, writing letters,
Had paused, and without disrespect made
Obscene gestures, cynical about the degrees
Of comfort administered by gold braid.
But, trusting that there were better
Times ahead, since they could not be worse,
Had strewn the air with flowery curses,
What might pass for thoughts, unsaid.
Whether they had yet been spotted
Was now for each the relevant
Question, framed on waking
To the bo'sun's mate on his way round shaking
Reliefs, surfacing in damp fug
To a reality they could not shrug
Easily off. Thoughts were painstaking.

Had they? Possibly, south of Iceland,
By a Focke-Wulf, while *Obdurate* obtained
Contacts and dropped depth charges,
And alarm reports came in from Norway.
But nothing definite save messdeck buzzes
Travelled through frozen spray.
Huddled on 'B' Gun, furred as a husky,
Roley Wilson dreaming of the sun,
A great one for Tombola, dwelt upon
Those green calm nights and that
Auspicious occasion when Doctor's Chum,
Number Nine, and Royal Salute, Twenty-one,
Came up to win him the House,
And the sun liquified, quiet as a mouse
The sea, and all night in,
After the Last Dog, he cuddled his money.

Each man waiting was two men,
The man with Pay Book and number,
A rank and a duty, Sick Berth
Tiffy, Torpedoman, Tanky
And Stoker, and another man inside

With a healthy fear for his own skin,
Reading month-old local papers,
What the Stars Foretell, the News
Of the World in which he was scarcely in,
Except by proxy. These two
Travelled a parallel course,
The man of ice outside,
The dreaming man within.

No longer comforting planes or the friendly gulls
Garrotting the sky and dipping their wings
In salute or farewell. Not since Jan Mayen,
Passed to port a day or so back, had the sea
Done other than boiled, hissed, spewed
With emptiness, rattling its boredom from horizon
To horizon, something none would ever again want to set eyes on.

Next day, the thirtieth, noon, ten were present
Of the fourteen, *Vizalma* catching up
And the Commodore increasing to nine,
Then slowing to allow stragglers to return,
Obdurate hustling them in on the first
Fine afternoon when ice could be chipped,
A smile be made without lips freezing.
And Captain (D) at 1630 saw slipped
Into formation the last of his charges,
Observing the crisis approach like a doctor
His patient's temperature, reckoning the chances,
As now between the ice and German Norway,
South of Bear Island, he felt his way.

Final dark, convoy and escort aware
Of each other, not knowing their relative
Positions, but simply that somewhere
Each followed a similar course,
A helmsman bringing the wheel to midships,
Steering 090, Wind Force 3,
North-westerly, and sixteen degrees of frost
Hardening on the steel deck, radar
And Asdic and RL85 slowly revolving,

W/T silent, gunlayers solving
Hypothetical problems, and the hammocks
Settling in a subsiding swell.

Dreams were dreamed, as well
They might, of child and grate,
Of eyes opening their lashes
To meet their own, holding steady
That for which some were not ready,
Some were already too late,
And chided themselves, men with no
High opinion of their own behaviour,
But belonging somewhere, belonging,
Inarticulate even in their longing.

Courses crossing, like lines on a hand,
Darkness disintegrating, and throwing up
Into the net of the morning, like fish,
A stranded sea of vessels, ignorantly
Approaching, British and German.

II

Not dawn, for dawn means light,
And from this light sun was withdrawn,
But eventually it was not night
Any more, and a sardine-coloured sea
Tipped into clouds torn
Here and there, the dull grey
Glinting, as if turned to metal.

And *Hyderabad* sighted them first,
On a bearing of 180°, two destroyers
She believed to be Russian
So did not report, her captain
Being of a trusting nature,
And they continued awhile, until *Obdurate*
Closed them, and was fired on,
The enemy retiring to the north-westward.

And, ahead, in *Onslow*, Captain (D),
W/T silence now being broken,
Signalled his destroyers, Join Me,
My course 280, Speed 20,
And the destroyers, breaking
Out of line, heeled over,
Increasing revolutions, like the spokes
Of an umbrella being opened,
Spray icing the look-outs,
Forming up in line ahead.

On 'A' Gun Smithers, settled behind
The gunshield, shook from his eyes
Pieces of dream, the unkind
Sea walling him in, spattering the wrists
Lately in fancy she had kissed.

In the engine room Stoker Davies
Of Merioneth said Hell loudly,
Giving all of the six l's full value,
And wiping his hands on waste,
Unctuously as a stage doctor,
Fussed over his gauges, proud as if
Playing at Cardff Arms Park,
The eyes of all Wales on him.

And *Onslow*, with *Orwell*,
Obedient, *Obdurate* taking up station
Astern of her, ordered the Commodore
East, an emergency turn
Of 135°, *Achates* laying smoke between,
And they closed the enemy.

Northward, an hour distant, Burnett,
Flying his flag of Rear-Admiral (D)
In *Sheffield – Jamaica* in company –
Turned on a course of 170°,
Making haste to that grey
Chessboard of ocean, on whose invisible
Squares ships related
The possible to the impossible.

Now in *Onslow* was sighted to starboard
An unknown vessel, approaching at speed,
Opening fire on *Achates* with six-inch guns;
And *Onslow*, altering to a parallel course,
At a range of 9000 returned her fire,
Identifying the enemy as the cruiser *Hipper*,
And made ready torpedoes, which *Hipper*,
Declining to receive, retired from
In smoke, desultorily shelling.
Which was the decoy, *Hipper* or those
Other destroyers, now numbering six,
That lurked in attendance, like
Male nurses round some gross invalid,
Expectant yet afraid?

More than one course was open,
But Sherbrooke, preying on the enemy's
Fear of torpedoes, pursued him,
Orwell astern, ordering *Obdurate*
And *Obedient* back to the convoy,
The best he could do for it
In the way of defence, while he himself
Went after *Hipper*, peppering her,
Tracers like bridges of fireworks
Linking over distance, and the slow
Grey swell heaving itself up,
Collapsing and breathless.

Hipper and *Onslow*, sea-horses
Entwining, as one turned, the other
Also, on parallel courses
Steaming, a zig-zag raking
The forenoon, as two forces,
From each other breaking,
Manoeuvred for position.
Like squids squirting their ink
In defence, ships smoked sky
Round them, camouflaging.

Herringbone waters, and the cold
Drifting south, narrowing
The escape routes, icing breeches;
A slow confetti of snow
Made bridal the gun teams,
Aiming awhile their dreams
At the blizzard of *Hipper*.
Who rounded, small flames
Pricking her, the stronger
Animal, able no longer
To stomach indignity,
Firing broadsides on *Onslow*.

Onslow to *Obdurate*: Have been hit
Forward and in engine-room.
Onslow to *Obedient*: Captain (D) wounded,
Take over for time being.
Onslow to Rear-Admiral (Destroyers):
Am retiring on convoy making smoke-screen.

Onslow to *Obedient*: Forward magazine
Flooded, fire in boiler room.
Am proceeding to southward of convoy.

The lamp flicked out the messages.
While below, on Port wave,
A Leading Telegraphist gave
Such information to Murmansk
As was necessary, repeating
To Force R what was relevant.

And *Obedient* took over, *Onslow*
In flames retiring, relinquishing
Seniority, a private ship
Fighting her private battle.

'A' and 'B' Guns unable to fire,
Radar destroyed, aerials ripped,
And, forward, the sea stripping
The Mess decks, spilling over tables,
Fire and water clinching like boxers

193

As the ship listed, sprawling them.
Tamblin, his earphones awry, like a laurel wreath
Slipped on a drunken god, gargled to death
In water with a noise of snoring.

Slip, slop, slip, slop, a boarding house slattern
In carpet slippers answering
The door, a telegram from 5 Mess
Refusing to come home, Gone Whoring
After a sleazy mermaid with tin fins,
Eyes rheumy with salt, shins
Barked on a stanchion, a pattern
Only too familiar, only this time
It was for good, not evil.
That the old devil
Was absent, and it was the sea
Slip slopping, no woman, over his property,
Ditty Box, Taxi case, bag and hammock,
Glazing his eyes under whose lids
Passed no parade of marriage,
But the sightless accountancy of one
Shocked out of debt, owing no one.

Ammunition party hurled into attitudes
Of early morning after a wild night,
Smith going for'ard trod and stumbled
On Aistrop's belly, which forever rumbled,
And now put him off balance,
Its last chance at assertion.
Passing buckets, not the buck,
From hand to hand, and heart to heart,
'X' and 'Y' doors clanging shut,
And merciful Arctic sliding at last
Its cold arms round the flames.

The human chain bent, passed,
Bent, passed, bent, passed,
Simmons forgetting his fibrositis
And Donkin, his four-eyes swept overboard,
Entered Heaven in a blur,
Which was as well, for little was left of him.

194

Mess traps banging, with a double issue
Of rum to all hands, ignorant
Now of the situation, apparent
Or real, but at all events
Warm, hearing steel shudder,
Noticing movements of rudder,
While smells of anaesthetic
Seeped for'ard, an Arctic
Stew was served of spuds
And corned dog, and the First
Lieutenant's voice coolly organized
What needed to be organized,
As if it was Sunday Divisions
And the Base Captain was coming aboard.

So *Onslow* rejoined in falling darkness,
Having aided the elements' cancellation
Of each other, fire and water
A litany henceforward for all
Who had use of litanies,
Her captain sightless in his sea cabin,
Having ordered the battle, wounded
As Ahab, and no less dogged.
Smythe, a CW candidate
With an eye on the future, smoothed
His beard, felt his neck
To confirm it was still there,
And ventured on deck,
Having a mind to recapitulate
The action, test the weather,
And generally nose out the future.

He saw, as he held to a ladder
For support, (the angle of list
Being forty-five degrees), *Achates*
Laying smoke astern, though holed
Forward, once more straddled
By *Lützow*, now up in support
Of *Hipper*; and slowly,
Northern Gem taking off survivors,
Doing the obsequies, she sank.

195

He saw, the convoy steaming sedate
As swans on a river, his own ship
Flying pennants of smoke,
Obedient and *Orwell* and *Obdurate*
To port, from time to time
Making sorties on a horizon
Of gunflash, returning to the rhyme
Of escort after passages of free verse.

And he learned soon how *Sheffield*
And *Jamaica*, surprising the enemy
On their disengaged side, had set fire
To *Lützow*, and finding fine
On the bow a loafing enemy destroyer
Had incidentally removed it –
A salutary lesson, inflicted
With the minimum of effort
And a courteous lack of ostentation
Entirely in keeping
With the traditions of the Service.

Beneath the ice-floes sleeping,
Embalmed in salt
The sewn-up bodies slipping
Into silent vaults.
The sea of Barents received them,
Men with no faults
Of courage, for the weeping
Would be elsewhere,
Far from its keeping.

Seamen of *Onslow, Achates*,
Travellers without warrants or visas,
It was All Night In
On that long Watch that encompasses
The Dogs, the Middle, the Forenoon,
The Morning, Afternoon,
And First that shall be the last,
That shall be forever.

A sea littered, and *Onslow*,
Collision mats in place, holes stopped,
Leaning on a falling ocean,
The wind dropped
As if not to disturb the dreaming
Of blanketed Wardroom forms
Gently up estuaries steaming
Bearing no names.

And the Buffer would remember
The date, the thirty-first of December,
When the forward fire
And repair party disintegrated
Before his eyes,
Leaving him an undelivered bottle
On his hands, an expression of surprise
That remained there for days.

Heads floating like lilies,
Pulled under by currents, or surfacing
To take no part
In the tactical situation,
To appraise which was an art
Dependent on survival.
This water-garden of the fo'c'sle,
These statues of the heart.

And if you had brought
To the attention of Dinwiddy,
A three-badge AB, notorious
For the kindness of his soul,
The foulness of his language,
His captain's intuitive appreciation
Of a situation fraught with ambiguity,
Six enemy destroyers off the starboard quarter,
A pocket battleship and a heavy cruiser
Approaching on the port bow,
And the necessity of drawing fire
Away from the convoy, yet not deserting it,
His head would have reeled,

197

His tongue licked out obscenities,
His heart hardened, though even as
He blasphemed, simulating fear,
And voicing the popular opinion
That for a destroyer to engage
An eight-inch cruiser was a form
Of insanity credible only
In one wanting a double layer
Of scrambled egg on his cap,
He would have grown most
Marvellously cool and unfussed,
As loyal to the concepts
Of sacrifice and duty
As to his often, and fastidiously expressed,
Devotion to his own self-interests.

For the ears, the thud of gunfire,
The thunderous shudder of impact,
The hissing of charred wood,
The clanging of steel doors;
And the faint voice of the Gunnery Officer,
Relayed over earphones,
'Short' – 'Over' – 'Straddle',
The thin bird-cry of a man
Pinioned under shells, and the endless
Injections of the surgeon.
For the nose, smell of burning,
Clove sweetness of anaesthetic, the acrid
Odour of cordite.

For the eyes, smoke
Stinging, disarrangements
Of the familiar, Rita Hayworth
Stripped from a locker lid, dice
Rattling in a tea cup, and Reid's
Severed arm cuddling a hammock.
The slow grey heave of waters,
A Focke-Wulf cruising,
Predatory as a shark.

The cold seen almost as a colour
– Ice-grey, gelatinous, glass-edged –
And that rose-shaped explosion of fire,
Booming over bruised sea,
Which those on deck or bridge
Saw as either doom or rescue
And had to guess which.

Enemy withdrawn, and convoy
Proceeding to Kola. This night
Of New Year, sea moderating,
Darkness scattered its largesse,
Though the close escort, not
Knowing the enemy's movements,
Had small feeling of escape,
Merely of being afloat,
Of inching forward into dawn,
Eastward round the North Cape.

Course 226°, Wind Force 2,
And at noon, on January 2nd,
Position 69° N, 35° 30' E,
Land was sighted ahead.
The convoy in three columns,
White Sea to starboard,
And nosing through fog patches
The minesweeper *Harrier*, in company
With two Russian destroyers,
Joined on the port beam.

Kildin Island, and *Seagull*
In position, Syet Navalok Light
Blinking its welcome that spelled
Quite simply 'It is over
For the moment, you are half-way
Home, you are half-way.'

And *Obedient* leading,
The convoy, in line ahead,
Slipped down the inlet behind her,
Onslow already along side,
Having discharged her wounded.

199

From snow into snow. A kind
Of deliverance, an unloading.
As skies, snow-heavy, are lightened
By the falling of flakes, the mind
Also is eased of anxieties.
The rattle of anchors, whiff of fish,
And Lyons, after a run ashore,
Tucking in the ears of his Rabbits,
Or so he imagined himself,
Gazing at low hills like snow-clouds,
And snow-clouds like low hills.

Arrived, the deck stationary, bulkheads sweating.

East Coast Routines

WE WERE SOMEWHERE off Flamborough Head, going north. The convoy stretched out for three miles behind us, each ship making smoke straight up like a chimney embedded in water. The coastline, where it looped out, was sensed rather than seen, a smell of English summer parallel to the port bow. The sea was thick green, flinted with light. The sun had left it as if strummed by an invisible finger, the notes beginning to die away though some vibrancy remained in the air. The water spilling on our beam was heavy and milky.

A few engine-room artificers, a stoker, a couple of Afternoon Watchmen were on deck, smoking. The pump of the engines was restful once you were out of the sweating, oily inferno below, and they were glad of the pure air.

The ERAs stood together talking; another hour and they would be below again. Tonight, however, was fairly slack. E-Boat alley was behind them, they had had no trouble, and after midnight, when they would put some of the convoy off at the Tyne, they would be free. By dawn the escorts would be going full speed up the Forth and into Rosyth. For the watch ashore it was the nearest thing to heaven that they knew.

Petty Officer Dicks was a stout, complacent, serene man, who only spoke to reassure himself of what he already knew.

'Them civvies ashore set their bloody clocks by us, I shouldn't doubt,' he said, addressing no one in particular. Willis and Denton, the other ERAs, grunted.

'That bastard pig'll start going round the convoy just as soon as I get started on my bangers,' Denton said. 'I'd like to set 'is bloody clock for him, it'd never bloody strike again.'

Willis nodded morosely. He had a poor stomach, ate little and only waited for the day when his internal complaints would get him out of the service. He went on picking his teeth, unmoved by the fact that shortly the Captain would decide to make his evening inspection of the convoy. This was as a rule carefully timed to coincide with the crew's supper, a move which, involving an increase in speed from their normal eight knots to thirty, succeeded in breaking crockery, putting everyone in a bad temper, and relieving the Captain's feelings.

Dicks puffed on his pipe, fatalistic as ever. He would take his supper later. Feeling the need for a change of company, he drifted off to where Winston and Reeder, ABs of No. 5 Mess, were dhobeying.

Dicks pretended to fancy Winston, a young, fresh-faced boy who had delivered newspapers until a few months ago. Winston's conversation consisted of catch phrases copied from his naval elders, and long-winded, largely invented dramas of his own sexual exploits.

'Hullo me lovely lad.' Dicks beamed over Winston's glistening head. His hair, regularly oiled, was combed about every two hours, its creases streaming back in ploughed furrows from the bow wave on his forehead.

'Get stuffed, you fat bastard,' Winston replied, without looking up from the bucket in which he was squeezing out the soap from a blue jean collar.

Reeder, formerly an assistant in a radio shop at Dagenham, whinnied like a horse, an animal he much resembled.

'That's not the way to talk to yore winger, Ronnie boy,' he said. 'Smile nicely and the PO will give you a piece of nutty. Give *us* in fact a piece of nutty, I knows my price.'

'Watch aboard this boiler – clean, aren't you, Bash?' Dicks went on. He knew this to be so, for the fact that they were both Starboard Watch had frequently lent edge to the jokes which became painfully heavy after they had been on leave. Winston came from Lincoln and Dicks lived in Dover but nobody bothered about that. 'Get plenty?' Dicks was always asked when he came back aboard. 'Your winger looks as though he's been put through a mangle.'

'Yes, I bloody am,' Winston replied to Dicks's question. 'And it's not for love of you, Grandad.'

'What about a nice run ashore, you and me, Wings?' Dicks persisted, unabashed by the tone of Winston's reply.

'Think I want to bag off with you? I'd rather have "Blood" Reid, that I would,' Winston retorted. 'Blood' Reid was the Captain's servant, a misanthropic walnut-faced AB with a mad cackle. 'Any case I got a party, works in the Canteen, all lined up, lovely grub.' He fumbled in his overall pocket and brought out a wallet from which he carefully extracted a small, harshly-lit photograph.

'All right, Dicks?' he said, passing up the picture.

Dicks, still beaming, looked down at the starched features of an ageing blonde, a clinging jersey moulding her breasts, but naked from the waist down. She tottered precariously on high heels.

'Had a bash at her yet, Wings?' Dicks asked blandly.

'A bash at 'er! 'E doesn't know what it's for.' Reeder, wringing out a vest, wiped his hands on his overalls and said:

'Pass 'er over, Bash.' He picked up the photograph and began to study it with the same solemnity he gave to a hand of cards.

'Where did you get this from, Ron,' he said at length, with a slow-dawning grin. 'A big rough sailor give it you?'

'You filthy brown-hatters,' Winston said amicably. 'It's wasted on you lot.' He licked his lips. 'Wait till I slip 'er a length, she won't know whether she's going or coming.'

'It won't be coming, Ducks, from what I seen of you,' Reeder cackled. 'Never mind, Winnie boy, dinner's up, let's get stuck in.'

They got up and, pail in hand, went for'ard back to their Mess. Dicks started to re-light his pipe, then, thinking better of it, walked aft and down the steel ladder to the ERAs' mess.

'The course of true love never runs smooth, Mate,' Denton called after him. 'Roll on my twelve.'

He looked quizzically at Willis and was about to speak when

the sharp clang of the ship's telegraph rang down from the bridge.

'There 'e goes, strike a light,' he said, moving his long thin face up and down and making a sucking noise with his teeth. 'Restless bugger. Gord 'elp 'is ole woman.'

The destroyer began to shudder and throb. Willis could hear the Captain's voice coming down the voice-pipe from the bridge:

'250 revs. Hard a' starboard.'

His stomach winced as the ship keeled sharply over. One minute he was gazing mournfully at a gently bruised, violet sea, the next at pale green sky and the evening star.

He steadied himself and holding firmly on to the handrail went down into the engine-room.

The ship completed its wide circuit and leaving behind a crescent-shaped wake, bumped down into a sea now running against it. The bulky merchantmen, for once keeping good station, began to flow by, a small smudge of foam on each bow, like cotton wool on a lip cut by shaving.

For'ard, the crash of benches, the rattle of crockery, the bellowed oaths from the galley, competed against the barrage of the engines. The ship began to plunge and the First Watchmen coming out, in dufflecoats and gloves, to take up station on guns and as look-outs, took the spray straight in their faces as they climbed up to the fo'c'sle.

No. 5 Mess, to which I belonged, was at supper, except for those now on watch. We were about half-way through the convoy on our way back, having slewed round the last mer- chantman, giving it the usual encouragement through the loud-hailer to keep up, and had begun to work up at full speed to the head of the convoy again.

The crockery on the mess tables shook in the orange light. On each side of the for'ard part of the ship wooden lockers con- verged to meet in the bows by the cable locker. Alongside these, wooden trestle-tables, three to a side, were fixed to the deck. Each trestle-table constituted a Mess for twenty ratings presided over by a Leading Seaman. The lockers contained No. 1 uniforms and private possessions, and above them, after Darken Ship had been sounded, hammocks would be slung. At present they were stowed in a pile by the door, except for two which were slung over the table and in which two First Dogwatchmen were asleep. The portholes were closed and the only light came from bulbs fitted into the sweating bulkhead. The men now eating supper at the six mess-tables wore vests and pale blue overalls turned down and knotted round their waists.

'There's a buzz that we're taking on new radar fittings during boiler-clean,' Moulson, the leading hand of 5 Mess, said. Moulson, who had his ear to the ground, was always the first to pick up and spread any rumours that were going.

It was always bad news or else Moulson would not have bothered with it. Usually it concerned the postponement of leave or the diverting of the ship to unpleasant areas. On the rare occasions it proved accurate Moulson basked in his prescience. If it was wrong Moulson pretended he had been joking. Since he himself never went on leave it was all the same to him. He was Active Service, not Hostilities Only, a grey dignified man who, like most regular sailors, looked years older than he was. He walked perpetually stooped, coughed continuously, and only changed out of overalls when essential. He was a father figure and 5 Mess was his territory.

'I heard that too on the bridge this forenoon,' Smithy said. 'The pigs were talking about it.' Smith was the second senior of the four Active Service ratings in the Mess, a lean red-faced man with sandy hair that hung diagonally across his forehead. He had retired from the Service after doing twelve years but within eighteen months was back at sea again. Most of his time off watch he spent writing long, laborious letters to his wife on thin, lined pads of notepaper.

He spoke now with apprehension in his pale blue eyes. Any change of circumstances that might interfere with the regularity of his leaves caused him evident dread.

'You two old men are always hearing something.' Winston, stuffing bread into his mouth with one hand and drinking tea from a thick white china cup in the other, jeered at them. 'You don't know nothing, the pair of you. Break your bloody heart if we ever lost this run, Moulson, that it would.'

'Up your pipe,' Moulson answered evenly.

''E's saving it for Dicks, the brown-nose. Aren't you, Winnie Boy?' Tosh Ellis, red-bearded and piratical, grinned across at Winston from the bottom end of the table. He, like Moulson, rarely went farther ashore than the dockyard canteen, but, never without a newspaper, had some opinions on almost everything.

Reeder, sitting a little way up the table from Ellis, said:

'What about a game of uckers when I've got washed up, Tosh?'

'George'll play,' Ellis replied, indicating Moulson with his head. 'I've got some dhobeying to do and then I'll get turned in, I think. That bloody Shiner Wright talked all night when we was closed up and then I had the morning.'

'All right, George?' Reeder asked but was interrupted by Winston saying

'Dhobeying, Tosh? Not going ashore are you? Christ, you sailors 'ud drop down dead with excitement if you was ever to leave the dockyard.'

'See you get the washing up done, Winston, and the dinners kept hot for Blood and Haggis,' Moulson said, limping off to the Heads like an elderly crustacean.

'Blood and Haggis can get stuffed,' Winston said. 'Them buggers are never here at proper time and they never bloody dish up for me.'

'You're never on watch at mealtimes, you cowson,' Reeder chipped in. 'What d'you have to give the Buffer to make you his Messman?'

'I work ruddy 'ard, I do,' Winston grunted, his mouth half-full, 'more'n what you do sitting reading in that 298 all day.'

'Come on me lads, get finished up,' Smithy said, getting up from the table and putting his cap on. 'Some of us wants to get our 'ammicks slung. Who's Officer of the Watch, Tanzie?'

'Blackbeard.' Tanzie Lee who was fishing about in his locker looked up. 'Never spoke a word all last watch 'Aggis said.'

'Blackbeard' referred to Lieutenant Jago, the Navigating Officer, who had risen from the ranks. His sallow Mongolian features, with slanting up eyebrows, were lent a Mephistophelian air by a small pointed beard. His character, in fact, had none of the inscrutable calculation of his features, and his monosyllabic, cryptic utterances, followed frequently by a short, harsh laugh, disguised simplicity.

'I'll lay that crafty sod knows something,' Smithy said. 'Totman, let me get at me ditty-box.'

Totman, putting treacle on a thick hunk of bread and butter, raised his behind slightly, enough for Smith to lift up the lid of his locker and get out the small wooden box containing his writing materials. Totman, a tall black-haired builder's mate, lived in the Seven Sisters Road. Now he said:

'Smith, you'll be home this time tomorrow –' but instead of finishing his sentence he shook his head uncomprehendingly and went on spreading his bread. Then he began to sing as he frequently did:

> 'You make fast
> Kiss my arse
> Make fast the dinghy . . .'

Totman never sang more than three lines of this song. What we had in common – and he now turned to me to discuss one of the players – was that we were both Tottenham Hotspur supporters who had seen Willie Hall and George Hunt in their heyday. You could scarcely have a closer bond.

I had by now been back in *Vivien* eighteen months. This was my last trip before leaving for *HMS King Alfred*, the officers' training establishment at Hove. Despite everything, I was going to miss the inhabitants of 5 Mess and their totally predictable conversation and habits. East Coast convoys were routine affairs, their moments of drama calculable. Every week we mustered a convoy of twenty to thirty ships in the Methil Roads off Rosyth and escorted it to Sheerness. At Sheerness we had an evening ashore and then sailed at midnight with a northbound convoy.

The first night out from Rosyth and the second night out from Sheerness were likely to be peaceful, while the other two nights we would be closed up at Action Stations.

In E-boat alley 'Headache' came into its own. E-boats, in packs of four or five, had the habit of coming across at dusk from their bases in Holland to lurk on the edges of the swept channel. Usually they waited alongside buoys, so that if the escorting destroyers got a radar contact they might, knowing the position of the buoys, tend to disregard it.

Once the E-boats sighted the convoy they would start to chatter, the flotilla leader giving coded instructions about which target to aim at, the estimated speed and course of the convoy, and his own intentions.

The moment of interception never lost its excitement. Usually it was the first indication of an enemy presence, and once notified to the bridge resulted in immediate sounding of Action Stations.

From then on I could relay to the bridge each E-boat signal almost as it was made. Sometimes by getting merchantmen to take evasive action, turning hard to port or starboard, we could steer them out of trouble. Sometimes they were simply too cumbersome to manoeuvre quickly enough and got hit.

On occasions the E-boats made minelaying forays into the swept channel. This was more nerve-racking because although we usually intercepted their cross-talk and drove them off we could not always tell exactly where they had laid their mines.

I must have made over a hundred trips through E-boat alley and the thrill of the contact never faded. First, the careful, deliberately enunciated conversation suddenly coming up loud and clear into one's earphones, as if one had got a crossed line on a telephone call; then the estimating of range and distance, the acceleration from convoy speed to full speed. Sometimes the voices faded, drifting into unintelligibility, at others they began faintly, then steadily increased in strength. If it was the latter, then radar contact was soon made and we would peel off in pursuit, opening fire as we closed. The E-boats just about had the legs of us, but we easily out-gunned them.

Weeks would go by without any contact at all, either because it was too rough, or the E-boats were licking their wounds. Then, on a still night of a particular kind, there would be a feeling in the air, an instinct of something about to happen.

Rarely was this anticipatory quickening of the senses misplaced. One attack – either by torpedoes, or by the laying of magnetic, moored or acoustic mines – was usually the signal for a flurry of activity on successive nights, German aircraft joining in.

There were only two other CW candidates on *Vivien* during my time there. One was George Butcher, who was with the Woolwich, and the other was Charles Wiskin, a Bank Manager. Neither made it to *King Alfred*. Butcher was a voluble Marxist, a pear-shaped man with a bloodhound's face and a squeaky voice which went up several octaves in moments of stress. A copy of the *New Statesman* usually protruded from his duffle coat pocket. Butcher and I became friends but he was teased mercilessly about his political views and it was soon plain that his sea-lawyer's knowingness and questioning of authority, not to say endless moaning, would not get him far. Wiskin, whose main interest in life was choral music, went about the ship with a martyred expression, and it did not need much imagination to foresee that he too would go no further.

Wiskin hadn't eaten anything since they'd sailed. He sat behind the windshield of 'B' gun, only eyes and a square of grey face with dripping blue nose visible from under balaclava and duffle coat hood. The forenoon watch had been on for about an hour. They had trained the guns, and now settled down to keeping as warm as possible. It was only just beginning to get light. Adams was humming tunelessly on one side of him, Butcher hunched up on the other.

He tried to avoid looking at the sea as it rose right above him, grey and surly and swollen, and then cut away to leave sky equally grey before his eyes. He fixed his gaze determinedly on the stained, pale green volume on his lap, *A Seaman's Pocket Book*. He felt dirty and stale, too weak and tired when he got up to wash, and now he felt the dry sweat all over his body. He could smell, too, the remains of vomit on his duffle coat and as it came to him in waves he contracted his stomach and clenched his knuckles. The sweat began to form on his forehead but he held on, forcing his lips together.

The crisis passed and the print on the page in front of him cleared and had a meaning again. He repeated the paragraph headings to himself, his lips moving silently as if in prayer. *Anchor dragging: An anchor is said to be dragging when it is not holding in the ground. This is dangerous.* The words conveyed nothing to him, except something so obvious that he felt they could not mean that. He looked across at Butcher, who returned his gaze with completely expressionless eyes.

'Like to hear me?' Wiskin said.

'All right.'

He handed over the book to Butcher who dropped it.

'What do you want me to hear, anchors and cables or boat work?'

'Anything.'

'All right. Let me see. Various terms used in cable work. What is "to snub"?'

'To snub is to arrest the cable suddenly by applying the brake.'

'Right. Kedging?'

'Kedging is moving the ship by means of small anchors and hawsers.'

'What do you know about growing?'

'A cable is said to grow in the direction in which it is lying.'

'Correct. And when the captain asks "How does the cable grow?" what is the proper answer?'

'The cable officer on the fo'c'sle indicates the direction with his arm.'

'Good. Ten out of ten.' Butcher handed the book back to Wiskin who had been answering with his eyes shut.

'How does your cock crow?' Adams leered, looking at Wiskin. 'That lot ain't no good, mate. What you needs is to learn the job. All you sprog WCs mugs up stuff from books, then you come aboard and don't know a fender from a funnel. Give me straight stripers any day, you know where you are with that lot.'

He shook his head derisively. 'Anyone wettin' the tea?' he asked. 'That'll settle your stomick, Wiskin boy.'

'Have a heart, Adams.' Fenton, the leading hand in charge of the gun, gave Adams a kick on his sea boots. 'I can remember when you first came aboard, your hammick slit in Pompey barracks and all, and your first couple of runs. Christ, talk about a pig lying in his own shit.'

'All talk, Adams, you miserable member of the depressed classes. You poor old proletariat, always got something to say except when it's needed,' Butcher squeaked at him. 'In any case, a civvy like you, what do you want straight-stripers for?'

'So as not to have jack strops like you, Butcher boy,' Adams said. 'If some cowson Jerry battlewaggon's coming at me, I'd sooner someone who knew his job were at the helm, and I tell you that straight.'

'What makes you think it's all that difficult? If you had any sense, you'd know it was only those who couldn't get a job in anything else who joined the services in peacetime.'

''Ere, Wiskin, 'ave a look at these.' Adams fumbled in his duffle coat pocket and began to pull out an envelope.

'I don't want to see them, thank you, Adams,' Wiskin said. His face was a raw pink from the cold and a drop had begun to form at the end of his nose.

'How do you know what I'm going to show you?'

'Because I've seen you show them to other people.'

'You bin rummaging in my ditty box, that's what. I'll get you run in.'

'Don't be silly.'

Adams drew the envelope out of his pocket and pulling up the flap slid some photographs into his hand.

On the plank Collins, a coloured West Indian from Cardiff, Winston, Ellis and myself jostled for position. Moulson was leaning over the ship's rail talking to Ellis.

'Got nothing to do, you tired cowson?' Winston stopped hammering and looked up from the dented orange paint in front of him. 'Like to do my whack and let me get me 'ead down?'

'What you got to be tired of?' Ellis asked.

'Not much,' Winston answered scornfully. 'Bagged off at the Naafi with that party last night. Lovely grub.'

'You never,' Moulson spoke witheringly. 'Don't give me that, Winnie. I see you up in the fo'c'sle with Dicks.'

Ellis's eyes lit up. 'Get a feed?'

He turned to Collins:

''Ear that, Snowball?'

'Got a fag, Tosh?' Collins rarely had cigarettes and his conversation, on the occasions when his opinion was invited, was frequently turned into the request for one.

'Chop! Chop! you two,' Winston said, 'I don't want to be standing 'ere all day. Mail in, George?'

'Ain't nothin' for you. No, it ain't.'

'Wot Pusser 'ave to say last night?'

'Says 'e seen a draft chit for you to go on Russian convoys.'

'Wouldn't mind at that. Shake your old woman if you was on too.' Winston shook the guy-rope that held the plank, nearly knocking Ellis and me off, though we were each tied to the rail. Collins's legs swung free over the grey water. Then he regained the plank.

'Typical wet sprog's trick,' Moulson said from above. 'Might have ditched the lot.'

'Got nothing between the ears, that's 'is trouble,' Ellis grunted.

'Nor between –'

'You shut yer bloody mouth, Moulson, you wouldn't be the one to find out any road.'

'Let me get up,' Collins said. 'Think I'll 'ave a drag in the Heads. Seen the old Buffer go ashore.'

He pulled himself over the side and disappeared into the messdeck.

'Bit more room with the old nigbo gone,' Ellis said. 'Don't take 'im long to shamper off when he feels like it.'

'You nearly 'ad the poor bugger in the hoggin, Winnie.'

'Serve 'im right, 'e'd scrounge the drawers orf of 'is granny if 'e 'adn't nothink to blow his nose.'

'Wot you got against 'im?' Ellis asked, in between chipping.

'Nearly 'ad me in the rattle last trip. Bastard, went down to piss and then when the Buffer found 'im orf of watch said I 'adn't relieved 'im.'

'So he relieved 'imself,' Moulson said indulgently. 'I suppose you was late as usual.'

'Later than that,' Ellis said. 'Never get up to watch on time do you, Winnie? Not proper, is it?'

'You ought to be in the Service peace time, Bash,' Moulson said. 'Cor, you'd never be out of the rattle.'

'I'd be sorry for you, Winnie,' Ellis began.

'Well, you can keep yer bloody sorrow for yourself, you won't see me when this little lot's finished.'

'What'll you be doin', Winnie?' Moulson asked.

Winston pushed his cap carefully back over his furrow of oiled hair and considered:

'Let's see. Saturday. Knock off early at shop, get me dinner and then watch Brum beat one of your fancy London teams.'

'You ain't never watched a football match, 'ave you?' Ellis asked. 'Who plays in goal for Brum then?'

''E thinks it's Hibbs,' Moulson said to Ellis.

'Only player you ever 'eard of, I suppose,' Winston said scornfully. 'Suppose you think W. G. Grace still plays cricket.'

'Wait till Pompey play 'em. I'll take you to Fratton Park, Ron, and give you a free lesson,' Moulson said, 'that is if they ain't been relegated.'

'Which I doubt,' Ellis interposed. 'Better come up White Hart Lane and see the wizards.'

'You pore old men won't be seein' anything. 'Ere's the Buffer.' He began to work away at the ship's side.

The Buffer, Petty Officer Radley, who was in charge of all seamen, a small, compact man with a sharp face, came over to where Moulson was standing.

'You working, Winston?'

'Yes, Buffs.'

'Well, fall in on the fo'c'sle. Captain's coming aboard. News for you.' He turned to Moulson. 'Going aft? Tell the bo'sun's mate pipe hands to fall in amidships. Winston, put your cap on straight or you'll find yourself in the rattle.'

He walked away, his boots ringing out on the steel deck.

'Bloody hell,' Ellis said. 'Just on tot time.' He called after Winston: ''Ere, tell that nigbo get up orf his arse and take his chipper up.'

The Captain, his trousers flapping like dead skin, did have news for them. The Duty Watch gathered in a semi-circle, port and starboard, round the Carley floats amidships, while the officers stood behind him. He spoke for some five minutes, in detached, short sentences, while he looked impersonally round at his crew or out at the launches moving between boats at anchor downstream.

They listened respectfully to him, staring down at the deck, occasionally looking up. The sun had begun to fade, the racing clouds shading over more solid patches of blue.

The Captain did not say much that you could hang on to,

except that they were going to have a break in routine. Some new equipment was coming on board, they would do working up trials, a shoot. Their period in harbour might be longer than usual, but no extra leave would be given. They must be extra careful about security.

While he was speaking Collins charged out from the galley-flat with a cigarette stub behind his ear, then, taking in what was happening, rapidly retreated.

The Captain paused, beginning to enjoy himself like an actor. His officers and crew did not know what he knew and even that was not much. But they got the message, vaguely but forcibly, and when he dismissed them even Collins, hurriedly lowering his trousers in the Heads as the Buffer came past, knew something was up.

I watched Moulson, 'Blood' Reid, Totman and Reeder playing a game of uckers. I had seen them play hundreds of times but a feeling of great sadness came over me as I realized this would be the last time.

'Gor, stone a crow, strike a rat,' Blood exclaimed delightedly. 'Double six, sets me barrier up and sends you back to the womb, Reeder boy.'

Moulson, unlike the others, never gave the game more than half his attention. Now he commented on some lawn mowers going cheap in the ad. section of the Portsmouth *Evening Argus* he had posted to him every week. He had an imaginary future worked out and he spent all his off-duty hours planning the details. The only trouble was that it would break his heart if he ever had to realize it. On board ship nothing could surprise or disconcert him, and in 5 Mess he was not only the longest resident but the arbiter of taste and behaviour. The idea of him setting up home on his own ashore was unthinkable.

I left them to it, and went out on deck. Half the convoy had turned off at the Tyne, the rest were mere smudges in the darkness. Our mast-head swung gently between two stars. From the bridge the voice of the Officer of the Watch drifted down, giving slight alterations of course and speed, his words returning in a muffled echo from the wheelhouse. The crew on the 4.7 for'ard crouched still as poachers behind the cowling.

Soon we would be closed up, but on this last lap of the journey it was mostly formality. No attacks had ever taken place this far north, a long way from the E-boat bases in France and Norway.

On such nights the war seemed quite unreal, a period of reflection and self-education. During the time I had been in *Vivien* I had managed to get through several novels a week, so that by the time I left I had read the complete works of virtually every contemporary English and American novelist of consequence. They were nearly all first editions, bought for a few shillings, but unfortunately the whole stock was destroyed when a flying bomb hit the Officers' Club in London where they were stored. All I managed to salvage was the poetry – Owen, Graves and Sassoon, Eliot, Auden, MacNeice, Spender and Day Lewis, bought as they came out.

John Lehmann's *New Writing in Europe* had recently been published and a telegraphist called Flint and I took it in turns to bring back from leave a selection of the books mentioned. Thus we worked our way through Aragon, Chamson, Giono, Malraux, Montherlant and Saint-Exupéry, as well as Silone and Jünger. Eventually, the Captain began to take an interest in what we were reading. We passed on the books to him, and he grew increasingly greedy for them.

Towards the end of the morning watch, at first light, we took leave of the rest of the convoy. For'ard, the scuttles had been opened for the first time for days and some badly needed fresh air was thinning out the general fug, composed mainly of smoke, sweat, seaboots, rotting cabbage, condensed milk and tea.

At the five washbasins serving over a hundred men queues began to form. Few people bothered to shave at sea, so this was big business. Others, naked, soaped their almost indecently white bodies under the showers, legs splayed to offset sudden lurches as we altered course.

Nothing later could ever equal the exhilaration of steaming at full speed into port after a successful patrol. Euphoria spread through the ship like a drug, though there was a sharp division between those who were going on leave and those who were not. For the latter there would be a couple of runs ashore, to Edinburgh or Dunfermline, but no chance of going home. Instead they had to stay on board while the dockyard mateys set about the routine tasks, liberally interspersed with card games, involved in a boiler clean.

Alongside in Rosyth, I was summoned by the Captain and given his blessing. One day, correcting Confidential Books in his day cabin, I had picked up from the deck a note written by his wife, a sturdy pekingese-faced blonde remarkably similar in feature to himself and whom he had only recently married. It read 'When you're soft you're lovely, when you're hard you're brutal.' Whenever afterwards I saw her silk-stockinged legs descending the ladder from his cabin I would wonder what games they had been playing. I saw the rather monosyllabic Captain, a former merchant navy officer who had transferred to RN, in an altogether cosier light.

I said goodbye to No. 5 Mess – Moulson, Smithy, Totman, 'Blood' Reid, Tanzie Lee, Tosh Ellis, and Haggis – and went out on deck. Half a dozen 'V and W' class destroyers lay for'ard and aft of us in the pens. Gulls dived and squawked on the oily water and trains shunted along the quay.

Across the estuary a shallow sun brought the greenness out of the hills. It was hard to believe I was seeing it all for the last time, for even if – as seemed quite likely – I failed the course, it would not be to *Vivien* that I returned.

That same evening, having said my farewells to the Edinburgh family that had befriended and fed me, and spent one last afternoon in the bed of the girl who had given me something to look forward to on my runs ashore, I took the night train to London. Whatever happened next, a part of my life was over.

U-Boat in the Arctic

From seas that had been dull
For days, white horses like real
White horses with startled eyes grew
Out of troughs and with slew
And heave of flanks like seal
Or whale the slack liquorice hull
Of a U-boat surfacing. Then
It becomes merely a matter when,
And through the angled periscope who.

Messdeck

The bulkhead sweating, and under naked bulbs
Men writing letters, playing ludo. The light
Cuts their arms off at the wrist, only the dice
Lives. Hammocks swing, nuzzling in tight
Like foals into flanks of mares. Bare shoulders
Glisten with oil, tattoo-marks rippling their scales on
Mermaids or girls' thighs as dice are shaken, cards played.
We reach for sleep like a gas, randy for oblivion.
But, laid out on lockers, some get waylaid;
And lie stiff, running off films in the mind's dark-room.
The air soupy, yet still cold; a beam sea rattles
Cups smelling of stale tea, knocks over a broom.
The light is watery, like the light of the sea-bed.
Marooned in it, stealthy as fishes, we may even be dead.

Morning Watch

Staggering on deck and filthy
I watch the first stealthy
Feelers of light, the sky torn
And spurting, like blood from a thorn.

Nothing as fabulous as this
Has existed, the imperceptible kiss
Of sunlight on ice, on faces,
Withdrawn as it melts.

These black ships and welts
Of saffron streaking our mess,
Crate up and cradle all we possess,
Sunroses strewn over white horses.

Destroyers in the Arctic

Camouflaged, they detach lengths of sea and sky
When they move; offset, speed and directions are a lie.

Everything is grey; ships, water, snow, faces.
Flanking the convoy, we go through our paces.

And sometimes on tightening waves at night wheel,
Drawing white moons on strings from dripping keel.

Cold cases them, like ships in glass; they are formal,
Not real, except in adversity. Such deception is normal.

At dusk they intensify dusk, strung out, non-committal:
Waves spill from our wake, crêpe paper magnetized by gun-metal.

They breathe silence, less solid than ghosts, ruminative
As the Arctic breaks up on their sides and they sieve

Moisture into messdecks. Heat is cold-lined there,
Where we wait for a torpedo and lack air.

Repetitive of each other, imitating the sea's lift and fall,
On the wings of the convoy they indicate rehearsal.

Merchantmen move sideways, with the gait of crustaceans,
Round whom like eels escorts take up their stations.

Landfall, Murmansk; but starboard now a lead-coloured
Island, Jan Mayen. Days identical, hoisted like sails, blurred.

Counters moved on an Admiralty map, snow like confetti
Covers the real us. We dream we are counterfeits tied to our jetty.

But cannot dream long; the sea curdles and sprawls,
Liverishly real, horizon and water tilting in to walls.

Murmansk

The snow whisper of bows through water
Asking and answer in their lift
And screw, ceremonials
Of salt and savagery,
Burial of man and mermaid.

On those last ski slopes
Voices still murmur
Ciels de Murmansk, ceilings, sea-eels,
Water-skiers with lovely backs
Arched before breaking.

I remember the thirst of Murmansk
The great eyelids of water.
Can one ever see through them?

Captain's Fur Collar

Stained and wet as shot rabbit
And his eye clinging to a thread
Like spit, a bullseye that might
Be swallowed whole, taking sight
With it.
            Hiding his forehead
He picked his way from the bridge
With the indifference of a waiter.

We found him hours later,
Bolt upright on the edge
Of his bunk two decks below,
Eye dangling like a monocle, face like snow.

Soft Objects

Sea to his waist, thick boots
Muffling all feeling, he is a rubber
Man encased in blubber,
At an angle to reality, without roots
Or ceiling. And it's as well,
As he reels in the swell
Of swollen water, eyes red
From smoke, that he can't tell
Whether he's stumbling against dead
Bodies or hammocks fallen from racks –
Simply soft objects lying on their backs
In a Mess he'd recently inhabited.
What he'd never forget was the feel
Of the non-feeling in the heel
He ground on a face as he vomited.

Night-Train Images

I

The train takes you where you have to go.

Eyelids like blinds coming down on darkness,
War atrophies in musty gas-masks.

The train takes you where you have to go.

The airless carriage sweats through loosened dress,
Our faces sag in flesh that never basks.

Each makes the wish obliterate the fact,
Imagines the loved face, not the unlovely act.

The train takes you where you have to go.

Outside, Lincolnshire is deliberate with aerodromes;
Passengers are forced to become their own homes.

The carriage jolts; the lemon light unfolds a bed
Whose occupants still sleep or appear dead.

But now look up, half nod and mask a yawn;
Night grows soft with rain and streaks of dawn.

The train takes you where you have to go.

II

The uniforms conceal identity, make
Conversation the exchange of counters,
Though experience helps us now to fake
Responses in our false encounters.

The make-up glistens on a face,
The look might be of lust or love;
But opposite the mirror shows
The leopard speaking through the dove.

223

Survivors

With the ship burning in their eyes
The white faces float like refuse
In the darkness – the water screwing
Oily circles where the hot steel lies.

They clutch with fingers frozen into claws
The lifebelts thrown from a destroyer,
And see, between the future's doors,
The gasping entrance of the sea.

Taken on board as many as lived, who
Had a mind left for living and the ocean,
They open eyes running with surf,
Heavy with the grey ghosts of explosion.

The meaning is not yet clear,
Where daybreak died in the smile –
And the mouth remained stiff
And grinning, stupid for a while.

But soon they joke, easy and warm,
As men will who have died once
Yet somehow were able to find their way –
Muttering about their food and pay.

Later, sleepless at night, the brain spinning
With cracked images, they won't forget
The confusion and the oily dead,
Nor yet the casual knack of living.

Night Patrol

We sail at dusk, the red moon
Like a paper lantern setting fire
To our wake. Headlands disappear,
Muffled in their own velvet.

Docks dwindle, rubbed out by mists,
Their cranes, like drunks, askew
Over jetties. Coal is unloaded
Under blue arc-lights.

Turning south, the mapped moon
Swings between masts, our aerials
Swollen and lurching. The bag
Of sea squirts black and sooty.

Flashes of gunfire, perhaps lightning,
Straddle our progress, a convoy
Of hearses. The bow-waves of gunboats
Sew us together, helplessly idling.

The watch changes, and changes
Again. We edge through a minefield,
Real or imaginary. The speed of a convoy
Is the speed of the slowest ship.

No one speaks, it might be a funeral.
Altering course, the moon congeals
On a new bearing. The telegraph rings,
And, at speed now, clouds grow visible.

We're on our own, making for harbour.
In tangerine light we sniff greenness,
Tremble like racehorses. Soon minesweepers
Pass us, continuing our business.

Fog

The sea warmed glass, pink milk,
Such an evening of lull,
Of abandon. Men write letters
On deck, lean on the rails smoking.

Suddenly, out of nowhere, faint ripples
As if huge fish were fluttering
Their fins, shivering. A chill breeze
Shaking out clouds like nuns' habits.

In minutes the miraculous dusk
Has become clammy, umbrellas
Of white wool round mastheads.
Visibility is down to a cable.

And we are left with the bleating
Of sirens, a whole convoy
Scattered like toys thrown down
By some petulant child, haphazardly.

Waiting for it to clear,
Anchored, one becomes aware
Merely of black looming
And fading, the great cliffs

Of bows that any second
Might split you, clean
As a fish, between lighting
A cigarette and inhaling.

Naval Base

Waiting in the bar for the war to end,
Those who for the second time saw it begin
And, charting the future, watched death crawling
Like a lizard over the lidless eyes of the sun.
The shaving glass shows them now
The face and features that they find appalling.
Reflections of launches move across the mirror,
Destroyers and corvettes swinging round buoys, sweepers
At anchor. But here the voyages begin and end,
Gin-time stories which they note, like keepers
Of lightships, as they wait for friends –
The same routine, continuing the war until it ends.

Radar

Distance is swept by the smooth
Rotations of power, its staring
Feelers multiplying our eyes for us,
Marking objects' range and bearing.

Linked to them, guns rehearse
Calculated obedience; echoes of light
Trigger the shadowing needle, determine
The arrest of night.

Control is remote; feelings, like hands,
Gloved by space. Responsibility is shared, too.
And destroying the enemy by radar
We never see what we do.

Côte D'Ivoire

Wearing grey like a second skin,
Sea, sky, camouflage, an onion
Crew peeled to show more onion.

Voyages breed strange fantasies,
That the sea is become
Green fields, a grass home

We can roll in like foals.
There's a name for it, this unequivocal
Madness of the deep.

Leaning over rails week
After week, the bleak
Waters create a tropical

Vertige, we have to hold each other back.
Until, at last, nearing landfall,
A low estuary of green moiré

That is no more than scrub on hills,
We can reconcile the real
And the imaginary – a coastline we peel

Of its trappings, discovering there
Rain forests, trinketed women, lemurs,
An East Anglian *côte d'ivoire*.

(

Sensations of Land

Sometimes, miles out, you get
A sensation of land, as if somewhere
Deep down a valley was surfacing –
The sea seems to heave contours
Of green out of itself
And you watch fields and forests
Being salvaged like wrecks.

I imagine a man whistling
To his dog, someone pruning shrubs,
The sounds of a cricket match.
A pub door shuts on faint music.

It is just such fantasies that mean
England is not after all
A figment of our deprivation,
But a landscape with outriders
Bringing real consolations.

Indigo dusk. Stokers, wiping grease
From their fingers, take the night air,
Throwing waste to the gannets.
Indiscriminate in their appetites,
They dive, as deprived as we are.

Angel of Harwich

She was usually good for a fuck
If she liked you, or just felt
Like a change from long hours
At the bar at the mercy of bores –
She'd flick you a look, then turn on her heel,
Legs in black nylon the colour of rail,
Making for the shed by the siding
That backed on the quay. Soon you would feel
The hardening thrust of those low-sliding
Breasts as she pressed and then knelt
As she liked and bucked as you felt
She was starting to come. She'd wail
Gently, straighten and then tuck
Her blouse back into her skirt, kiss,
And, slightly unsteady, trot her way back,
Humming. You marvelled at your luck.

Better than to scorn is to bless
Such promiscuity, the 'angel of Harwich'
Who made love as a nurse
Might minister to the suffering, eyes
And legs wide, but with so rich,
So tender a compassion only fools would despise.
At sea, it was her you'd most miss.

Leave Train

Yellow as daffodils as wax fingers
Yellow as death as a mandarin
Rosyth with eyes like a stranger
Rosyth with the pallor of dawn.

Shunting of engines in sky torn
Like a curtain, shunting of objects
In memories divested of features.
Without you without you without you

The bell of the blood in a deep sea
Drowns, the hood of the face is eyeless.
An emptied body in a warm room
An emptied body in its own tomb.

Dawn tricked out with sick stars
Dawn curdled with smoke
Yellow as fog as this compartment
Yellow as dogs' eyes as a death's head.

Without you without you without you
Branches are naked and wracked with fever
Rosyth is a terminus evil as an adder
Rosyth is absence that goes on forever

Yellow as dead flowers as a shared south
Yellow as desire as face to face
Dawn with a handful of spare hours
Dawn with hangover and a taste in the mouth.

Second Front

I NEVER IN FACT went on board *Vivien* again, though the following winter I was often nearby when she was passing through E-boat alley. It was unlikely anything had changed. Totman, Ellis, Reeder, 'Blood' Reid would be playing uckers, Winston dhobeying and bridling under innuendo, Smithy writing his long laborious letters home. I imagined Moulson studiously going through the Jig and Tool ads in the *Argus* and trying to convince himself that life out of the service would be an improvement on 5 Mess. For Butcher and Wiskin the end of the war, which still seemed a long way off, could scarcely come too soon.

Only with Flint did I continue to communicate, sharing reading lists and discoveries, until one day he got a draft to the Med and that was that.

Within four months I was back on the East Coast, though no longer based at Rosyth. *King Alfred*, at Hove, had gone better than I had thought possible, and although fifty out of our class of eighty fell by the wayside I was, miraculously, not one of them. Some were deemed not to have 'officer-like qualities', others to be too stroppy. A few could not manage parade ground work, the remainder failed at navigation or gunnery or signals. I discovered, to my immense surprise, that I enjoyed long marches and doing rifle drill, still more making others do it. Morse and semaphore came easily, navigation was a challenge, and gunnery I mugged up at the last minute and immediately forgot. None of it would be much use to me since I was going back to the same job, only as an officer, but it was good for morale to know that I could do it.

I don't think I have ever felt so well as I did that summer. The sea air, the physical exercise, the need to do everything at the double, resulted in exhaustion by the end of the day, but it ensured wonderful sleep.

There was, too, a constant, stimulating – or debilitating, depending on how it took you – nervous tension, for no one, having got this far, particularly wanted to go back to sea as a rating, and it needed only one blunder – a social faux pas or a misdemeanour of some kind – to have you packing your bag and hammock. Failure to salute was a serious offence, so that one was saluting in one's dreams, in one's pyjamas on the way to the washrooms, to anyone at any time. Making dates with waitresses in Brighton was dangerous and taking a light from another person's cigarette was fatal.

Though looking and acting the part of a naval officer was an ingredient of success, it was not the only one. 'When you give the order to present arms,' the First Lieutenant, who was an English lecturer at Glasgow University, used to rasp out, 'I want to hear the tones of the damned in the Inferno of Dante Alighieri, not a crow's croak.' Those unable to deliver needed to be pretty good at the rest to get by.

The Commander of the establishment had been wounded when his ship had gone down early on in the war. One of the results had been a speech difficulty that made him unable to articulate certain words. He had particularly asked for his present job as therapy because it obliged him to address hundreds of men at divisions morning and night. For those of us on parade it was often agonizing, since in the middle of a prayer or in the process of dismissal he would suddenly be rendered speechless. No matter how long it took – and sometimes it was minutes – we waited absolutely motionless as if everything were normal. It was a courageous performance, though nerve-racking for all concerned.

While this was going on the Second Front had started up. The night I was commissioned I went up to London, changed out of my gleaming new uniform into battle dress, and went on the prowl. The prowl must have been successful, which was just as well, because when I got back in the early hours to the

Regent Palace, it was to discover a bomb had fallen on it. Nothing was left of my room and my uniform was in shreds.

After a week's leave and then a month's refresher course on German signals at Wimbledon I was appointed Assistant Intelligence Officer on the staff of Captain (D), 16th Destroyer Flotilla, based at Harwich.

Captain (D) was Captain J. D. S. Salter, who flew his flag in *Mackay*, and then later in *Eglinton*. My own lodging was in *HMS Badger*, a pre-war floating brothel which used to anchor outside limits and doubled up as a Casino.

The prefix HMS seemed particularly absurd in her case for she was an ancient North Sea packet-boat now tied up along-side Parkeston Quay and no more likely to go to sea than to the moon. She was, however, a congenial home, providing a cabin overlooking the Harwich estuary and agreeable company, notably a traditionally boozy surgeon and an Irish chaplain with a taste for the hard stuff. I don't know if *Badger* returned to her civilian occupation, but she did very well by me.

Whereas *Vivien* did the donkey work of escorting convoys the whole way down from Rosyth to Sheerness and back, the ships of the 16th Destroyer Flotilla, based nearer the heart of the matter, provided additional cover only during passage through E-boat alley. *Vivien*'s job was primarily defensive, the 16th DF's to seek out and sink any interfering enemy, E-boat or U-boat. Although I now went to sea for only two or three nights a week, when I did go something was usually expected to happen. Nominally appointed to *Mackay* 'additional to staff for Special Duties' I did not belong to her as part of ship's company, nor did I always sail in her. Instead, depending on weather condit- ions, the position of the northbound and southbound convoys, and the likelihood of attack, I was free to attach myself to the senior escort going on patrol on any particular night. Mostly, they were Hunt class destroyers, but we also worked with frigates, and sometimes I went out in them. Each ship had its own 'Headache' operator, but I was there to keep them happy and share watches with them on busy nights. When not at sea it was my duty to lecture to the operators of the flotilla on any recent changes of code or developments in signalling. Every morning we would have a dummy run of some sort, in which I simulated an attack on a convoy, inventing a whole series of coded signals which they had to pick up on their headphones and decipher. When at night the real thing took place it was often alarmingly like these imaginary encounters and difficult at first to take seriously.

My immediate boss at Harwich was 'Dreamy' Coates, an RNVR Lieutenant who had taught languages at Marlborough. His engaging, vague, gregarious personality, evidenced by his punctiliousness in paying social calls on ships of the flotilla at drink time, had made him a legendary figure. In appearance and manner rather like a musical comedy actor, Dreamy leant backwards when he walked. Years of teaching inattentive pupils had resulted in his, rather like Joce, not appearing to take anything too seriously and the slight haze through which he viewed naval life made him welcome relief wherever he went. In due course he returned to Marlborough where I imagine he looked back on the war as a convivial interlude.

The night patrols we did from Harwich were short and sharp, with none of the monotony of convoy work. Also, unlike in *Onslow*, 'Headache' was of demonstrable value. Usually we sailed at dusk, sometimes working with MTBs based across the bay at Felixstowe, and, if E-boats were out, were in action by midnight. By dawn we were finished, and sliding in between green hills as we sailed up the estuary at first light was a marvellous feeling.

Apart from our regular forays into E-boat alley we made occasional sorties in support of the landings in Europe. Shortly after I arrived at Harwich, Antwerp fell, its port, unlike those on the French Channel coast, quite unscathed. The Germans, however, were still installed on the banks of the Scheldt and until they were removed from there, and from the island of Walcheren at the mouth of the river, Antwerp was useless.

It took nearly two months for the 30,000 strong garrison at

235

Walcheren to surrender, and then only after inflicting heavy casualties on the Marine Commandos and supporting naval craft. While the assault force went ashore we steamed along the coast bombarding German positions and driving off the E-boats and human torpedoes that made high-speed attacks from their base at Ijmuiden.

The seaward approaches to Antwerp were heavily mined and often we acted as cover to the minesweepers. With over a hundred miles to sweep, the minesweeper flotillas came under constant attack. Fifteen merchantmen went down but we sank increasing numbers of ships and the attacks dwindled away. We took a number of prisoners, whom it was my business to interrogate. It gave one a curious sensation, after months of listening to Germans talking to one another, to hear one of those voices in the flesh. Mainly we were concerned to discover where mines had been laid, but if the information was not forthcoming there was little we could do about it. Troopships carrying thousands of soldiers would be following us up the Scheldt, so it was essential for the channel to be clear. Luckily for our prisoners, and for us, the mines were usually detected and blown up.

By December 1944 the first convoys were able to reach Antwerp. Thereafter the Rosyth-Sheerness convoys became of less importance and for the rest of the winter I alternated between the destroyers, frigates and minesweepers that patrolled the sea lanes into Antwerp.

It took an effort these last few months of the war to realize that the Arctic convoys, attacked now by U-boats, were still making their way through to Murmansk. They were rarely in the news, but the conditions were frequently no less awful than they had been in my *Onslow* days.

Swarms of U-boats now began to appear off Western Approaches. Simultaneously, with fierce fighting taking place in Europe, a new menace appeared off the Dutch coast. These were the *Seehunde*, midget submarines who burrowed into the traffic lanes and then made off at great speed. E-boats and the

Luftwaffe continued to lay mines and though it was at last obvious the war would be won, a lot of people were still going to be killed.

A period of comparative calm after Christmas, when it began to look as if the German Navy was resigning itself to the inevitable, was followed in March by a violent renewal of activity. E-boats, the Molch and Biber class human torpedoes, and explosive motor gun boats, *Linsen*, combined in a furious last-ditch assault. It was impossible to prevent these 40-knot suicide squads getting through, even if few of them got back, for they had only a short distance to travel and the traffic into Antwerp was as dense as Piccadilly.

Night after night on patrol we heard and saw merchantmen blowing up around us on mines laid by E-boats. Generally, we could prevent E-boats attacking by torpedo, 'Headache' often providing useful information about their intentions, but there was little we could do about the mines laid by them and by the Luftwaffe.

In mid-April, by which time more than forty merchantmen had gone down since the New Year, mainly on mines laid by E-boats, we had our final skirmish at the mouth of the Scheldt.

A fortnight later the Germans surrendered. On 4 May Doenitz ordered all U-boats, of which there were over a hundred in operation, to return to port. Four days later I left Harwich, and *Badger*, for good. All German U-boats had been required on 8 May to surface and report their positions to the Admiralty, where by now I was installed, my pleasure to direct the surrendering captains to proceed, flying black flags, to British bases. It was the first tangible sign of the transformation in relationships that was to take place.

A number of U-boats were reluctant to accept either Doenitz's orders or our own, and repeated signals, followed by threats, had to be made. In dribs and drabs, however, they trickled in from the Atlantic and the North Sea, from the Norwegian coast and the Baltic. Nevertheless, although we had

237

a hundred and fifty in our hands within a week, over two hundred scuttled themselves in German waters.

It seemed, that first summer of so-called peace in Europe, that one was not going to be killed after all. It had always been on the cards during the winter, as I watched ships going down on mines in the Scheldt.

At Harwich, in my cabin on *Badger*, I had begun work on JW51B, the impressionistic battle poem about the *Onslow* action that I published several years later. Since I scarcely knew my messmates in *Onslow* I substituted for them characters from *Vivien* – Moulson, 'Blood' Reid, Totman and Smithy among others. The names were not, in this context, important. What I wanted to convey was the outward shape and narrative of the convoy, reinforcing this with atmospheric fragments of messdeck life.

At the same time I started a series of poems based on incidents and memories of my time at sea – poems about Iceland and the Arctic, about East Coast convoys, night patrols, fog, and those rare summer afternoons in the North Sea when you could sense the coast and the missing England of trees and grass and village greens. On those days, with the ship steady and the engines shuddering hypnotically, it was impossible to tell twelve miles out whether the smell of land was real or whether it was an hallucination. Either way the memory haunted me for years, as idyllic as the smell of stewing tea and toast was repellent.

In the rush of leaving Harwich for the Admiralty my poem notebook got lost. It surfaced later, but it took nearly twenty years, and a return to wartime places, for me to be able to put the poems of that time together again.

The main problem in writing poetry with war as its subject – and I knew about little else – was that of finding a tone and style that approximated to the experience: the experience itself, a mixture of fear, farce and tedium, and worst of all, the absence

238

of any real feeling at all, was hard enough to define. One relied on luck, cunning, patience and the skill of others to get one through. The excitements when they came were their own reward. What I could never get out of my head, though, from my *Onslow* days onward, was the incredible courage and initiative of men in extreme situations, especially R.N. officers who in other circumstances often had little to say for themselves or spoke in clichés.

To do justice to these was not easy. No one seriously thought the war would have been better unfought or was being gratuitously prolonged by bungling politicians and generals, so acceptance rather than protest on the Sassoon and Owen level was the only valid response. This perhaps made for a poetry of less vehemence and satiric force, but anything else would have seemed false.

The time was against inflation of feeling, certainly against rhetoric, even in those who had political licence. There were, in truth, heroes enough – Spitfire pilots, destroyer captains, commandos, submariners, bomb disposal experts – quite apart from the anonymous and unsung ratings and other ranks, but they were in the main practical men who would not have thanked you for drawing attention to them. Hillary's *The Last Enemy* was the product of an essentially romantic temperament, a disfigured hero in love with death, but his book is a search for meaning not an anti-war polemic. During my time at Harwich the poems of Roy Fuller, Alun Lewis and Keith Douglas, the three most considerable poets of the war, began to appear. It was not until long after two of them had been killed – Douglas in June, 1944, in Normandy, Lewis three months earlier on the Arakan front, possibly by his own hand – that their work in anything like its full extent was available. But, in my cabin in *Badger*, on those lucky nights when I was able to detach myself from the padre and the doc, I had time enough to read what was coming out by them in magazines.

Inevitably, I tried to relate my situation to theirs, but if, up to a point, everyone in wartime shares similar experiences, the details of our day-to-day lives and our attitudes towards them were totally different.

In my experiments with writing I had to learn as I went along. If I had little ideological commitment, and scarcely any experience of relationships except on the most superficial level, at least I had the asset of three years at sea. Just as much later I set myself the task of trying to write properly modern poems about sport, examining techniques, so I now spent evening after evening trying to find the poetic equivalent for my days in *Onslow* and *Vivien*, while they were still fresh. The details were real enough, but my own feelings towards them were vague.

I came to know nearly all Roy Fuller's poems by heart and it would have surprised me then, reading admiringly on my bunk in *Badger* before whisky took its toll or the padre hauled me out for a nightcap, if I had known he was to become one of my closest friends. The poems of separation from his wife and son which he wrote then came to touch me as if I had known them in real life as well as on the page. With such subjects as 'Waiting to be Drafted':

> It might be any evening of spring;
> The air level, twilight in a moment
> Will walk behind us and his shadow
> Fall cold across our day

or 'YMCA Writing Room':

> A map of the world is on the wall: its lying
> Order and compression shadow these bent heads.
> Here we try to preserve communications;
> The map mocks me with dangerous blues and reds

I was familiar enough, but it was the disgust at what war was making of relationships that gave the poems their force. Ironic, self-mocking, Fuller captured in a poem like 'The Middle of a War' the datedness of death – how it belongs to a precise moment, the one hanging over us, but already become the past:

My photograph already looks historic.
The promising youthful face, the matelot's collar,
Say 'This one is remembered for a lyric.
His place and period – nothing could be duller.'

Its position is already indicated –
The son or brother in the album; pained
The expression and the garments dated,
His fate so obviously preordained.

Such poems as 'Saturday Night in a Sailors' Home', in which
'The coughing goes on all the night', and 'The End of a Leave'
became part of my subconscious:

Suddenly our relation
is terrifyingly simple
Against our wretched times,
Like a hand which mimes
Love in this anguished station
Against a whole world's pull.

By the time I read most of these poems Roy was already in
Africa, on a Fleet Air Arm station near Nairobi. The poems in
A Lost Season which he wrote there made an even greater
impression on me. The African landscape and its animals –
giraffes, lions, monkeys near the mess

Most sad and tender
They clasp each other and look round with eyes
Like ours at what their strange captivities
Invisibly engender'

– are used to mirror the human situation and at the same time
reflect the distance between the writer and all that is most real
to him. Going up on deck before turning in – destroyers and
frigates riding at anchor in the estuary – it was often with Africa
in my head.

Reading Keith Douglas, who was only two years older than I
– he left Oxford to join up as a cavalry trooper the term before I
went up – was a reminder of a different kind of Africa, the Africa
of the desert war. By the time I was reading Douglas's marvellous poems of 1942-3, such as 'Mersa':

I see my feet like stones
underwater. The logical little fish
converge and nip the flesh
imagining I am one of the dead',
and 'Vergissmeinnicht'

'For here the lover and killer are mingled
who had one body and one heart.
And death who had the soldier singled
has done the lover mortal hurt

– he was, unknown to me, already dead, killed near St Pierre,
commanding a tank troop of the Sherwood Rangers Yeomanry.

His poetry had the smell of death in it, as did Hillary's prose.
They had similar backgrounds, overlapped at Oxford and were
killed within a year of each other. They possessed the same kind
of dash, though Douglas was the more introverted and complex
character. Of all Douglas's poems the one that I found most
typical and evocative was 'Aristocrats', its source a note written
by Lt Col J. D. Player, who was killed at Enfidaville, directing
that £3000 should be left to the Beaufort Hunt and that the
incumbent of the living in his gift should be a man 'who
approves of hunting, shooting and all manly sports'. Douglas's
poem ends:

How can I live among this gentle
obsolescent breed of heroes, and not weep?
Unicorns, almost,
for they are fading into two legends
in which their stupidity and chivalry
are celebrated. Each, fool and hero, will be an immortal.

These plains were their cricket pitch
and in the mountains the tremendous drop fences
brought down some of the runners. Here then
under the stones and earth they dispose themselves,
I think with their famous unconcern.
It is not gunfire I hear, but a hunting horn.

That seemed to me to get the tone and style just about right.
'Le Crève-Coeur' and 'Les Yeux d'Elsa', Louis Aragon's

poems from occupied France, had recently reached England and the contrast between the impassioned verse of the Frenchman – communist, surrealist, patriot – with its echoes of Apollinaire and Baudelaire, and the cool irony of Douglas was indicative of more than national temperaments.

Introducing 'Le Crève-Coeur' to English readers in 1942, Cyril Connolly remarked: 'Nowhere else has the situation called forth the man, or the intellectual poet (and the poet who is not an intellectual today is at a technical disadvantage) been able to liberate in himself the music for which so many are waiting. Considered in relation to the war Auden is an oracle in a cave, and Eliot a philosopher on a dark mountain. Aragon, at first neither a pacifist nor a patriot, yet obtained inspiration from the crass stupidity of war, and then from the apathy of defeat. Why should only he be the singer of that heat-wave when France fell, he alone of the men at Dunkirk write a good poem about it.'

The two poems of Aragon's that famously expressed the heart-break of the Free French were 'Les Lilas et Les Roses':

> O mois des floraisons mois des métamorphoses
> Mai qui fut sans nuage et Juin poignardé
> Je n'oublierai jamais les lilas ni les roses
> Ni ceux que le printemps dans ses plis a gardés

and 'Zone Libre':

> Mon amour j'étais dans tes bras
> Au dehors quelqu'un murmura
> Une vieille chanson de France
> Mon mal enfin s'est reconnu
> Et son refrain comme un pied nu
> Troubla l'eau verte du silence

In due course they were published in *Horizon* in translations by Louis MacNeice, and it is probably true that at this stage there was no comparable war poetry being published in England. Not one of the established poets of the Thirties was serving in any of the Armed Forces – all of them were some years younger than Aragon – and those who were later to write the poetry of the war had yet to get started.

Nevertheless, poems began to get written that made ordinary war-time experiences memorable, often in jokey fashion. For example, Henry Reed's 'Naming of Parts':

Today we have naming of parts. Yesterday,
We had daily cleaning. And tomorrow morning
We shall have what to do after firing. But today
Today we have naming of parts. Japonica
Glistens like coral in all of the neighbouring gardens
    And today we have naming of parts.

and Gavin Ewart's 'Officers' Mess':

It's going to be a thick night tonight (and the night before was a
    thick one)
I've just seen the Padre disappearing into 'The Cock and Bull' for
    a quick one.
I don't mind telling you this, old boy, we got the Major drinking
You probably know the amount of gin he's in the habit of
    sinking –

At Harwich, even in late 1944, there was no sense that the war in Europe, let alone the one in the Far East, was anywhere near over. Ensconced in *Badger* I imagined myself, if my luck held, settled there indefinitely, going out on nightly patrols, lecturing, getting mildly drunk with the padre, reading and writing poetry. Good poems were coming in from the Middle East, Hamish Henderson's 'Fort Capuzzo', for example:

One evening, breaking a jeep journey at Capuzzo,
I noticed a soldier as he entered the cemetery
and stood looking at the grave of a fallen enemy.
Then I understood the meaning of the hard word 'pietas'

and Norman Cameron's 'Green, Green is El Aghir', with its mirage-like title.

Alun Lewis's 'All Day It Has Rained' became one of the best-known poems of the earlier part of the war but by the time his poems from India and Burma were being printed he, too, was dead. Looking back now, the survivors among poets – F. T. Prince, Roy Fuller, Bernard Gutteridge, Charles Causley, who later wrote some of the best naval poems of the war, Gavin Ewart, Hamish Henderson, Vernon Scannell – appear barely to outnumber the casualties – Sidney Keyes, Drummond Allison, Keith Douglas, John Jarmain, Alun Lewis, at any rate those, among them, who promised most and were publicly mourned. 'Farewell, Aggie Weston, the Barracks at Guz,' wrote Charles Causley, 'Hang my tiddley suit on the door / I'm sewn up neat in a canvas sheet / And I shan't be home no more.'

I had seen my fair share of sailors sewn up in their canvas sheets, but when I read Douglas's 'Living in a wide landscape are the flowers – / Rosenberg I only repeat what you were saying –' and Jarmain's 'El Alamein' 'There are flowers now, they say, at Alamein; / Yes, flowers in the minefields now,' it was to be moved in a different way. At sea one dreamed of fields, and the poetry of the desert war revolved round landscapes and places. The names of ships called up echoes of their own, but sea battles were rarely linked to specific areas, spilling over from one ocean to another. Seasons at sea related to degrees of roughness and temperature, to mood and not to cycles of growth and decay. In the mind and memory the sea, in contrast to the variety of the land, was an unchanging metallic grey, the land an hallucination. All the more, therefore, did the names of towns in North Africa and Normandy, Burma and Italy, the map suddenly brought alive and given a tragic or heroic dimension, link one to the tangible war whose ebb and flow and ultimate advance were at last discernible to everyone.

I felt during these months my own lack of involvement with anyone acutely at times. In my paybook, under a youthfully grave photograph of myself, only dark blue jersey and blue jean collar showing, my number seemed more important than my name. That I had no family ties, unlike most of my messmates, reinforced the feeling that if anyone was expendable it was I.

I threw away all the half-finished poems I had addressed to a mythical girl. When eventually I came to write what I wanted

245

about those years I stuck to what was real – life on board a destroyer in wartime, as I experienced it. No more, no less.

That summer, after the war in Europe ended, I spent mostly in London, a habitué in off-duty hours of the Wheatsheaf in Soho, where Julian Maclaren-Ross reigned. My route from Soho to the Admiralty, where I was working at night, took me every evening down Rupert Street at the corner of which a voluptuous tart, like a mechanical toy operated by proximity, opened her fur coat to reveal her ripe nakedness to every promising passer-by. For the first week of this I found it hard to concentrate on signals and ciphers but in due course familiarity led to acquaintance and we used to have a quick drink to cheer me on my way and to fortify her against the cold.

My war-time leaves had been given point by the friendship of John Lehmann, then living in Carrington House in Shepherd Market. He had published my first poems, sent in from *Vivien*, in Penguin New Writing, and at his flat I met well-known writers for the first time – Rosamund Lehmann and Cecil Day Lewis, Louis MacNeice, Laurie Lee, and Henry Green among others. There, too, I met the painters John Minton and Keith Vaughan, then just beginning to make their names. Through John Lehmann I met Edith and Osbert Sitwell, my friendship with whom survived until just before Edith's death when I published an article on her poetry by Julian Symons in the *London Magazine* which greatly wounded her. The Sitwells did not take to criticism and Edith, in particular, often so generous in other circumstances, became transformed by malice and vindictiveness whenever she felt slighted, often without reason. She was kind and encouraging to me, and had I known she was seriously ill I would have held up Julian's critical but not unfair article for a more propitious moment. I made numerous appearances at Sitwell soirées or tea parties, usually held at Sesame House in Curzon Street, but in my sailor's uniform felt rather out of it among the Sitwells' smart and famous friends. On one notable occasion I found myself climbing the stairs with a slight, dormouse-like figure in a raincoat who turned out to be

246

E. M. Forster. 'Where have you come from to-day?' he inquired politely. 'Portsmouth,' I replied, 'and you?' 'Cambridge,' he said – we had now reached the buzz of the party and a wall of backs – 'and I think I'm going straight back there.' Whereupon, his head having darted rapidly from left to right across the crowded room, he disappeared down the stairs again.

My real, as opposed to social, life on land centred on the Wheatsheaf. There were other pubs, such as the Fitzroy and the Highlander, and slightly up the scale there were the marble-topped tables of the Café Royal, but it was at the Wheatsheaf that one could be certain, no matter how long one had been away, of finding familiar company. It was not always congenial, but it was certainly not anonymous.

The most consistent customer, one who I don't think missed an evening from the time of his demobilization to VE Day, was Julian Maclaren-Ross. He had published stories of army life in *Horizon* and *Penguin New Writing* and recently a collection called *The Stuff to Give the Troops*, which made him a bit of a celebrity. He was certainly a 'figure', tall, with dark wavy hair, a kind of bohemian version of Jack Buchanan. He smoked from a long holder, wore a Teddy Bear coat and carried a cane. He was often to be seen in dark glasses and sporting a carnation in his button-hole. His voice, from his reserved position at the far end of the bar, was nasal and relentless. In his day – which encompassed the decade before the war – Julian had lived in France, been on the dole, sold vacuum cleaners, and worked in films, and each of these activities, combined with his army service, contributed to his bearing and turnout. He impressed newcomers and so always had an audience, but his egocentricity and determination to act out the dialogue from obscure films, his total recall of plots in minor novels and insistence on recounting them, required a continually fresh turnover. The old hands kept their distance, other than giving and returning nods. The only person I have ever known to talk more was Neville Cardus, the music critic and cricket writer. I was once, many years later, dining at the Garrick and made the mistake of asking Cardus a question as he was going out, having finished his own dinner. My guest and I had not yet started, but we had eaten our way through three courses before Neville could be persuaded to depart; he remained standing throughout, talking non-stop, impervious to the attempts of waitresses to budge him.

Among other regulars in The Wheatsheaf was Nina Hamnett, painter, author of a lively autobiography, *Laughing Torso*, and one-time model and bed-companion of Modigliani and Gaudier-Brzeska, to name only two. Nina was by now in her late fifties, her unconventional features mottled by drink, her country voice fruity. 'Modi said I had the best breasts in Europe,' she was wont to remark, apropos of nothing, hauling up her striped jersey to demonstrate. 'You feel them, they're as good as new.' They certainly were good, needing no support, but the rest of Nina was disastrous. She carried what little money she had in a tin box, rattling it from time to time for contributions, 'Got any mun, dear?', a leper-like noise that soon got on one's nerves. Nevertheless, with her endless stories of Parisian low life and studio anecdotes – dancing naked for Van Dongen, working for Aleister Crowley, drinking with Picasso – she was a true whiff of Bohemia. No matter how depleted her finances or how humiliating her circumstances – drunk American GIs and sailors she had picked up late at night littering the floor of her flat – she carried herself with style. Her father had been a Colonel and one of her grandfathers, I forget which, a General in the Salvation Army.

After months of 5 Mess conversation, Nina and Julian were a relief and until they had exhausted their repertoire and were embarked on repeats, they were exotic companions for a sailor on leave. Once Julian took me to dine in his regular eating place, one of the cheapest in Soho, where he behaved as if it was the Connaught. The décor was basic, the menu a grubby, gravy-stained sheet with little on it. Julian, however, studied it as if the alternatives were endless and unfamiliar to him. We finally settled for soup and roast beef, whereupon Julian launched into tediously detailed instructions to the bored and solitary Greek waiter as to how rare the beef should be and exactly how the vegetables should be cooked. The waiter listened long-sufferingly and when it was over walked across to the hatch and bellowed 'Roast and two veg for His Nibs and his mate'. Similar consideration was given to the matter of the wine, at the end of which House Red was selected with the same deliberation that others might have given to a rare Mouton-Rothschild.

Such vanities were engaging, initially anyway, since they testified to a regard for standards even in the least likely circumstances. They were not common among either the regular or floating inmates of Soho pubs, most of whom were servicemen – British, Poles, Norwegians, Americans – or fringe art-world figures, anxious only to get drunk.

Maclaren-Ross's *Memoirs of the Forties*, published in 1962, provides a cast list of wartime Soho: the Scottish painters Macbryde and Colquhoun, usually drunk and quarrelsome, George Barker, whimsical and evasive, in workman's cloth cap, the painters John Banting, Keith Vaughan and John Minton, Dylan Thomas on occasion, Fred Urquhart, all of them, like myself, victims of what Tambimuttu called 'Soho-itis'.

Soho-itis: the Marquess of Granby and the Wheatsheaf, the Fitzroy and the Black Horse, The Burglar's Rest and the Highlander, magic cobbled area after months at sea, where the beer spilled and fists occasionally flew, but where the bearded Paul in his kilt and sporran, dirk and gold earrings, banged on the piano and girls with long hair materialized out of the shadows. There was nowhere else where I ever wanted to be, certain that it was here that life had real meaning, that art and literature and sex all came magically together among friends, even if no work ever seemed to get done.

Some work, of course, did get done, but least of all by those two Ceylonese who were Soho's dark and idle princelings: M. J. Tambimuttu and Alagu Subramaniam. Tambi in those days was in his pomp, shamelessly indulged by his employers,

Nicholson and Watson, publishers of *Poetry London*, and looked upon with favour by such as T. S. Eliot. Where all else, through wartime necessity, was shifting, Tambi, surrounded by girls, secretarial and literary, poets on leave, and hangers-on of various categories, was a permanent fixture, holding court at either the Hog in the Pound or the Wheatsheaf.

Rising late in his squalid New Row quarters off St Martin's Lane, he would arrive in his office in Manchester Square at opening time. A cursory glance at the mail and he was off to the Hog. After two hours drinking and a curry lunch he would return to the office, sometimes to take a late afternoon bath. On occasions, before leaving, he would sweep up a pile of manuscripts to be read elsewhere and often lost. By now it was time to take the evening trail, beginning at the Wheatsheaf.

Tambi ate little, but drank copiously, though with few obvious lapses from sobriety. He was painfully thin, had long wavy hair, dazzling white teeth and a tongue that flicked about in his mouth like a snake's. He cracked his knuckles, wore a long overcoat and laughed continually. In dark Rossetti-like fashion he was, in those days, rather beautiful. There was no doubting Tambi's feeling for poetry and he could recite the most obscure poems that for some reason had taken his fancy. He encouraged good writers and bad equally, the former, such as Keith Douglas and David Gascoyne, out of a genuine regard for quality, the latter out of laziness.

Tambi became, before long, a caricature of himself and very arrogant, not least about his allegedly noble ancestry. But to someone like myself, turning up out of nowhere, without warning, he was immensely welcoming. In the first place he provided girls, to most of whom he would behave like a pasha. 'Take your clothes off immediately,' he would bark out in New Row to some poetic acolyte. 'My friend has been at sea and hasn't seen a woman for three months. Come on, hurry, hurry.'

Although amiable, Tambi was also touchy, and days in his company could seem long, simply because of their aimlessness. Subra, larger, fleshier, and even more physically indolent than

Tambi, was one of those people noticeable only as one of a group. A barrister by training, Subra had published one or two short stories, but there was as little energy in them as he had himself. No one could dislike Subra, for he was intelligent, courteous, good-tempered and infinitely patient. When the war came to an end and Soho lost all its excitement and most of its literary personnel, Subra returned to Ceylon.

Tambi saw the war out in Soho, prestige and charm dwindling. *Poetry London* folded, re-started, and folded again. Various innocent American matrons dished out large sums of money to Tambi for new ventures but, predictably, the results were negligible. He married and departed for America, but eventually, sadder and wiser, returned. Drink and drugs had taken their toll and his last years in London were drab. Nevertheless he remained, to the last, never short of devoted women willing to minister to him, convinced of his genius and tolerant of his irritability and scorn. Dying in 1982, he outlived all but a handful of those who, wary of each other, nightly made the rounds of war-time Soho. Suicide and drink removed the best of them as well as the worst and it now all seems a century ago.

Still not cured of Soho-itis, I went on another course in Wimbledon, which was handy for Roehampton where my friend Bill Purkiss was lying badly wounded in hospital. Bill had taken a History scholarship to Hertford and played at Lord's for Oxford the year after I had done. Then, as a Lieutenant in the Northumberland Fusiliers, he had been blown up by a mine in the very last days of the advance on the Rhine. The waste seemed to me unbearable but he remained, superficially anyway, marvellously composed and cheerful, despite the long months ahead of learning to walk on new legs. In due course he gallantly started playing cricket again for the next village to mine in Sussex. Bill was that rare thing among schoolboys, a medium-fast inswing bowler of great accuracy, whose array of close onside fielders, an unusual sight outside County and Test cricket, took many catches and was rarely endangered. Bill was a correct and fluent opening batsman and most counties would have been glad of him.

By 1945 the photographs of my Haileybury and Oxford XIs scarcely bore looking at. My two Haileybury captains, 'Hopper' Sheppard and Alec Sheldon, had both been killed in 1944, Hopper as a Captain in the 9/12th FF Rifles, Alec in India as a Captain in the 14th Punjab Regiment. Crawford Boult, a Harrovian fast bowler, who had captained Oxford at Lord's, had been killed in the desert. Michael Cassy, our opening batsman, was killed at much the same time. There were others who died of wounds or who had simply disappeared.

I learned of these things mostly by chance and sometimes long after the event. Of those who were in my two Haileybury XIs I saw only three ever again, and from my Oxford XI only one, Jimmy Burridge, who had been at Haileybury with me, and who, after years in the Sudan and as a solicitor, became a successful breeder of racehorses. Those who remained had lost touch and were scattered all over the world.

I played some cricket for the Navy that summer and the next, but it was hard to take much interest in such spasmodic appearances. I hankered after the agreeably competitive cricket of Haileybury and Oxford, and even, from time to time, resumed my dreams of playing for Sussex. Very courteously, on the recommendation of Bert Wensley, the Sussex Secretary offered me some games at the end of the 1946 season, but I could not, when the time came, get leave. I had taken part in one or two matches on the county ground at Hove while I was at King Alfred, but it was a makeshift place then and not the sacred arena of memory. We knew, in any case, we would shortly be on our way to Germany, for it had been agreed by the Allies that the Royal Navy would handle the dividing up of the German fleet, mostly now returned to their bases and awaiting dispersal. The Sussex cricket that had sustained my adolescence and war, and since bred such durable images – Tate swinging the ball in a typical Hove sea-fret, James Langridge leaning a half-volley into the rugs of the Colonel's ladies – would have to wait for the time being, if not for ever.

PART IV

Occupying Germany

In the late summer of 1945 I was appointed to the staff of Rear Admiral Hutton, Flag Officer, Western Germany, then at Wilhelmshaven. We sailed up the Scheldt, disembarking at Antwerp, where for the first time in my adult life I trod European soil. After war-time England the smells of Belgian cooking emphasized what we had been missing. The night of our arrival I went out with some of my new colleagues to dine at a restaurant near the hotel where we were billeted. The hopelessly drunk Belgian owner was sitting at the next table, tears pouring down his cheeks behind thick glasses. He pointed to a handsome young waiter and said ''E has been my lover all these years and now 'e only go with woman.' The Black Market resulted in many curious relationships, abruptly terminated when conditions changed.

We stayed only a few days in Antwerp, moving off in convoy to the bleak German naval base at Wilhelmshaven. Just off shore lay the East Frisian islands of Wangerooge, Norderney and Borkum where E-boats had often lurked before setting off for their assaults on our East Coast convoys. Due north was the fisherman's island of Heligoland, a honeycomb of U-boat shelters flattened in one devastating raid by Mitchell bombers. Luckily, our first Headquarters was in the village of Sengwarden a mile or two inland, in rolling farming country. East Friesland is largely treeless and flat, with little else but cows and sea to look out on. The crews of E-boats and U-boats, tucked away in their camouflaged pens, must occasionally have been relieved to go out on patrol.

On blue September evenings, though, walking down farm lanes along the edge of rippling cornfields, the sense returned of a Germany untouched by Nazism and war. Labourers returning from haymaking touched their caps as they rumbled past on

255

carts and tractors, and if there had been a village green anywhere with a cricket match going on one might have mistaken it for Sussex. Before the autumn was over, in the shadow of a church spire, we provided one.

Sometimes we passed groups of German officers walking out from their barracks. They were obliged to salute and did so reluctantly. Radio music drifted out into the fading dusk, Zara Leander singing *'Abends in der Kaserne'* or *'Ich bin nicht noch nie so geküsst'*. In Wilhelmshaven I bought an old wind-up gramophone and a stock of records by Lala Andersen, Maria von Schmedes and Ilse Werner, unfailing reminders years later of those farm-smelling East Frisian evenings, in that first summer of European so-called peace. The records themselves seemed to reek of woodsmoke, the husky voices with their obsolete messages of longing and hope already consigned to an obliterated past.

This rural idyll did not last long. Within a month we were moved on, this time fifty miles due east, to what had been the palatial Headquarters of the German Navy, *Nord-West*. Buxtehude was a small, undistinguished village an hour's drive west of Hamburg. The village sloped each side of a cobbled street, at the top of which, its entrance gates guarded by sentries, an impressive modern barracks climbed to the skyline.

From the wardroom you looked down over a valley with dense pinewoods on the far side. Although the Elbe, twenty miles down river from Hamburg, was within easy reach, there was no sense here of the sea, still less of a naval headquarters.

Those early months at Buxtehude, with the summer slipping away, were concerned mainly with interrogating specialist German officers on technical matters. Whereas at sea I had to deal with coded signals relating to navigation and gunnery, now I had to familiarize myself with every aspect of warship equipment, from mine-laying gear to boilers. I spent a week visiting German gunsites in Holland, many of which had been mined or booby-trapped. Some of these still contained relics of occupation, liqueur glasses, empty packets of cigarettes, pin-ups.

The German naval officers, uncertain what to expect in the first months after surrender, soon lost their apprehensions. Those not required for specific purposes remained in huge camps awaiting classification. Questionnaires were issued, *Fragebogen*, and their answers on every detail of their service life, their involvement in politics, membership of the SS etc, assessed. It turned out for the most part a waste of time, for the Americans, in particular, already had other enemies in mind.

It was in these camps that the *Werwolf* organization, dedicated to the underground continuation of the war and the perpetuation of Nazi ideals, first revealed itself. Before the Germans laid down their arms on 8 May huge stocks of arms, money and equipment had been hidden away.

From time to time we had reports, conveyed secretly by anti-Nazis in the camps, about *Werwolf* activities and their ringleaders. The use of such agents, professing anti-Nazi convictions, required discrimination, since overnight it turned out that almost no one had been a Nazi except under compulsion. Nevertheless, by establishing certain credentials, it became possible to form a judgment.

We had one particularly valuable contact, quite different in calibre from others, whose main purpose seemed to be to ingratiate themselves rather than to denounce an oppressive brotherhood. One day this man, having signalled the urgent need for a meeting, failed to keep the appointment. Our meetings with him, necessarily, had to be concealed or given a mundane purpose. When we arrived at the camp, having hastily organized what purported to be a routine inspection, there was no sign of him. His body was found two days later in the surrounding woods, by which time a senior officer, already under suspicion from information smuggled out, had disappeared. He was rounded up in the Harz mountains after an exhausting chase and eventually brought to trial. No doubt, in the changing atmosphere of the winter, he was acquitted.

One of the problems of these camps was that, because of the numbers involved, they had to remain nominally under the command of their own senior officers. Since these tended to be high-ranking SS, it was understandably as dangerous for a genuine anti-Nazi in a camp as it had been while the war was still on.

The experiences of those first months in Germany gave me some idea in reverse of elementary problems of occupation. Were those who co-operated loyally with us entirely admirable or were they precisely those opportunists who would have made the most of any situation, regardless of what was involved?

The process of bringing war criminals to trial was long and complicated. In the case of the concentration camps, like Belsen, for example, the trial of whose commandant and staff in Lüneburg I attended, the issues were comparatively clear cut and the evidence and witnesses on hand. Yet so impartially was the case conducted – to the amazement of the German public – that individual responsibility was hard to determine.

In the majority of such trials the accused relied on the simple defence that he was acting under orders, and that refusal to carry them out would merely have resulted in his replacement by someone with no such scruples. Their SS ranking generally determined their acquittal or conviction.

Some time later that winter I was detailed to escort a German Admiral who was to be tried at Nuremberg. He was a bluff old seadog, a professional sailor with beautiful manners and country interests. Everything about the Nazis was plainly hateful to him but he accepted his share of responsibility as a serving officer with dignity. He was sent for trial because during the period of German atrocities in Greece he was the senior officer in the area, even though he rarely set foot ashore and the Navy was not specifically involved. He was found guilty, as were many others in similar situations. If the principle of senior officers being held responsible, however little personally accountable, had not been upheld, only those who did the actual processing – at a much lower level – would ever have been convicted.

Long before most cases came to court, after laborious gathering of evidence and witnesses, enthusiasm for revenge had evaporated. At the outset the instinct for justice lent an excitement to the chase, but as the months went by the heart went out of it. It required a degree of obsession, and a personal as well as professional commitment, to take any pleasure in the proceedings.

One of the Navy's heavier responsibilities in Germany was the dismantling and re-distribution of the German fleet. After top-level decisions had been reached as to who should get what, individual ships were to sail under their German crews to their allocated ports. The crews would then be guaranteed safe conduct home.

The procedure got off to a bad start. The first ship to sail, part of the Russian draft, turned east through the Kiel canal and docked at Tallinn in the Gulf of Finland. Here the crew disembarked, having handed over to the Russian Navy. They were never seen again.

Not surprisingly, once their disappearance had become common knowledge, the other crews refused to sail their ships to Russia, announcing that they would prefer to scuttle them. Since the Russians still expected their full quota, this presented a problem. We therefore made a night swoop on the docks, removed the crews from every ship, and made a thorough search of them. The crews were then taken back, and under a Royal Navy officer with an armed guard sailed under sealed orders. Not until we were well out to sea was the destination disclosed and the course set accordingly. There was no more trouble, though all ships travelling through the Baltic in future had British escorts.

Slowly winter set in. Although Buxtehude was undamaged as a village it had its share of returned servicemen, empty sleeves folded into grey jackets or hopping about on one leg. The German naval officers whom we had to deal with on official business tended to be rather dashing and glamorous, anxious to let bygones be bygones and to re-establish the camaraderie of the sea. Their assumption of equality was both understandable and irritating, for recognition of it made nonsense of the whole war, turning it into a game.

It had been no game for the wretched members of the Wehrmacht now streaming westwards. Once or twice a week we drove through the rubble of the suburbs into what was left of Hamburg. The Atlantic Hotel was still miraculously standing; so, too, on the other side of the Alster, was the *Vierjahreszeiten*, from whose underground ballroom William Joyce had made his Lord Haw-Haw broadcasts.

In the Long Bar at the Atlantic, once the haunt of celebrating U-boat officers, it was possible briefly to forget the desolation outside. Now it was for Allied officers only, grateful survivors only too happy to drink their last weeks in uniform away. The expertly-made Alexanders frothed and champagne flowed and no one thought it other than just that six years of war should have yielded some spoils. In relation to what the Germans had inflicted there was no cause for feelings of guilt, certainly not then.

It was, nevertheless, an appalling experience to wander the streets of the city. Not only was the destruction, except for isolated pockets, almost total, but the swarms of refugees, picking amongst the rubbish for scraps or pushing their pathetic hand carts and prams containing their worldly goods, were a heartbreaking sight. Many of these had fled from the east before the Russians, and had nowhere to go. Others were residents of Hamburg or the cities of the Ruhr, whose homes had been flattened. In England, even at the height of the bombing raids, there had never been devastation on this scale.

Except in country villages, where nothing much had changed, the whole population seemed on the move. They were not going anywhere, because they had nowhere to go to, but they couldn't stay where they were. So they simply pushed on, finding shelter where they could, sleeping rough and searching for the soup kitchens set up by the British in the larger towns. Since there was little food – no meat, coffee or tobacco, bread and potatoes only at impossible prices – the Black Market thrived.

In our barracks at Buxtehude we saw little of all this. The days were fully taken up with work, and as they shortened, the winds from the Baltic whistling through the pinewoods, so we made our own entertainment. Non-fraternization with the Germans was strictly enforced, so that a pattern of life almost as non-sexual as being at sea developed. As far as we were concerned, there was no shortage of food or drink. Vast quantities of champagne and fine wines had been taken over with the barracks, and they cost practically nothing. The catering was in the hands of the First Lieutenant, a huge, bearded RNVR Lieutenant Commander whose piratical appearance was exaggerated by the wearing of a single gold ear-ring. His name was Ronald Chesney, and often he was my partner at bridge.

Chesney's duties, in relation to those of the staff, were purely administrative. His job was to see that everything ran smoothly, from catering to transport. He dealt with discipline, as far as ratings were concerned, with the employment of German civilians, and with maintenance. If you wanted anything, from a car to make a private visit or champagne for a party, you got it from Chesney. There seemed nothing he could not provide and he managed it all with an airy, breezy manner, as if it were the easiest thing in the world. The only things that detracted from this impression were the meanness of his piggy, watchful eyes and the way his head, with its short back and sides, narrowed to a point above the forehead.

It was easy enough to get on with Chesney superficially, but he was one of those people whose manner and mood seemed sometimes at variance. We had no contact during the day but every evening, in the wardroom before dinner, there he would be at the bar, larger than life and roaring with laughter.

Since Chesney was one of the few officers whose normal day to day duties required him to deal with German civilians of

261

both sexes, both for the obtaining of supplies and the domestic routine of the barracks, his retinue caused no initial surprise. But in due course his foraging expeditions, ostensibly on our behalf, when he would be absent for several days at a time, and the constant presence in his quarters of one or more German women, occasioned comment.

No one was quite sure about Chesney's past. He had once, in the middle of an evening's bridge, when mention was made of a pre-war incident, blurted out 'Oh, that was the year I murdered my mother,' and giggled. It seemed a silly, tasteless sort of joke, but it happened to be true. As the weeks went by Chesney's star shone more and more brightly, he gave select parties for his German friends, and he visibly grew in power and opulence. In anything to do with the barracks he was a law unto himself, and the Admiral, soon to retire, seemed content to let him be so. There could be no complaints about the food and drink, or indeed over the general discipline and appearance of the place. It was a honeymoon period for him, great in its way while it lasted. Then, suddenly, it was all over.

Bridge Partner

This man with huge belly and gold earring
Through black whiskers produced a high whinny.
He murdered twice. Now he's my partner
At bridge, a Commander with a penchant
For finesses. He's costing me a fortune.
He makes psychic bids and has pig's eyes.

Generous with loot, he passed on
Krug by the caseful, arranged girls
(His own tastes ambiguous), fixed transport –
Himself riding a Mercedes, waving through cheroot smoke.
His was the way of the conqueror, if only
It could last! But he died by his own hand,
Bankrupt like the rest of us, Nemesis upon him.

A Bad Man

CHESNEY'S STORY EMERGED, bit by bit, over the next few years. His name was not, in fact, Chesney at all, but Donald Merrett and he had been born in New Zealand. After his parents had separated, his doting mother brought him to England and Merrett went first to Malvern and then to Edinburgh University. In Edinburgh Merrett began systematically to cheat his mother by forging cheques in her name, the proceeds being spent on drink and dance hostesses. When she eventually discovered what had been going on and challenged him, he shot her. When the police came he told them that his mother had got into financial difficulties and had attempted to take her own life. She regained consciousness but died within weeks.

The verdict after the post mortem was that death was consistent with suicide. The police, however, were not entirely satisfied and pieces of evidence, relating to the forgeries, began to accumulate. Six months went by before they were ready to pounce but then Merrett was arrested, hauled back from London to Edinburgh and charged.

The trial, which began on 1 February 1927, was front page news. It lasted for seven days and Merrett chose not to give evidence. Three things saved Merrett's neck: the long time-lapse between the offence and the charge, the conflicting statements of the maid who was in the kitchen at the time, and the performance of Sir Bernard Spilsbury, the Home Office pathologist, who disputed the prosecution's conclusion about the impossibility of suicide or accident from the nature of the wound.

By a majority verdict of ten to five the jury found the charge of murder 'Not Proven'. On the charge of uttering false cheques Merrett got twelve months. 'I knew I would get off,' he told me one night in England, long after we had left Germany.

Between leaving prison and the war Merrett, who had by now taken the name of Chesney, lived the rackety life with which he was only too fond of regaling fellow naval officers. Within a few months of release he had married the daughter of a bogus 'Lady' Menzies and got himself back in prison for fraud. At twenty-one he inherited £50,000 from his grandfather, bought a country house and an open Bentley, and started the pattern of lavish entertaining that continued whether he was in funds or not. He gambled most of his money away over the next few years, but not before he had equipped himself with a small boat and a two-seater aeroplane, both bought with a view to smuggling.

In due course Chesney shifted his activities to the Mediterranean, smuggling drugs and arms on a run that took in Malta, North Africa and Spain. Most of what he made he lost in French casinos. The outbreak of war was a relief to him.

The tales of those days, embroidered with accounts of wild parties and hair-raising encounters with customs and police, were available to anyone who had the time to listen, though Chesney was a shrewd judge of his audience and was scrupulously deferential to senior officers. He had a child-like desire to shock but was usually careful not to offend. In his stories he always presented himself in a favourable light; taking on authority, living it up and chancing his arm. Only an occasional lack of expression about the eyes or petulance to the mouth suggested that this open-handed raconteur was anything other than the genial adventurer he suggested. Since no one knew anything about him, he was free to invent as many outrageous episodes as he wished. There was enough truth in his stories for them to be convincing.

No one at Buxtehude had served with Chesney during his naval career. His criminal past never came to light and his sailing experience soon got him a commission. He was given the command of a gunboat and then, in 1941, of a schooner based in Alexandria, whose duties included the taking of supplies into

Tobruk. Chesney quickly acquired enough surplus for profitable private deals to be made at each end of his trip. Later, describing his experiences at the helm of the *Kheir-el-Din*, he made it all seem a lark, dicey sometimes, but an opportunity not to be missed. The idea that there was anything reprehensible about his activities he would have laughed to scorn. He was totally amoral.

Despite his trading activities Chesney still managed to get into debt. He managed to avoid the consequences of a steady stream of bounced cheques by getting taken prisoner, the *Kheir-el-Din* being sunk under him in Tobruk harbour.

There was no reason to doubt Chesney's courage, a brand of bravado that made him appear indifferent to consequences. He did a good job with the *Kheir-el-Din* by all accounts and he was a spirited prisoner, the last of several attempts at escaping landing him in an Italian camp. Here, his vast bulk much reduced, he managed to feign illness and eventually got himself repatriated.

Chesney saw out the war at Scapa Flow, having acquired the command of a fishing boat and been promoted Lieutenant Commander. Once again his extravagance and gambling debts far exceeded his means. His posting to Germany, with its opportunities for looting and smuggling on a larger scale than even he had ever imagined, came in the nick of time.

By Christmas 1945 Chesney's undercover concerns, carried on in league with various German contacts, had extended from food, drink and cigarettes to petrol, cameras, drugs and jewellery. Although there was no way he could conceal the vast quantities of goods he had acquired and which he disposed of at night, few people realized that he was trading on behalf of himself. He bought off German civilians and sailors alike and since he never behaved in a remotely secretive or guilty fashion there was no reason to suspect him of other than minor offences.

His association with a German girl had now become blatant. Not only had he installed Gerda Schaller, the sister of a telephone operator working in the barracks at Wilhelmshaven, in his quarters but he gave a lavish party for her. He was persuasive in his efforts to get officers to accept her, making out, plausibly enough, that it was priggish not to do so. What most people minded was not Chesney's private relationship but his elevation of Gerda to official status, largely at naval expense.

In January Chesney and Gerda had a serious car accident and were lucky to survive. With Gerda in hospital for several weeks and badly scarred Chesney appeared faintly lost, but his worried appearance was caused less by Gerda's condition than by inquiries from Special Branch police into his dealings.

In the spring Chesney went on leave. The HQ work of Flag Officer, Western Germany, was tapering off and reserve officers were gradually being released. When Rear Admiral Hutton was posted to the Admiralty I left Buxtehude for Minden, for special duties on the staff of Admiral Sir Harold Walker, British Naval C-in-C, Germany. Had it not been for a fluke I might never have heard of or seen Chesney again.

In Minden I got occasional news of him. After demobilization he had returned to Germany as a member of the Control Commission. He had been seen in Paris by someone and there was a rumour that he had been arrested, no one seemed quite sure on which of many possible charges.

The charge turned out to be the minor one of appropriating a naval car, something so ludicrous in relation to what Chesney had been up to that it sounded like a joke. Nevertheless he got four months, for which he was sentenced in Hamburg and which he served in Wormwood Scrubs.

In proper Chesney style, within twenty-four hours of his release he was at the wheel of a Rolls-Royce, bought with diamonds smuggled in months earlier. Now, with Gerda as companion, he made weekly trips from his base in Liège to all parts of Europe, the luxuriously converted van he had acquired stuffed with contraband.

He was heard of next in Algiers and not long after that a report appeared in the French press of his being sentenced to six months in the Santé prison in Paris. During the two years following his release he was in and out of jail; weeks of high life, champagne and casinos alternating with arrests for currency frauds and drug smuggling. Gerda did a spell in prison, too, for travelling on a forged passport.

During that period I saw Chesney twice, by accident; once in a Chelsea pub, the Antelope, surrounded by sycophants and making free with the drinks, and once in the old Allies Club in Hamilton Place, where he sat at the bar alone, brooding and sullen. On the first occasion he was full of talk and good humour, elaborating on his adventures in the Mediterranean and in gaol, reminiscing over the old days at Wilhelmshaven and Buxtehude. He had, he told me, bought an E-Boat and was going to use it for cross-channel 'activities'. I was welcome to a trip any time. At the Allies bar a few months later he ignored my greeting, other than by a nod of the head, and I knew the mood too well to hang around. Two days afterwards the morning papers contained a brief report of his appearance at Marlborough Street court and his sentencing to three months for importing nylons without paying duty. This time he was sent to Pentonville.

I heard no more of Chesney for a time; then, in May 1950, at Lewes, he received a sentence of twelve months, again for smuggling, and was carted off to Wandsworth. I thought that would be the last I heard of him but I was wrong.

In January 1954 Chesney rang me up and suggested a drink. He apologized for not having been friendlier on our last meeting, but he had things on his mind. He hoped soon to be able to pay off an old debt. Years ago, in Buxtehude, he had taken advantage of my absence on leave in Copenhagen to confiscate a privately-owned Mercedes that had been entrusted to me, explaining that it had been called in for use in the officers' car pool. In fact he had driven it himself to Brussels and sold it.

I had long given up hope of Chesney ever acknowledging, let alone repaying, any debt, though in funds he was always a lavish host. It was uncharacteristic, therefore, that he should bother, nearly ten years later, to mention the matter. He was not exactly bubbling over in the way he sometimes did, and there was something unusually deliberate about the way he spoke.

We met in the Pier Hotel in Chelsea. I was surprised by his appearance, amazingly hale and hearty compared to the shifty, seedy creature he had appeared at our last meeting. No good reason for this particular summons emerged, except that Chesney was at a loose end and wanted to pass a convivial hour or so with an old colleague. He told me that Gerda had left him but that he now had an even younger German girl, Sonia, whose family owned a greengrocer's shop in Cologne. He made great play of his own performance behind the counter in striped apron and straw hat. He intimated that the E-boat run had proved less profitable than he had hoped and that his wife, whom on a previous occasion I had been prevailed upon to telephone to make excuses on Chesney's behalf, was causing him a lot of trouble by refusing to divorce him. Her reluctance to part with any of the marriage settlement he had made on her, some £10,000, in the first flush of his pre-war inheritance, continued to irk him. She and her ancient mother, the self-styled 'Lady' Menzies, were apparently running an old people's home in Ealing, and Chesney, curiously, in the circumstances, was staying the night there. Mention of his wife usually resulted in an immediate change of mood in Chesney and the appearance of his mean, vindictive expression. This time was no exception but the cloud soon passed and we parted amicably. The only puzzling thing was why he had bothered to ring up in the first place.

I soon discovered, because not many days later his face, bearded and ear-ringed and I think under a jauntily-worn naval officer's cap, appeared on the front page of the Evening Standard. Vera Chesney and her mother had been found murdered at the house in Ealing and after a process of elimination suspicion had fallen on Chesney.

Although at first there appeared to be no motive, investigation revealed the existence of the marriage settlement, the survivor taking all. Chesney, however, was known to be in Germany. Nevertheless, his description was circulated and immediate efforts via Interpol made to trace him.

Once investigations began, facts about Chesney's past accumulated: the murder of his mother, his string of prison sentences, even his attempts to bribe fellow prisoners to get rid of his wife.

More and more lurid details started to appear in the popular papers, but there was still no sign of Chesney. Five days after the murder his body was found in a wood outside Cologne. He had shot himself through the mouth. At the Ealing inquest on the two dead women the jury found that both had been murdered by Ronald John Chesney, once John D. Merrett.

Two years after Chesney's death Tom Tullett, a former CID detective turned journalist, published a biography of Chesney, *Portrait of a Bad Man*. In this, with the help of Scotland Yard, he convincingly reconstructed Chesney's movements during the last week of his life. But for an unexpected piece of bad luck Chesney might well have got away with another murder.

When Chesney had rung me up he was in the process of establishing, to as wide a circle of acquaintances as possible, his presence in England at that particular period. His reason for doing so was that if he should subsequently have been recognized (on the visit he planned to make later on a forged passport), anyone questioned would be unlikely to be able to differentiate clearly between the two dates. Many people could testify that they had seen him in London early in February and there would be passport proof that he had returned to Germany and was there on the night of the murder.

It turned out that Chesney, some months before, had met a Chelsea photographer, Leslie Chown, whose resemblance to himself had startled him. He had immediately conceived the idea of passing himself off as Chown, coming to London, killing Vera, and then returning, he himself having officially been in

Germany all the time and therefore having a perfect alibi.

With this in mind Chesney applied for a passport in Chown's name, having forged Chown's signature and that of his own doctor's, the latter's testifying that the photographs attached were a true likeness. Since Chown was clean-shaven and wore glasses Chesney removed his beard and earring and acquired a pair of spectacles similar to Chown's.

With his new passport safely hidden away Chesney returned to Germany and bided his time. In February, when I met him, he was here in his own right and lodging at Ealing. He returned to Germany via Harwich, making sure that his presence was remarked on at crucial points of departure and re-entry into Germany.

After forty-eight hours in Germany Chesney flew from Amsterdam to London under the name of Chown, arriving on a KLM plane in the early evening of 10 February. Sometime later he must have made his way to Montpelier Road, Ealing, waiting in the bushes until all the lights had gone out in the old people's home.

Satisfied that he had not been seen, Chesney then made his way into his wife's quarters, separated from the rest of the building. He had brought a supply of gin with him, and Vera, an increasingly heavy drinker for many years, was not one to turn down any opportunity, even one so unexpected. At some time during the next two hours, when Vera was sufficiently drunk, Chesney carried her to the bathroom, filled the bath, and held her under. It was the classic method used by George Smith in the Brides in the Bath case, the accounts of which were known to have made a great impression on Chesney.

Satisfied that Vera was dead, and that everything would point to her having accidentally drowned after an even larger intake of alcohol than usual, Chesney prepared to leave. His plan was working like a dream. He had been seen by no one and he had a perfect alibi.

Unfortunately for him his mother-in-law, the bogus Lady Menzies, had been unable to sleep and was on her way down from her room in another part of the house to make a cup of tea. They must have met in the hall.

With the prospect of all his efforts suddenly coming to nothing Chesney set about removing the only witness. His mother-in-law, old and frail though she was, put up a terrific fight, but Chesney, having struck her down, then strangled her with one of her own stockings. This had been no part of his intentions, but in the circumstances he must have felt he had no alternative. Having done what he could to remove any traces of his own presence, Chesney left. By the time the bodies had been discovered and the police informed, Chesney/Chown was safely back in Germany.

Did Chesney still imagine he might get away with it? Certainly, there was as yet no proof of his entry into the country, but it must have become plain to him over the next few days that his time was running out. He had no money to go far afield and there was nowhere in Europe where he was welcome. His picture was on the front page of every newspaper in connection with the murder and when he tried to get in touch with Sonia her father refused to let him see her.

During his last forty-eight hours Chesney wrote letters to his solicitor, to the public trustee authorizing release of the marriage settlement funds, and to Sonia. Unable to face the prospect of a trial and yet another prison sentence he must in despair have decided to take the only way out. It was the one unconvincing thing he had ever done, and for years afterwards, whenever I chanced upon a huge, heavily jowled and dark-bearded man, a shiver ran through me. Chesney, I felt in my bones, would have had some last trick up his sleeve, and the man with a gunshot wound in his mouth found in that Cologne wood could not have been him. At the funeral there was only one mourner, Gerda Schaller, loving accomplice in so much of Chesney's life since that first post-war winter in Buxtehude we had all shared.

Hamburg by Night

White boats on the Alster like confetti,
Slate sky, and a sense of diminishing
Returns, the handcarts smaller and emptier.

Women have cloth faces, will exchange
Anything for anything, though in St Pauli
Wrestle naked in mud during dinner.

As you watch them, children grow thinner,
Their eyes huger. Is it for this we came,
To go whoring and give defeat a name?

Wilhelmshaven Dockyard

Acetylene lamps spark mauve parasols on paintwork,
Raede Schleuse and Nord-West Hafen, docks
Almost immortal, illuminated and banging. But rats
Have returned now, custodians of litter,
Eating into uniforms, scavenging through messdecks.
A fleet laid up is a field-day for them.
Here the captured crews write letters,
Sailors with streaked hair and on their caps
Leipzig, Lützow, Nürnberg, Emden,
Myths taking on the dustiness of moths.
It's hard, though, to work up much interest,
Ships atrophying around them, reduced and irrelevant.
Our feelings are like end-of-term; half euphoric,
Half regretful. *Theirs* like staff under notice.

273

Sengwarden Barracks

Something (but what?) could be made of this,
Two U-boat officers turning to piss
In swastika shapes against a wall.

These level fields are Wehrmacht grey,
Friesians chew cud all the way
To the Baltic, camouflaged as pillboxes.

From the barracks a horn gramophone
And Ilse Werner singing *Abends*
In der Kaserne, a long way from home.

Here gold eagles rust like the sky.
We paint out glory and forget how to fly.

German Gun Site

A year passed and the emplacement empty.
The Vierling trains on immune sky, and shells,
Discarded like old cigars, yellow in the stamping sun.
All round, weeds ripen into fibrous bells.

The blown bridge hangs a vacant sleeve,
A mocking image in the river's scum
Where pairs of limbs now fold in ones.
Bleached wrists grope a petrol drum.

Pinned on the wall, a smiling and naked girl,
Embellished now with bush and name.
Tin specs grow moss on rusted frames,
And, like liqueur glasses, glass mines curl.

Hotel Albert 1er, Ostende

Ochre sea, the Quai des Pêcheurs awash.
Through loops of your hair sails
Drip heliotrope, cinnamon, rust.
Beyond the lighthouse the breakers crash.

In bed we are warm and entwined.
For this it was all worth it.
We shed war like our clothes,
In each other are confined.

French Zone

Zone of Black Forest and blown bridges
Zone of blue mountain and ice ridge
The future hangs from a precipice
The future is the turned-back past.

Zone without petrol and *de rien*
Zone without fags or *pâté*
Heads shaven under the *tricolore*
Heads paying off an old score.

Zone of *poilus* and *képis*
Zone of Arletty and grog
France growing out of resentment
France tied to revenge like a dog.

Zone of wristwatches and cream cheeses
Zone of Pernod and short thighs
Winter dreams on an empty stomach
Winter grows into men's eyes.

Zone of snow and mulled fears
Zone of swagger and coarse wine
Today with scenery and no tears
Today with handouts and no love.

275

Fräulein

As for my predecessor,
Leutnant von R, whom times have laid
Aside, you mend and press
Uniforms. On request, undress,
Share the bed you made.

As for my predecessor
You came, in a manner
Of speaking, with the room.
We both got a bargain.
Neither can complain.

Autumn in Hamburg

Two nights running in the early hours
I've woken to imagine their footsteps
Echo past the Jungfernstieg. They round
The Alster like black scarecrows flapping arms,
The woman with such puffy eyes
The man in homburg and smoked glasses.

They seem to swivel with ugly shoos and laughs,
Herding me off the pavement like an animal
Into traffic. Once vaguely pretty
In languid southern fashion, she smells
Of scent and doughnut, smiles black ice.
His coat is fur-lined, reaching to his calves.

It's hard to reconcile their malice.
Or did I witness once, in squalor,
Their nightly scavenging for rations,
The dustbin trips, like werewolves on the prowl?
Or meet him in his palmy days,
A Commandant's corset on his banker's body,
The double-lightning on the turkey collar?

Interrogation

We fished him from the sea, eyes blurred,
And dripping. Stripped him, gave him rum,
Then hauled him like a prisoner to the dock,
Asked questions gently, kind. Playing dumb,
He gave his rank and number, smiled
Cynically as we probed for more. Riled,
Trying not to see his shrivelled cock,
We asked him where he'd laid his mines,
And when he merely said his rank
The captain, as if he hadn't heard,
Inclined politely, murmuring 'We'll see to that,'
And gave the Chief PO dismissal signs.
The Leutnant shrugged 'Ich bin Soldat.'

Grotesquely draped as though in furs,
His blanket half-slipped across one arm,
He shifted position, uncertain whether charm
And pride were his prerogative or ours.
'All right, Bo'sun, take him below,
We'll comb the area all bloody night
If necessary, and if we should hit
He'll be the first to go,
Can't be helped, sorry and all that.'
So we marched him below to the stokers' flat,
And altered course out of the zone,
Steaming in circles until his nerve broke
And he asked to come up and explain
The pattern of his mines 'for everyone's sake'.
By dawn our sweepers had got rid of them all,
And we sailed up the Schelde as if on a lake.
Troops followed us in; it was quite uneventful.

The Pied Piper

NOT LONG AFTER we had settled in at Buxtehude it was decided that the Command should have a magazine. I'm not sure now whether the initial purpose was anything more than light entertainment for the officers and ratings on the Staff, but *The Pied Piper*, as the journal was eventually called after much discussion, soon grew into a lively forum for debate. Fairly crude printing facilities existed in the barracks and there was a stock of low-grade paper. None of us had any editing or publishing experience but an editorial board was set up, with a managing editor, publisher, and business manager. I was appointed literary editor and Geoffrey Corden, a fellow Intelligence Officer, Humour Editor. After two issues the Managing Editor got his bowler hat and departed, Reg Noquet taking over my job and I the general editorship.

We enjoyed ourselves with *The Pied Piper*, bizarre misprints notwithstanding. Six issues were printed in all, covering the whole life of the Command, from September 1945 to March 1946. On the cover a Pied Piper was seen emerging from the entrance to Buxtehude barracks, followed by vast quantities of rats. The symbolism is obscure, but at the time the title seemed an inspiration.

It was never easy to get contributions; the ratings were consistently indifferent and the officers feigned pressure of work. Chesney promised an account of his adventures but failed to produce it. There is, however, a photograph of him in the last number, looking vast but spruce at the Wardroom Mess Dance. He is arm in arm with Miss Blundell, a senior functionary of the CVWW, a lady of similar girth to himself. The caption I wrote above this odd twosome was 'I'll Walk Beside You', but the dopey grin on Miss Blundell's face would have rapidly melted away if she had realized the nature of the man whose hand she was so chummily holding.

The format of each issue was roughly the same – stories, reminiscences, discussions of policy and the German character, reports of activities, poems, sports pages, jokes. There was even a mock Agony Column, 'Aunt Agatha's Lively Letter Box'. Looking through the main articles now is, more than ever, to be reminded of the dilemma in which the occupying forces found themselves. There was, on the one hand, the view put forward by the Security Officer, Lieutenant Commander J. E. Sheppard. The burden of his swan-song, as he called it, was that history often repeats itself. In 1930 we had marched out of Germany, five years before we were due to go under the terms of the Peace Treaty, with colours flying and looking very smart, but to a chorus of German whistling. Sheppard concluded: 'The Germans knew that with the occupying Army gone, the way was clear for the next war. This incident was never explained to the people at home and don't forget that up to the early days of this war – despite the pogroms, the blackmail, the absorption of Austria and Czechoslovakia, there were good secluded people in our dear island who said the Germans liked us. The reductions in the Armed Forces brought us not respect but only contempt . . . The contempt is still there despite our victories. Don't fall into the trap like those of 1930. They thought they were liked by a population that actually hated them. That gale of whistling that followed those predecessors of ours out of Wiesbaden was to me, an interested bystander, an unpleasant surprise. Hadn't the German fräuleins been ready to go out and about with our boys? However, that afternoon in Wiesbaden quite a number of these young ladies had their heads shaved by young Nazis who had already been preparing behind the scenes. Remember that we don't want another war when we are middle-aged and require our gravity beer, peace and quiet. German friendliness is used in the cause of Germany. Always be correct, and if they are friendly watch out for the secret motive.'

279

Sheppard, not surprisingly, was ruthless and tireless in his pursuit of war criminals and members of the SS on the run. But if his views were typical, in their wariness, of the majority, there was a serious attempt made by many serving officers and administrators to 'understand' the Germans and in doing so to achieve a balanced relationship towards them, without appearing to condone the crimes of the Nazis.

In simple terms we were being warned of the danger of acting like suckers or, alternatively, of creating the climate of disaffection that in itself leads to war by exacting retribution.

Walking this narrow tightrope was made no easier by the Germans themselves. Forgetful of the murder, oppression, exploitation and terror they had unleashed on Europe as conquerors, they were now quick to react and complain about the slightest affront to their dignity or restraint of their liberty. Far from expressing remorse or feelings of guilt, they seemed merely to regret that their plans for domination had misfired and that they had been misled to the very last by their leaders, who had encouraged the belief they were winning the war long after it was plain they were losing it.

G. R. Lavers, a pal of Chesney's and a slightly sinister but articulate Supply Commander, in the same issue as Sheppard's article put a quite different, and more subtle, case. 'There is something basically oriental in the German attitude,' he wrote, 'in its detachment of mind, in its power of resignation, in its infinite patience, and perhaps above all in its belief of the slight importance of the individual.' Lavers went on to contrast the British tendency to be importunate, 'to strike, to abandon duty for convenience and to seek always the day-to-day gain for themselves whatever the wider cost', with the German qualities of 'patience, of political subordination of private to public interest, and of unselfishness'.

These virtues were not apparent to everyone, but Lavers's view that the Germans were a deeply religious but not a Christian people seemed valid. 'Their profound feeling for natural beauty, their acceptance of basic higher laws of propriety, such as regulate their family life and are the basis of their discipline, and their mysticism, are all manifestations of a religious groping. They perpetually re-enact the drama of Faust – learning, seeking, betraying their own spirit, and then starting again'.

Lavers saw 'the call to repentance' of the New Testament, or 'the change of heart' in modern idiom, to be as necessary in London and Washington as in Berlin or Tokyo. For the Germans, it meant to change to 'something completely new and only partly comprehended – not just a swap from Nazism to Western Democracy'.

In fact, things turned out rather better in Germany than any of us, there at the start, could have anticipated. The 'obedient' mentality that allowed participation in the excesses of Nazism seemed to have been diluted by the emergence of a questioning and radical new generation, untainted by the crimes of their elders.

Apart from publishing discussions about our role in post-war Germany, *The Pied Piper* gave expression to individual views about such matters as 'non-fraternization'. 'Non-fraternization is a machine for expending such good will as may exist with a view to providing an adequate supply of enemies at a later date'. Lavers wrote in his regular column 'Window on the World'. Most of us would have agreed, if only because of the artificiality and unpleasantness of avoiding human contact in ordinary social situations. Nothing was ordinary, of course, but normal life and relationships had to start sometime. In practice, of course, the non-fraternization rule was virtually impossible to enforce and gradually, as it was officially relaxed, so did flirtations and acquaintanceships develop. Chesney's full-scale affair, however, was an exception.

In the first issue of *The Pied Piper* Geoffrey Corden described how the word 'Buxtehude' always raises a smile to Germans, 'nach Buxtehude' meaning something like 'pull the other one'. The expression 'Hier bellen die Hunde mit dem Schwanzen' –

Dogs bark here with their tails – is supposed in Germany to refer to the complacency of the inhabitants of Buxtehude, a fortified, medieval town that had been a prosperous fruit-growing centre since the thirteenth century, with its own monastery and woods, and a tributary of the Este ringing the old port like a moat.

Very few officers and almost no ratings spoke any word of German, and for all they knew about their surroundings might have been anywhere in Europe. We tried therefore in each number to print something about the country round about and local customs, as well as about the origins, work and development of our own Command.

In the January 1946 issue, A. C. McCarthy, a Sub-Lieutenant, observed sharply 'When we hear a man chattering in terms of Huns, The Master-Race, and "Why should we worry? They deserve all they get" we know that he is either a half-wit or a newcomer to Germany.' I find myself regretting, in the editorial to that same issue, the absence of so many familiar figures, around whom the character and atmosphere of the Command was built, and about whom *The Pied Piper* made jokes. Now they had been posted elsewhere or retired or demobilized, and we had to start all over again.

The jokes were made regardless of rank, and numerous officers, including Chesney, had their private activities – commercial or sexual – referred to, though rarely in the blunt manner of *Private Eye*.

In the editorial to the February issue I wrote: 'it is already evident that Britain is at heart the one great power with a feeling of social obligation in Europe and an abstract desire for justice'. This certainly represents what many of us felt to be the case, with the French pettily vengeful, the Americans cynically opportunist, and the Russians impenetrable.

Already, it appeared, lines were being laid down for the next engagement, with the Germans, as a buffer state, being alternately humiliated and bribed. From time to time MPs and war correspondents visited us, arriving with fully-fledged ideas about how the Germans should be treated and how the German problem should be solved. After a few days swanning around they returned with their varying prejudices confirmed.

My own contributions to *The Pied Piper* consisted, apart from editorials, of impressionistic pieces of prose, atmospheric in the manner of French films of the period, and bearing such titles as 'Dawn over Antwerp'; 'Hamburg Nights'; 'Moon on the Este'. They dealt in freighters unloading under arc lights, rain washing down cobbled quaysides, moonlight on anchored warships, and romanticized versions of port life in general. What *The Pied Piper*'s readers made of these clotted pages I can't imagine, but, if nothing else, they got something out of my system.

Putting *The Pied Piper* together, with a staff of five and our German printers in the neighbouring town of Stade, was good practice. It was a challenge to try and make officers express themselves on the subject of their work and the German problem, and to get sailors who had never written a word in their lives to attempt something, be it only an anecdote, a football report, a joke or a complaint.

When finally, in March 1946, we shut up shop, the pages of *The Pied Piper* had provided a fair summary of the history and work of the barracks. Its photographs recall the faces of many half-forgotten colleagues, seen daily for months on end and then, overnight, gone for ever. Only Chesney, I think, ever hit the headlines.

I had, needless to say, not the remotest idea then that I would spend the best part of my professional life working for a newspaper and editing a magazine. Had I realized, bearing to the printing house of A. Pockwitz in Karl Krause Strasse galleys on such subjects as 'Operation Silver' and 'Bird Life in Buxtehude', that I was engaging in a useful apprenticeship I would have been very happy. But fifteen years were to pass before such luck came my way and there were many periods in between when, although I knew more or less what I wanted to do, I had no idea how to set about it.

Last Performance

After dinner, the pines resinous and the lake
Topheavy with moonlight, a piper marches
Round the wardroom. Kilts swirl and the larches
Flicker with gold braid, gnats hum.
Now the fat major, tight as a drum,
Bites the cat's tail, a cacophonous fake,
Imitating the piper all round the lake.
And never outdone, the Colonel, a past
Master on Mess nights, swallows his brandy
Glass. He's a stockbroker, asthmatic and randy.
An evening like many. Only this time the last.

Demobilization

The entered world is like a sleep,
But men the self-same vigil keep.

The future offers dreams of pleasure,
But can we now employ our leisure,

Or have we let this fragile art
Become a spectre in the heart?

The river's limpid line surrounds
The dwindling morals and the grounds

On which we start afresh to prove
The valid images of love.

The pencilled eyebrows of the face
We gaze at conjure with the trace

Of familiar and objective fact,
As shadows merge into the act.

And we are half what luck contrives
In our one or other lives.

Off Brighton Pier

I saw him, a squat man with red hair
Grown into sideburns, fishing off Brighton pier.
Suddenly he bent, and in a lumpy bag
Rummaged for bait, letting his line dangle.
And I noticed the stiffness of his leg
That thrust out, like a tripod, at an angle.
Then I remembered: the sideburns, that gloss
Of slicked-down ginger on a skin like candy floss.
He was there, not having moved, as last,
On a windless night, leaning against the mast,
I saw him, groping a bag for numbers.
And the date was the 17th of September,
Seven years back, and we were playing Tombola
During the Last Dog, someone beginning to holler
'Here you are' for a full card, and I remember
He'd just called 'Seven and six, she was worth it,'
When – without contacts or warning – we were hit.
Some got away with it, a few bought it.
And I recall now, when they carried him ashore,
Fishing-gear lashed to his hammock, wishing
Him luck, and his faint smile, more
To himself than to me, when he saluted
From the stretcher, and, cadging a fag,
Smirked 'I'm quids in, it's only one leg,
They'll pension me off to go fishing.'

Night Porter

Perusing his Form Book in a glass booth,
Around him the familiar hum of generators,
A lift creaking like stores from the hold,
The smell of tea in sickly confinement,
He might be back in his reeking messdeck,
Never seeing daylight, on edge with ulcers.

With a kind of regret for the old days,
The slavish stink of condensed milk
And seaboots, the steeplechasing cockroaches;
When, among cronies, he surveyed an empire
Slung between stars and a sliding ocean
As softly sustaining as a silken pavilion.

Demob Suit and Bell-Bottoms

LIFE IN MINDEN during the early summer of 1946 was comparatively peaceful. I spent much of my free time walking by the river and working at night on the poems that later appeared in *Open Sea*. The Commander-in-Chief, 'Hookey' Walker, was a keen tennis player and it was an agreeable change partnering him at tennis after playing opposite the erratic Chesney at bridge. Since Hookey had lost his left hand, wearing instead a piratical hook, his partner had to throw the ball up for him to serve, a task not easy to perform to the Admiral's satisfaction.

From Minden I travelled over most of Germany: to Heligoland to inspect the U-boat installations; to Wilhelmshaven, where the captured crews wrote letters aboard the mothballed warships *Leipzig, Lützow, Nürnberg, Emden*; to the French Zone and the Harz mountains.

There was, for most of us, an end-of-term feeling: every month that went by saw the release of more officers. Germany, with its wrecked cities and desperate people, had an odour of defeat and sickness everyone wanted to be rid of. It was time to start another kind of life. Only the Chesneys of this world could find the heart to exploit a populace so stricken. The bartering of cigarettes and chocolate for sex among the occupying forces was another matter. 'Heute Schokolade, Morgen Promenade,' the girls used to say, but the sailors and soldiers reversed it. 'Heute Promenade, Morgen Schokolade.' In general, the exchange of chocolate for walk-outs of varying intensity was conducted amicably.

If those months in Germany became in memory evening rides through the pinewoods, fireflies going on and off in the dusk, and then, later, walks along the banks of the Weser trying to write poetry, the contrary images had much stronger initial impact. It requires an effort of will now to recall the composite face of Germany in defeat: Navy and Army officers trying to put a good face on it, anxious for respect; thousands of prisoners in their camps, dishevelled and downcast, not knowing what to expect; wandering bands of the one-armed and one-legged still in Wehrmacht uniform, whose ubiquitous presence seemed inevitably to be mocking the undamaged; the stink of corpses in a rubble that seemed beyond repair.

It was not until the late '6os that I could face Germany again; it had already become unrecognizable, in mood, prosperity, appearance. Out of the ruins of Hamburg a thriving port and handsome city had blossomed that had no equal in England. When I drove with my son to Wilhelmshaven and Buxtehude to show him the barracks where I had lived for a year, the place was enveloped in new housing and the people we asked for directions denied all knowledge of it. We found it in the end, but were refused entrance. Already it was as if the war had never been.

Despite everything, however, that triangle of north-west Germany – Lübeck, Kiel, Cuxhaven, Bremerhaven, Emden, Wilhelmshaven, Hamburg, down to the Lüneburger Heath and the woods separating Osnabrück from the shambles of the Ruhr, retains for me a curious attraction, almost erotic in quality. The husky voices and blonde hair of women in smoky night-clubs, all silk stockings and black leather, during those months when relationships were permissible and hostility had begun to melt, revived the excitements of Sally Bowles's Berlin. Within a year a healthy awe of German military might had been replaced by pity. If fear remained over the flat landscapes of lower Saxony it was not our own. Germany was a country of the dispossessed and one could take no pleasure in that. But it was also, however brutalized, the Germany one had read about in Goethe and Schiller, in Hölderlin and Rilke; the country of Thomas Mann and Herman Hesse, the youthful playground of Auden, Isherwood and Spender. The smell of it, a mingling of garbage and potatoes, of sauerkraut and scent, of farmyards and sea, never went away.

At the first race-meeting held in our part of Germany I won a small fortune on a horse called Mickey Mouse. It went in at 66–1 and was tipped to me by an authenticated anti-Nazi for whom I had done some trifling favour. The meeting itself was attended by red-faced farmers, refugees, wounded soldiers in their long, grey-green coats, Allied troops and Black Marketeers: the familiar mix of those first post-war German winters. Shortly afterwards the currency was devalued, a new Mark replacing the old and making my winnings negligible. I decided, while the going was good, to go on leave with one of my colleagues and two Wren officers to Paris.

In Paris there was little more in the shops than in Germany, but the cooking was better and we felt marvellous. I bought a brown velvet smoking jacket of the kind favoured by Sherlock Holmes and in which, on winter nights, I still wrap myself. I also acquired a bottle of Schiaparelli Shocking brilliantine, its torso-shaped container with the pink label and heavy exotic scent a recurrent reminder of that first taste of luxury and liberty.

If Antwerp, with its banana boats and brothels, its cobbled streets and aroma of coffee, provided the first whiff of liberated Europe, it was Paris that restored one to normal relationships. We drifted from one small bar to another, drinking Pernod and listening to Piaf. Plausible *patrons* in dove-grey suits and fuchsia shirts presided over chic restaurants that played Jean Sablon and Tino Rossi and a few months earlier had been serving, equally courteously, *soupe de poisson*, *entrecôtes* and *pommes frites* to officers of the Wehrmacht.

France was recovering its self-composure but it still exuded suspicion and sullenness. The euphoria of de Gaulle's triumphant return had been succeeded by protracted bitterness between Resistance and collaborators. Many had not suffered in Paris under the Germans, and now they were going to have to come up with good stories or pay for it. Allied officers and troops were not always made welcome either, disturbing a careful routine that required a violent switch in attitudes.

With what was left of my money I bought elegant editions of the poems of Eluard, illustrated by Picasso, and of Aragon, of Matisse drawings and Braque lithographs. One of my war-time heroes, Antoine de Saint-Exupéry, had failed to return in July 1944 from a reconnaissance flight from Alghero in Sardinia, and it was with some sadness that I bought his *Courrier Sud, Vol de Nuit, Terre des Hommes* and *Pilote de Guerre*. Saint-Exupéry, a former commercial pilot, whose pre-war books had described the opening up of air-routes in North Africa and over the Andes, was in his mid-forties when he died and only the losses of Richard Hillary and of the painter Eric Ravilious off Iceland had affected me as much as the news of Saint-Exupéry's disappearance.

During my brief period in the Fleet Air Arm, before 'Headache' hauled me away from Walruses and Swordfish, it was the romance and poetry with which Saint-Exupéry invested flying that attracted me. I doubt whether his mystical approach to it would have the same effect on me today, but in the early days of the war his conception of happiness as the acceptance of duty, his evocation of the techniques of flying and the camaraderie of the air, were inspiring. To create a naval equivalent seemed a laudable aspiration.

The pre-war writings of Ernst Jünger, a much-decorated German officer in the 1914–18 war, and of Erich Maria Remarque had a similar effect on me. German news bulletins still used the phrase *Im Westen Nichts Neues* – 'All Quiet on the Western Front' – which gave the title to Remarque's famous novel and I tried, on my first visit to Osnabrück, to locate the house where Remarque had been born. But Remarque, whose books had been banned in Germany since the Nazis had come to power – not only *All Quiet on the Western Front*, but *The Way Back* and *Three Comrades* as well – had become a non-person and his name meant nothing to the citizens of his birthplace.

The English writers who wrote with similar intensity of feeling about war and survived – Sassoon, Graves, Blunden – were too old to be involved again. Only Keith Douglas in *Alamein to Zem-Zem* achieved the same kind of elegiac dandyism and now he was dead too.

On board *Vivien* Flint and I had bought and exchanged the complete works of Conrad, had read Lowry's *Ultramarine* and Traven's *The Death Ship*. James Hanley, most of all, in his sea writings – *Broken Water, Stoker Bush, Boy, The Ocean, Sailor's Song* – had struck a responsive chord, but books about the war at sea that in any way aspired to literature seemed non-existent.

Flint and I, as ordinary seamen, took a vicarious literary pleasure at seeing ourselves, if not quite as victims of the system, then certainly as members of unprivileged society. You can't get much less unprivileged than at the bottom of the heap in the messdeck of a destroyer, and we even envied miners who were able to return to their families and their own beds at night. Hanley's sailors were exploited, suffering creatures, bound to the sea yet made wretched by it. The same applied to the sailors in Traven and Lowry. We, self-satisfied, shared their dilemmas.

It seemed impossible to write the same way as an officer and officer talk in any case is harder to render convincingly than the repetitive cursing and limited idioms of the lower deck. Saint-Exupéry's reflections about solitude and night skies, his introspective ruminations about the role of the pilot, were a way of avoiding having to deal with communal life. The later revelation that both he and Aragon were homosexual came as a surprise, nothing in their writing nor biographies having prepared one for it. I suppose if one had not known to the contrary one could have been equally surprised to have discovered that the loved objects in Auden's poetry were not girls, and that it was boys who took Isherwood to Berlin. Until well after the war had finished, ambiguity in the description of relationships, or more often disguise, was the usual and almost unavoidable practice.

In Paris, I had acquired leather-bound editions of Baudelaire and Rimbaud, of Lamartine, de Vigny, and Apollinaire, all read obsessively at Oxford but not looked at since. Re-reading them at night in Minden after days spent on Intelligence reports, the translation of boring documents and the interrogation of German naval officers, not only helped to pass the rest of that winter but made me wonder whether I should not perhaps go back to Oxford after all. The war in Europe had been over almost a year and the administration of Germany was passing into the hands of the Control Commission and civilians. In the end, I decided against it. What I wanted to do was somehow earn my living by writing and two more years at Oxford were not going to help me to do that.

The Navy had one more task for me. An exhibition had been mounted in Oxford Street called 'Germany Under Control', the function of which was to demonstrate in visual terms what was being achieved in the way of rehabilitation and de-Nazification in Germany and how the tax-payers' money was being spent. Each Service had its own section, with a liaison officer, who had himself been in Germany, to answer questions. I was appointed Naval Representative, my HQ a five-minute walk from the Wheatsheaf. It seemed a fitting way to see out the war.

I was released on 18 October 1946, exchanging my naval uniform for a grey herringbone demob suit, rather miserly in cut but not unwearable. Somewhere, I suppose, were the clothes I had been wearing the day I entered *HMS Royal Arthur* and put on bell-bottoms for the first time. That first day, unlike most of those that succeeded it, remains as clear in my memory as if it were yesterday. *HMS Royal Arthur* was a Butlin's Holiday Camp just outside Skegness and as we came through the gates in a truck we were greeted by cries of 'You lucky people', the trade mark at the time of Tommy Trinder. The sailors milling about between the lines of chalets looked like old hands, their blue-jean collars worn pale through years of scrubbing. It transpired that most of them had been in the navy less than a week, and that they had devoted every moment of their free time to rinsing and bleaching their collars in an effort to suggest long service.

Having been allotted a place in a chalet I went for a stroll round the barracks. It happened in fact to be my twentieth birthday. It had been raining earlier and there were puddles on the concrete paths. I had barely gone twenty yards when I heard a voice call out 'Bugger, I've got my bastard left leg wet'; an old salt of forty-eight hours seniority was bemoaning a splashed trouser leg. For some reason the remark remained in my head ever after. The fellow who uttered it had a fastidious, rather desiccated appearance, and the contrast between his appearance and his newly acquired vernacular, of which he seemed simultaneously proud and shy, was comical. I laughed and he laughed, too. Six weeks later we went our different ways and I heard no more of him. Sometime in the 60s a photograph in the evening paper rang a faint bell. The name under it seemed vaguely familiar and suddenly I remembered. It was my old friend who had got his bastard left leg wet and he was now a judge.

My draft was, except for myself and my chalet mate, entirely from Tyneside; either shipyard workers or miners. My hut 'oppo' was a ginger-haired Glaswegian whose civilian job was cleaning a skating rink. How he got into the Navy I cannot imagine because he had an appalling squint; perhaps he was put to cleaning something or other on shore. We neither of us could understand a word of what the other one said so after a day or two we scarcely bothered to speak. We were, in any case, so exhausted by doubling about from morning to night that we fell asleep the moment we reached our chalets. We learned to tie knots and we did several hours a day of boat-pulling and drill. The first evening, the Officer of the Day gave us a chilling lecture on VD. 'I have the impression,' he observed with an expression of distaste, 'that contraceptives must be growing on the trees of Skegness.' What with fatigue, liberal doses of bromide in our tea and the horrifying slides showing the effects of syphilis that accompanied the lecture, sex was something of which none of us felt in much immediate need.

After six weeks initial training in the bracing Skegness air I was drafted to *HMS Daedalus*, a Fleet Air Arm base at Lee-on-Solent. At that stage pilot losses were few and it was uncertain quite what my future was going to be. At my interview at Oxford six months earlier I had volunteered for Air Sea Rescue but there were no vacancies going. What were most in short supply then appeared to be naval cooks but the interviewing Commander, brilliantly perceptive, thought me unsuitable.

It was while I was at *Daedalus* that I got into trouble. It was the custom for those not actually engaged in flying training to do sentry duty on the aerodrome. This involved standing with a rifle outside a hut at the entrance to the airfield and checking all approaching vehicles. Officers of the rank of Commander and above were entitled, if I remember correctly, to a Present Arms and those below to a Slope. It was a tedious job, for most vehicles entered by the main gate and sometimes a whole four-hour stint would pass without a living soul coming near.

One Friday I had the afternoon watch, noon till four. It was my weekend for leave and I was proposing to catch the five o'clock from Portsmouth to London, where I had a much-anticipated date. My relief failed to turn up at the proper time and when another half-hour had gone by and there was still no sign of him, I had visions of my week-end going up in smoke.

There was a call-box just across the road so I stacked my rifle against the hut and nipped across to ring the main gate and report to the Master-at-Arms. There had apparently been some balls-up over week-end rotas for sentry duty and while this was being sorted out, a matter of perhaps two minutes, during which I was never more than fifteen yards from my place of duty, a service car swished up the approach road. I was reluctant to put the telephone down with the verbose Master-at-Arms on the other end of it and, by the time I had heard him out, the car was in through the gates and gone. Inside was the

Station Commander (Flying). I cursed but thought no more of it. Shortly afterwards my relief arrived. I handed over the rifle to him, collected my belongings, and set off for the barrack gates.

Having shown my pass I was about to board the liberty bus when the Petty Officer on duty called me back. 'Where do you think you're going?' he inquired, grinning wolfishly. 'Leave,' I said, 'week-end leave,' fishing for my chit. 'You're bloody not, you're in the rattle. The Commander wants to see you. Defaulters, Monday morning.'

I began to protest but he cut me short. 'It's nothing to do with me, mate, but he's hopping mad. You'd better keep out of the way until then. He's just telephoned through to find out who should have been on sentry when he came through and wants him put on a charge. No leave for you, old son.'

Furious, I went back to my mess. Later, when the watch changed, I tried my luck again and this time got through. But by the time I reached London most of the evening had gone and my date with it.

Back at dawn on Monday I crept in, washed and shaved, and duly presented myself at Defaulters. When my turn came I was marched in, the Master-at-Arms bellowed 'Off Caps', and I was face to face with Commander 'Flying'.

Commander P. had one of those conventionally handsome, thin-lipped, glowering faces it was impossible for a rating ever to imagine smiling. I stared at the gold peak of his cap. He was an unpopular man, totally at odds with the generally happy-go-lucky atmosphere of a Fleet Air Arm station. There were rumours that he had lost a destroyer in unsatisfactory circumstances and his present shore job, entirely administrative, must have represented a come-down.

He gazed sourly at me for what seemed several minutes, then suddenly barked out: 'You realize, don't you, the enormity of the offence for which you are standing here?'

I began to make deferential noises, about to suggest that there were mitigating circumstances and that my failure to present arms that afternoon was not entirely my fault. He cut me short.

'Perhaps you are unaware that your absence from your place of duty in wartime can be construed as desertion in the face of the enemy. Suppose some German parachutists had landed at that very moment and had found the aerodrome undefended. What kind of impression would that have given? Quite apart from the fact that when I pass a sentry in my own barracks I expect to be shown the proper marks of respect.'

I was in the process of mumbling suitable expressions of apology, backed up by the confident prediction that if any German parachutists had appeared dangling from the sky above the airfield I and my rifle would have been quickly united and more than up to dealing with them. But once more he interrupted, now glaring and red in the face.

'Do you know the penalty for your conduct? Do you know it?' And before I could speak he leaned forward and bellowed into my face the solitary word 'Death'.

It was so transparently absurd that I could not avoid a smile. I thought perhaps he was having a joke at my expense. But he wasn't. Seeming to have exhausted himself he now leaned back and remarked despairingly, 'You deserve a punishment more severe than anything I am empowered to give you. Commodore's report.'

The Master-at-Arms shouted 'On Caps. About Turn' and I was dismissed. As we got out of earshot the escort muttered, 'Jesus Christ Almighty'.

I now had to wait several days before coming up before the Commodore and this period I spent in the company of old lags similarly awaiting sentence. 'Commodore's report' meant almost certainly cells, the Commander not being able to dispense more than fourteen days No. 11s, 'Jankers', a punishment unpleasant enough in all conscience.

Joining the regulars in detention was like being admitted to an exclusive club, the other members of which had long ago worked out for themselves ways of ensuring maximum comfort and minimum obligation. There were, perhaps, half a dozen of us at a time, and the talk was almost entirely of the relative merits of food, accommodation, and recreational facilities in various gaols. Canterbury, Maidstone, Winchester, were discussed with the same degree of connoisseurship as others might bring to smart hotels, grand restaurants, and fine wines. My ignorance led me to being considered very unsophisticated in these matters, which I was.

What I learned was that habitual offenders, once so tagged, were happier accepting their situation than trying to avoid it. Some were compulsive deserters, some thieves, one or two could not face shipboard life or were afraid of the sea, a few were criminal racketeers. They had no hope of promotion from the lowest rank and therefore did their utmost to make their conditions tolerable and to avoid danger. Most of all, they did not want to be disturbed.

I had always been amazed at sea to observe to what lengths people like Haggis and Winston, for example, would go to avoid the simplest of tasks, putting themselves out infinitely more in the process. Dodging was a matter of pride.

My new companions were the same, bringing immense expertise to the avoidance of routine duties. I remember, years after the war, Chesney telling me a story about how he was once given a short prison sentence, in this instance for parcelling up a looted Renoir and addressing it to himself, care of the Admiralty, by hand of an innocent destroyer captain whom Chesney had persuaded it was something he had painted himself. After conviction he was handcuffed and escorted to Tonbridge gaol by two Marines. Chesney induced the Marines to remove the handcuffs so that they could all enjoy a slap-up lunch and champagne before reporting. Chesney took them off to the Ritz and by the time lunch was over both Marines were hopelessly drunk. In the end Chesney himself had to drive the van with the Marines lying unconscious in the back. When they got to the gaol Chesney beat on the gates, demanding admittance, shouting that there was a room booked for him. I wondered then

297

whether any of my Lee-on-Solent mates had been present at Chesney's arrival.

Apart from the novelty of the companionship my own situation was no joke. Cells, for however short a time, would have meant saying goodbye to any sort of naval career, certainly to becoming an officer. If one was going to have to spend years at sea, it seemed to me preferable to do so in comparative style. Not everyone took this view, some potentially admirable officers preferring the simple routines and quiet of the lower deck.

To the other occupants of Nissen Hut 'D' my situation was nothing more than one could expect. They wasted no energy on regret or recrimination. Totally fatalistic, they saw every day as a rotten hand dealt to them which they had to play as craftily as they could.

We had minimal duties, most of the time being spent on cards, smoking and dhobeying. This enervating existence was suddenly interrupted by a summons from the Commodore. I was surprised by this for I was not due to come before him until the next day. In any case, Defaulters took place in a different manner altogether, not by personal summons.

Commodore Thornton was a bluff, kindly man who had played cricket for the Navy in the Twenties. Admitted to his presence via a hierarchy of petty officers and a flag lieutenant, I was not prepared for what seemed a convivial atmosphere.

The Commodore waved the others away and motioned me to sit down. 'This is good news,' he smiled, waving a signal on his desk. 'It's a long time since we had a representative from this station.'

He handed me the signal which contained the names of those chosen to represent the Navy against the Army at Lord's in a fortnight's time. Ordinary Seaman A. Ross, Royal Naval Air Station, Lee-on-Solent was among them. Leave of absence was requested by the Admiralty from the Commanding Officers of the respective ships or establishments.

It was no good beating about the bush, so I explained that I was due to appear on the Commodore's report next day, and had no chance of being able to play at Lord's, whatever happened. I described the circumstances of my failure to present arms to Commander 'Flying' and the outcome of my subsequent appearance before him.

The Commodore listened patiently. When I had finished he sighed, picked up the telephone and asked his secretary to get him Commander 'Flying'. When the latter came on the line the Commodore was brief. 'Look here. Take Ross off my report, will you. You must deal with him.' He put down the receiver. Then he turned to me and smiled. 'I'm afraid I'll have to return you to the tender mercies of the Commander. Fourteen days No. 11s, I imagine.'

I re-appeared the next morning before Commander P. who looked grimly displeased to see me and took no time at all to inflict the maximum punishment at his disposal.

The weather had become hot and humid and my period of 'Jankers' was very disagreeable. Being required to report to the quartermaster at four-hourly intervals from 0600 to 2200 was no great penance, but on most occasions, until the Duty PO got bored, it involved some particularly pointless task like shifting coal from one place to another and then taking it back again. At 1800 those on No. 11s had to muster with full equipment and double round the parade ground with a rifle. After twenty minutes of this one's arm begins to ache unbearably and it seems impossible to continue. Luckily, the Master-at-Arms is obliged to make certain you don't actually collapse and die, though there were some near misses. Once I had got over the senselessness of the whole business I started to feel pleasantly martyred and by the end of the fortnight extremely healthy. As it turned out, I was on that occasion 12th man at Lord's; it was considered that I was lacking in match practice, which I certainly was.

I never saw any of the old lags again, dispersed shortly, in any case, to assorted prisons. They would have regarded fourteen days No. 11s as a very humiliating experience, much preferring the cosy and clubbable atmosphere of gaol. I kept out of Commander P's way as much as I could and before the summer was over I was out of the Fleet Air Arm and beyond his jurisdiction. That Commodore Thornton had himself been a Navy cricketer was certainly a bit of luck for me, though if I had foreseen the events of the next six months and known that I was to spend New Year's Eve in a crippled ship in the Arctic I might not have thought so.

Stateless Persons

They carry no shadow, the past like a slate
Rubbed out by a future that arrived too late.

Visaless and visionary, they travel to discover
Contiguous ruins that are all like each other.

New smells, new ghettos, reflect on their eyes,
But self-pity demolishes, conditions surprise.

Nothing is relevant, important or true. The message
Was too long delayed. They are part of their passage.

POSTSCRIPT

Such melody as wartime Oxford relayed to me faded like a signal, caught briefly in my RL85, but never recaptured. I could recognize the tune but not hold it. Sometimes on 'Headache' watch one picked up a confused background music, often jammed and indecipherable, but occasionally clearing to pure sound – Bach, Mozart, popular music from Hilversum or Luxembourg. It surged in and out of the set, as elusive and quickly evaporating as the scent of girls passed in the street, among whom there were some few at Oxford, contacts that were scarcely more than a raising of the eyebrows or a softening of the lips, but whose images hovered.

These pages describe an adolescence devoid of colonial guilt, but whose values became increasingly susceptible to challenge. By the time I set off for Skegness my India had gone beyond recall, though it was not then apparent to me. The concept of Empire, in the service of which I had expectation, was no longer morally or physically tenable. I had imagined myself heir to one kind of tradition only to find, almost imperceptibly, that I had acquired another. I had to shelve all notions of my former selves before I could, a decade later, catch up with the ghosts of them again.

Whereas Oxford comes back now as faint and distant traffic on a very high frequency, Germany increasingly invades the privacy of memory. Murmansk was mere months away from the last beers in the Lamb and Flag outside St John's. But the docks at Wilhelmshaven and the North Sea patrols, the Belsen trials, were a lifetime closer, the grey, endless sieving of the sea obliterating what had been between.

I get out my old wind-up gramophone, only tangible reminder of those months, and put on Zara Leander. At once I am back in blonde cornfields ruffled by gentle breezes into

watered silk, the cows ruminating along the edge of the peri-
meter, as wise to defeat as to victory and indifferent to both.
What her voice brings back is not simply the landscape of
annihilation and distress but the shedding of naivety, the
renewal of seasons, the continuity of existence. Whatever else,
we were survivors, the Europe that till then had merely existed
in books, lay ahead of us.

A slinky and tawny-haired girl is scrubbing the floor in front of
me, the back of her tussore dress riding up her thighs and
revealing her lovely buttocks. She is as aware of her nakedness
as I am, of her sunburnt legs stained with blackberry juice and
cut by stubble, the blonde hairs just visible between her legs on
this most sweltering of mornings. She goes moodily about her
business, cleaning, as she is required to do, an English officer's
cabin. What goes on in her head it is impossible to fathom. She
means to provoke but whether only to rebuff, in a situation
where she is inviolable and it is more than my life is worth to
touch her, I am uncertain.

She gets up, her eyes flashing at me briefly, and makes to
collect her bucket and brush. The silence between us seems to
crackle with static, as if the RL85 had been on too long. After a
few seconds she looks up, I nod at her and smile, she swings her
curtain of hair and clanks out of the room.

With slight variations – sometimes she wears brief pants,
more often nothing, under her dress – this scene is repeated
almost daily for weeks, then abruptly stops. It belongs with the
voice of Zara Leander, part of an unresolved ritual that has no
particular claim on my memory, since nothing ever happened.

It merely is a reminder that, in the wake of an unremarkable
song of the time, it would be possible to resurrect an alternative
life to the one recollected here; recording not simply, as in this
case, a promise that never materialized, but a completely
different set of events, equally real, that chanced to have slipped
my memory.

No doubt if I tried hard enough I could conjure up a parallel interior existence quite as convincing to myself and to everyone else. The frail child wracked by undissolved fears and fevers who landed from India on a farm in Cornwall, the adolescent consumed by a passion for cricket, the undergraduate and the poetry-obsessed ordinary seaman, the twenty-three-year-old staff officer taking his first steps in a ravaged Europe, must presumably have something in common, though what I am conscious of is the pure chance that turned one into the other and which might have set up a totally different chain of circumstances.

My father lights a cigar and takes his solar topi from the bearer. At the car door the mali proffers the carnation for his buttonhole. My mother sits with a *chota peg*, the smoke from her holder drifting off the verandah towards the tall palms that shield us from the Alipore traffic and the Hooghly sirens.

Tomorrow is race day. That more than anything is what I look forward to. There will be time enough later for the imaginary and imagined life, the train beating westward across India, its whistle slitting the darkness.